LATIN AMERICAN FOREIGN POLICIES
BETWEEN IDEOLOGY AND PRAGMATISM

Edited by
Gian Luca Gardini and Peter Lambert

palgrave
macmillan

327.8
GAR

First published in 2011 by
PALGRAVE MACMILLAN®
in the United States – a division of St. Martin's Press LLC,
175 Fifth Avenue, New York, NY 10010.

Where this book is distributed in the UK, Europe and the rest of the world, this is by
Palgrave Macmillan, a division of Macmillan Publishers Limited, registered in England,
company number 785998, of Houndmills, Basingstoke, Hampshire RG21 6XS.

Palgrave Macmillan is the global academic imprint of the above companies and has
companies and representatives throughout the world.

Palgrave® and Macmillan® are registered trademarks in the United States, the United
Kingdom, Europe and other countries.

ISBN: 978–0–230–11095–3

Library of Congress Cataloging-in-Publication Data

Latin American foreign policies : between ideology and pragmatism / edited by Gian Luca
Gardini & Peter Lambert.
     p. cm.
   ISBN 978–0–230–11095–3
   1. Latin America—Foreign relations—1980–   I. Gardini, Gian Luca. II. Lambert,
Peter, 1948–
   JZ1519.L385 2011
   327.8—dc22

                                                                    2010035729

A catalogue record of the book is available from the British Library.

Design by MPS Limited, A Macmillan Company

First edition: March 2011

10 9 8 7 6 5 4 3 2 1

Printed in the United States of America.

LATIN AMERICAN FOREIGN POLICIES

CONTENTS

Acknowledgments

We could not have completed this project without the help of a number of individuals and institutions. We are extremely grateful to our editor, Robyn Curtis, for having faith in this book, for her advice and encouragement, and for her first-class editorial work. Our colleagues in our department in Bath, especially Richard Whitman and Adrian Hyde-Price, deserve a mention for their support and for engaging with and challenging some of the material. The same goes for our students, whose interest in Latin American International Relations spurred us to produce a book that might answer some of their thoughtful and challenging questions about foreign policy in the new millennium. We must also thank the many scholars who very generously shared their thoughts with us during the development of this volume, not least the contributors to this volume, who we would also like to thank for their enthusiasm, as well as their patience when dealing with our constant demands and requests for further amendments and changes. We are also deeply indebted to the Society for Latin American Studies (SLAS) and the Political Studies Association (PSA), both of which allowed us to host panels that not only stimulated debate and helped our ideas, but ultimately resulted in this volume. Gian Luca Gardini would specifically like to thank the British Council, the Banco Santander, and the University of Bath for generously supporting his research. He would also like to thank George Lunt for his encouragement and Maria Regina Soares de Lima, Gelson Fonseca, José Raul Perales, and Olivier Dabène for their comments on earlier drafts. Peter Lambert would like to thank the British Academy for its generous support for his fieldwork in Paraguay in August 2007, as well as José Rivarola, Mati da Costa, and Fernando Masi for their help and advice during two separate trips to Paraguay in 2007 and 2009.

Last, but by no means least, we must thank our families for their support and patience. In particular, Peter would like to thank Felix, who patiently put up with his dad's obsession with a seemingly endless editing process during the first three months of his life.

Gian Luca Gardini & Peter Lambert
University of Bath
August 2010

NOTES ON CONTRIBUTORS

Larry Birns and **Alex Sanchez**, Council on Hemispheric Affairs
Larry Birns is the Director of the Washington-based Council on Hemispheric Affairs. Educated at Bates, Columbia, and Oxford, he has published hundreds of articles on U.S.-Latin American relations. After a career in college teaching, he was appointed public affairs officer for the U.N. Economic Commission for Latin America in Santiago de Chile.

W. Alejandro Sanchez is a Research Fellow for the Council on Hemispheric Affairs. His work focuses on security, military issues, and geopolitics.

Dr Ronald Bruce St John
Ronald Bruce St John obtained his MA and PhD in International Relations from the University of Denver. He has acted as a consultant for a variety of Fortune 500 companies, U.S. government agencies, the Associated Press, *Washington Post*, and *The New York Times*. Working as an independent scholar and foreign policy analyst, he has published over a dozen books, contributed to many others, and written more than 300 articles and reviews, including his latest book, *Toledo's Peru: Vision and Reality* (University Press of Florida, 2010). His areas of expertise include Andean America, the Middle East, and Southeast Asia.

Prof. David Close, Memorial University of Newfoundland
David Close is Professor of Political Science at the Memorial University of Newfoundland, Canada. He has specialised in Nicaraguan politics for more than 25 years. In that time he has written two books, edited or coedited three others, and produced numerous articles and chapters on the subject.

Dr Ana Covarrubias, Colegio de Mexico
Ana Covarrubias is a faculty member of the Centre for International Studies of El Colegio de México. She obtained her BA in International Relations from El Colegio de México, and an MPhil/DPhil from the University of Oxford. She teaches Latin American international relations,

Mexican foreign policy, and theory of international relations. Her research focuses on Mexican foreign policy, principally toward Cuba and Central America.

Prof. Joaquín Fermandois, Catholic University of Chile

Joaquín Fermandois is currently professor of Contemporary History at the Catholic University of Chile. He obtained his PhD from the University of Seville, and in 1989 he was awarded a prestigious Guggenheim Fellowship. Prof. Fermandois was visiting scholar at Georgetown University, Hamburg University, and the Free University of Berlin. He is the author of *Mundo y fin de mundo. Chile en la política mundial 1900–2004*.

Dr Gian Luca Gardini, University of Bath

Gian Luca Gardini is Lecturer in International Relations and Latin American Politics at the University of Bath, where he is also Deputy Director of the European Research Institute. Dr Gardini obtained his MPhil and PhD in International Relations from the University of Cambridge. His research interests cover the international relations of Latin America, Argentine and Brazilian foreign policy, regional integration, and international relations theory.

Prof. Miriam Gomes Saraiva, University of the State of Rio de Janeiro

Miriam Gomes Saraiva is Professor in International Relations at the University of the State of Rio de Janeiro, Brazil. She did her PhD in Political Science, at the Complutense University, Madrid, and she was visiting fellow at the European University Institute (2002–2003). Her publications and research lie in the field of regional integration and foreign policy.

Prof. Antoni Kapcia, University of Nottingham

Tony Kapcia is currently Professor of Latin American History and Director of the Centre for Research on Cuba (and the Cuba Research Forum) at the University of Nottingham where he is also Head of the Hispanic and Latin American Studies Department. Prof. Kapcia has researched and written on Cuban history and contemporary politics since 1971, and in 1999 he was appointed *Profesor Invitado* at the University of Havana. His research interests focus on Cuban politics in the twentieth century and Cuban revolutionary ideology.

Dr Peter Lambert, University of Bath

Peter Lambert is Senior Lecturer in Latin American Studies at the University of Bath. Having worked in Paraguay as a political researcher for an NGO, he obtained his PhD from the University of the West of

England (UWE), before moving to the University of Bath to set up the Spanish and Latin American Studies program in 2000. He has researched and published extensively on contemporary Paraguayan politics and history, and carried out consultancy work on Paraguay. He was President of the Society for Latin American Studies (SLAS) 2007–2009.

Dr Andrés Malamud, University of Lisbon
Andrés Malamud is currently an assistant research professor at the Institute of Social Sciences of the University of Lisbon. He obtained his PhD in Social and Political Sciences from the European University Institute, Florence. His research interests focus on regional integration, comparative political institutions, and Latin American politics.

Prof. Diana Raby, University of Liverpool
Diana Raby holds the title of Professor Emeritus in History at the University of Toronto, and is currently a Research Fellow in the Institute of Latin American Studies at the University of Liverpool. Her research interests concentrate on contemporary politics in Latin America and in particular on the Bolivarian Revolution in Venezuela. She is the author of *Democracy and Revolution: Latin America and Socialism Today*, published by Pluto Press in 2006.

Prof. Stephen J. Randall, University of Calgary
Stephen J. Randall was Dean, Social Sciences (1994–2006) and is now Professor of History and Director of the Latin American Research Centre. He is the author of more than a dozen books on foreign policy and inter-American relations, including between Colombia and the United States.

IDEOLOGY AND PRAGMATISM IN LATIN AMERICAN FOREIGN POLICY

GIAN LUCA GARDINI AND PETER LAMBERT

SCOPE, AIMS, AND OBJECTIVES OF THE BOOK

The emergence of center-left and left-leaning governments throughout Latin America, the so-called Pink Tide, has been a striking feature of the Latin American political scenario in the first decade of the new millennium. Due to the progressive character and discourse of the majority of current Latin American leaders and governments, one would expect a more assertive approach to foreign policy. Indeed this has been the case, and Latin American foreign policies have become increasingly effective in defense of national interests. Yet, what is striking is the original synthesis between ideology and pragmatism. These two elements are integral components of political behavior in general, but what constitutes an innovative element is the considered and calculated variety in intensity, circumstance, purpose, and arena of the mix of ideology and pragmatism. They appear to coexist well in contemporary Latin American foreign policies, and represent an evident tenet of the highly heterogeneous approach to international relations that characterizes almost all current Latin American administrations.

This book aims to analyze and explain the foreign policy of 11 Latin American countries in light of the perceived tension between ideology and pragmatism. These two elements are used here as conceptual devices to understand apparently contradictory choices and behaviors. For example, the Brazilian government under President Lula Da Silva has presented itself as the champion of the developing world in many international arenas; yet Brazilian positions in multilateral forums coincide more often than not with those of the industrialized world.[1] In spite of President Chavez's strong anti-U.S. rhetoric and several high profile disagreements, ten years of Chavism have not altered the fact that the United States remains Venezuela's foremost commercial partner.[2] These apparent contradictions are not necessarily a sign of incoherence or inconsistency. Instead they reflect a dynamic tension between ideology and pragmatism, the desirable and the achievable. In the current historical phase of transition, this dyad may even represent evidence of diplomatic acumen and autonomy.

The focus of the contributions to this volume is on contemporary administrations and the relevant past. In other words, the intention is to focus on current developments within the past decade or so, but with appropriate attention to the historic context in each country. While the primary objective of the book remains the study of current foreign policy trends, a complementary objective is to understand whether contemporary foreign policies in Latin America represent a clear break from the past or whether certain states have policies that are consistent over time, or indeed whether aspects of change and continuity coexist. The book also intends to analyze trends and tendencies in the present and past in order to look ahead and explore to what extent current choices, decisions, and approaches are contingent or enduring.

We believe that the geographical scope is both ambitious and well focused at the same time. The range of case studies is broad, but does not attempt to be a full coverage of the region. The aim is to cover appropriate case studies in order to outline patterns, comparisons, commonalities, and differences among the foreign policies of the countries analyzed. We feel that although the full coverage of all Latin American countries may have enhanced the descriptive nature of the book, it could also have diluted the analytical force, and the clarity and effectiveness of the arguments. Therefore, the selection of the 11 country case studies (Argentina, Bolivia, Brazil, Chile, Colombia, Cuba, Mexico, Nicaragua, Paraguay, Peru, and Venezuela) is inspired not only by their relative regional importance, but also by their significance to the theoretical model and conceptual tools adopted in the book, both in terms of support for and challenges to our theoretical arguments. Since regionalism is an increasingly important feature in Latin American foreign policy and epitomizes tensions between ideology and pragmatism, the country case studies are complemented by a chapter on competing visions of regional integration in the region.

BETWEEN THEORY AND PRACTICE: ANALYTICAL INSTRUMENTS, IR THEORY, AND AREA STUDIES

The choice to employ the terms *ideology* and *pragmatism* to define and analyze Latin American foreign policies comes from both theoretical discussion and empirical observation. On the theoretical side, political thinkers have long perceived a tension in the conduct of political affairs between the pursuit of ideals on the one hand, and attention to the (practical) consequences of action on the other. Equally, as Max Weber observed, ethically oriented conduct may be guided by "fundamentally differing" maxims, which he termed the "ethic of ultimate ends" and the "ethic of responsibility."[3] By a similar token, equally rational social action can be "value-rational" or "instrumentally rational" oriented.[4] Ideology and pragmatism are in our opinion eye-catching, almost intuitive, labels that capture the aforementioned tensions underpinning much deeper and more profound analyses. Furthermore, after decades of attention to ideological confrontation, International Relations Theory has recently shown a renewed interest in pragmatism, both as a method of enquiry and as a coherent theory of thought and action.[5]

On the more practical and empirical side, ideology and pragmatism are the concepts that in our view best capture, reconcile, and potentially make sense of apparently divergent (and often seemingly incoherent) rationales, agendas, and policies in contemporary Latin American international affairs. What we argue here is not that the use of ideology and pragmatism is new to foreign policy, or more restrictively to Latin America, but that the observable combination of the two elements in the past ten years or so is qualitatively different from the past, and is hence highly characteristic of the administrations currently in power in what has been termed the "Pink Tide." The book aims to investigate the key features and explanatory causes, and hence make sense of the differing combinations of ideology and pragmatism characterizing Latin American foreign policies in the first decade of the twenty-first century.

Indeed, each nation and even regime has combined the two elements in its own way, at times balancing the two, at times with one element prevailing over the other. In a Cold War scenario, for instance, the Argentine military junta (1976–1983) was strongly opposed to communism and leftist subversion in terms of its ideological stance, which it used to justify the infamous "dirty war" at home. Yet, the same regime pragmatically conducted business with the Soviet Union in terms of sales of cereals, which helped delay the impending economic disaster in Argentina and prop up the military. At the apogee of neoliberal triumphalism in the 1990s, all Latin American countries with the exception of Cuba broadly aligned themselves with the agenda and international preferences of the "winners" of the Cold War, the United States. This behavior was certainly the result of the prevailing ideological mood, but contained a significant degree of pragmatism too. Closer relations with the United States were considered the most viable option to pursue national interests in the fields of security, political democratization, and economic recovery and growth.

Paradoxically, since 2000, there appears to be a parallel rise of pragmatism and of ideological discourse, both employed to foster the national interest in a rapidly changing context. Three elements define this shift: the reassertion of Latin American autonomy and nationalism; the concomitant questioning of globalization and U.S. economic and political dominance; and the quest for redefinition of development models and international relations. These conceptual changes open the path to more pragmatic and less constrained international policies, while the various combinations of pragmatism and ideology appear to be employed to confront and challenge the remaining structural obstacles to the realization of these demands.

From the perspective of International Relations Theory, the choice of ideology and pragmatism as analytical lenses may raise some eyebrows. Realists may argue that the relation between ideology and pragmatism in foreign policy is not complementary but rather hierarchical. States are primarily concerned with survival and security, and only secondarily with questions of ideals or ideology. As a consequence, the international conduct of any state would be essentially and invariably pragmatic in the first instance.[6] However, in today's world, and in Latin America in particular, the vast majority of the foreign policy agenda is not concerned with questions of survival, but rather with issues such as economic prosperity, poverty alleviation, quality of democracy, human rights, and regional and multilateral cooperation in spheres other than security—in all of which ideology and pragmatism combine in different ways.

From the opposite end of the theoretical spectrum, constructivists would argue that reality and foreign policy are essentially constructed, stressing how identities, ideas, and values inform even apparently pragmatic behavior.[7] However, the reality of foreign policy practice demonstrates that coming to terms with reality and practical constraints is an exercise in both pragmatic and ideological accommodation, rather than a true paradigm shift or revision.[8] Furthermore, the dichotomy is by no means between value-free pragmatism and value-oriented ideology, as is further explored in Chapter 1.

This book rejects clear-cut, dogmatic theoretical divides. Despite our insistence on a unitary analytical framework, we have sought to embrace the richness that diverse theoretical perspectives bring to our understanding of issues as complex as foreign policy, in the belief that theoretical pluralism is intellectually stimulating, encourages further enquiry and innovative research agendas, and inspires open debate and richer analysis. This is even more important in an edited collection in which individual approaches and contributions are expected to add variety and value to the central research question. However, we would argue that theory needs to be applied to case studies and its propositions need to be grounded in empirical observation, situations, and problems if it is to have a practical value. In short, theory has to be relevant to and reflective of practice.

Although engaging with any single, specific region—such as Latin America—may be difficult and even problematic in terms of general analytical and theoretical categories of political science, it is, as Fred Halliday has argued, both feasible and desirable.[9] Key issues in International Relations such as patterns of relations between states and regions, causes of conflict and cooperation, and the place of ideology in foreign policy, are all relevant to Latin America and to the understanding of its international relations. In turn, the specific problems, issues, and realities of Latin America, such as regional integration, power asymmetries, or foreign policy formation, should be relevant to general IR concerns.

Furthermore, Latin America offers good reasons to justify the search for a "distinctive foreign policy approach" to the region's international relations.[10] Five such reasons stand out: first, the form and pervasiveness of U.S. influence in the region is unique to the Americas and yet, with the exception perhaps of Colombia, Latin America is a region where the impact of 9/11 and the so-called War on Terror has been less strongly felt;[11] second, the spread of the Pink Tide, while peculiar to Latin America, expresses globally felt aspirations and concerns; third, Latin American regionalism, in its singular hemispheric and subcontinental dimensions, is arguably the most sophisticated and enduring outside Europe; fourth, the absence of major international conflicts in the region since 1936 characterizes South America as an unrivaled "zone of peace" in the developing world;[12] and, fifth, with a touch of optimism, Latin America is a region steadily gaining a higher profile in international affairs by virtue of its oil and water resources, its economic and industrial growth, and the growth of its multinational corporations.[13] The idea that Latin America is somehow different from the rest of the world is prevalent within and without the region.[14] For all these reasons we believe that a book on Latin America informed by Foreign Policy Analysis and International Relations concepts and concerns is worth writing—and worth reading.

THE ANALYTICAL FRAMEWORK:
FIVE FACTORS FOR CONSIDERATION

The literature on comparative foreign policy stresses the importance of a unifying conceptual framework in order to analyze and compare foreign policies within a region.[15] Accordingly, the individual case studies of this book are developed within a common analytical framework, which proposes a systematic method to analyze and seek to explain the combination of ideology and pragmatism that different Latin American countries have adopted. Chapter 1 discusses at length the concepts of ideology and pragmatism as applied to foreign policy and provides a working definition of ideological and pragmatic foreign policy. It also analyses in detail five factors that can help us understand how and for what reasons ideology and pragmatism may coexist within a country's foreign policy.

The five factors are intended to serve as tools to explore the possible motives, locate the possible sources, and identify the possible agents of ideology and pragmatism in foreign policy.

(1) **Ends and purposes**: These are the objectives of foreign policy and the implications for the strategy to achieve them. In practical terms, a country that aspires to join the club of global powers, and a country that aspires to challenge the foundations of the existing order, will probably adopt different combinations of ideology and pragmatism. Also, the different audiences, domestic and international, to which foreign policy discourse and action are directed influence the combination of ideological and pragmatic elements.

(2) **Means available**: This refers to the country's capabilities (including traditional attributes of power) and would include the means available for a country to conduct foreign policy. If ideology is the main negotiating asset of a country, it may feature prominently in the resulting foreign policy style.

(3) **Agency**: The stature and quality of leaders and their worldviews and beliefs have a strong impact on foreign policy. As Snyder, Bruck, and Sapin's seminal study persuasively argued, human agency is fundamental in shaping political outcomes.[16] This is especially true in presidential systems, which are characteristic of Latin America. A leader's propensity to seek consensus or to provoke polarization has repercussions on the consistency of foreign policy and its ability to perform in the medium and long term.

(4) **Process**: The ways in which foreign policy is designed, adopted, and implemented, as well as the stakeholders involved in the process, affect the subsequent combination of ideology and pragmatism. This element would also include the rules and timing

of the process, as well as the effects of bureaucratic dynamics and political bargaining.

(5) **Structure**: The specific historical and political, domestic, and international context, clearly influences the use of ideology and pragmatism. The contemporary regional and international systems seem to offer greater variety and fewer constraints to actors, permitting a more favorable context for pragmatism than, for example, the ideological, political, economic, and military dominance and uniformity of the 1990s. As argued by the English School of International Relations, events and episodes have to be contextualized temporally, geographically and politically.[17]

THE DISTINCTIVENESS OF THE BOOK

Our aim has been to produce a volume that combines rigorous historical research with insightful political analysis, to offer a comprehensive and balanced survey of Latin American foreign policies in the new millennium. The book intends to contribute to the advance of knowledge across a number of disciplines (International Relations, Latin American Studies, and Politics) and subdisciplines (Foreign Policy Analysis, specific country politics, and history) on three different planes: analytical and conceptual tools, methodology, and content.

First, the use of the tension between ideology and pragmatism is well established in politics and also foreign policy. However, we have sought an original approach in two senses. First, the tension is applied not only to one case study or bilateral relationship,[18] but to a broad and coherent geographic region to capture the key feature of its foreign policies in a particular historical and political moment. Second, the analytical approach of the book is intended to make sense of this tension by identifying the underlying motives, sources, and agents. Pragmatism and ideology are therefore not only used to analyze current political affairs, but also to analyze longer term political processes.

Second, the methodological approach of this volume is inspired by the English School of International Relations in four major respects. All events occur within a specific historical, geographic, and political context, thus creating the need for contextualization. Both the analytical framework and the case studies thus adopt a historic perspective and method of investigation, in which theoretical systematization and possible conclusions are derived from practice and are not prepacked in order to be later applied to selected episodes. Moreover, the human factor is at the centre of politics, emphasizing the need for interpreting the thoughts and actions of the actors involved in international relations. Finally, both interests and ideas play a central role in politics, thus making necessary the analysis of norms and institutions, as well as the tension between order and justice (or pragmatism and ideology).

Third, this book seeks to offer a comprehensive and systematic overview of foreign policies in contemporary Latin America. In a single volume the reader will find up-to-date material and analysis of contemporary events and debates. The book, however, has a broader scope and potential for interest. The analytical framework provides a unitary and systematic tool for analysis, with the result that the case studies address fundamental questions that are of wider relevance to the complex relationship between ideology and pragmatism in foreign policy. Such questions include:

- Tensions between the genuine national interest and the administration's own objectives.
- Awareness of constraints (and possibilities) in terms of foreign policy due to factors such as size, level of development, and political system, as well as the systemic context.
- Tensions between rhetoric and practice, discourse and action.
- Tensions between change and continuity.
- The extent to which foreign policy stance, rhetoric, and practice are influenced by domestic politics.

This volume also aims to fill a gap in the existing literature in terms of the specific subject and time-frame coverage. Although the literature on foreign policies of specific Latin American countries is relatively abundant, there are only two comprehensive books on Latin American foreign policies, both of which have different scopes and aims from this volume, and cover different historical periods. *Foreign Policy and Regionalism in the Americas* by Mace and Thérien (1996) includes a collection of case studies with a specific focus on the relationship between national foreign policies and integration projects.[19] *Latin American and Caribbean Foreign Policy* by Mora and Hey (2003) is a large volume including 18 country studies and is based on the 3-level of analysis approach.[20] The former established itself as a major reference book on Latin American foreign policy in the early and mid-1990s at the height of pan-americanism and ideas about hemispheric regionalism. The latter is the reference volume for the passage into the new millennium, but importantly its analysis ends before the political shift to the centre-left had become apparent. Our work aims to establish itself as the reference book for the first decade of the twenty-first century with a strongly analytical approach and arguments applied to contemporary (and generally left-leaning) administrations. Our aim is to characterize and define a period, and establish the key areas for debate and research.

This book is the result of a long-term, carefully developed project, which we originally launched in 2007. Since then, ideas and concepts have been discussed with many scholars worldwide and have been presented in panels in two international conferences, namely the 2007 Political Studies Association (PSA) and the 2008 Society for Latin American Studies (SLAS). Feedback has been encouraging, has stimulated debate, and has prompted further discussion and adjustments to the theoretical framework and the contents. This book thus reflects the efforts, contributions, and enthusiasm of a wide group of scholars and students from all around the world over the past three years.

We are confident that a major strength of this book is the quality and variety of its contributors, whom we would like to thank for their commitment and their academic contribution in terms of both their chapters and their input into theoretical debates. All the authors have proven expertise in Latin American politics and an unquestionable passion for and extensive knowledge of the continent. They also reflect a variety of scholarly backgrounds and cultural approaches to Latin America and international politics, and come from different areas of the world, including Latin America, the United States, Canada, Britain, and continental Europe. This variety within a truly international team contributes to the richness of the volume in terms of pluralism, perspective, and analysis. Finally, there is a healthy and balanced mix of promising young scholars and more experienced and established academics and analysts, which we hope makes for a refreshing and fruitful approach to the subject.

The organization of the book follows a broad regional and geographical pattern. It begins with a fuller discussion of the analytical framework outlined above and employed throughout the volume. It then continues with analyses of countries in the Southern Cone, before moving north, through the Andean region and on to the Caribbean Basin, Central America, and Mexico. A chapter on regional integration elaborates on many of the issues previously discussed in the country-specific chapters, and provides an ideal bridge to our conclusions. In the last chapter, we summarize the principle issues, dynamics, and trends that emerge throughout the volume and identify four key conclusions and an open debate for broader and further discussion.

NOTES

1. Alfred P. Montero (2005), *Brazilian Politics*, Cambridge: Polity Press.
2. Miguel Angel Centeno (2008), "Left Behind? Latin America in a Globalized world." *The American Interest*, 3:3, pp. 12–20.

3. Max Weber (1948), "Politics as a Vocation," in H. H. Gerth and C. Wright Mills (eds.), *From Max Weber*, London: Routledge and Kegan Paul, pp. 77–128, 120.
4. Guenther Roth and Claus Wittich (eds.) (1968), *Max Weber. Economy and Society*, New York: Bedminster Press, pp. 24–25.
5. See, for instance, the excellent forum on Pragmatism in International Relations in the September 2009 issue of the International Studies Review: Gunther Hellmann (ed.), "Pragmatism and International Relations," *International Studies Review*, 11:3, pp. 638–62.
6. Stephen Walt (1998), "International Relations: One World, Many Theories," *Foreign Policy*, Spring, pp. 29–46. William C. Wohlforth (2008), "Realism and Foreign Policy," in Steve Smith, Amelia Hadfield, and Timothy Dunne (eds.), *Foreign Policy: Theory, Actors, Cases*, Oxford and New York: Oxford University Press, pp. 31–48.
7. See, for instance, Walt (1998), "International Relations," pp. 40–41. David P. Houghton (2007), "Re-invigorating the Study of Foreign Policy Decision-making: Towards a Constructivist Approach," *Foreign Policy Analysis*, 3:1, pp. 24–45.
8. Ernst Haas (1991), "Collective learning: Some Theoretical Speculations," in George Breslauer and Philip Tetlock (eds.), *Learning in US and Soviet Foreign Policy*, Boulder, CO, and Oxford: Westview Press, pp. 62–99.
9. Fred Halliday (2005), *The Middle East in International Relations. Power, Politics and Ideology*, Cambridge: Cambridge University Press.
10. Ian Manners and Richard G. Whitman (2000), "Introduction," in Ian Manners and Richard G. Whitman (eds.), *The Foreign Policies of European Union Member States*, Manchester and New York: Manchester University Press, pp. 1–16.
11. Russell Crandall (2008), *The United States and Latin America after the Cold War*, New York: Cambridge University Press, p. 247.
12. Arie M. Kacowicz (1998), *Zones of Peace in the Third World: South America and West Africa in Comparative Perspective*, Albany: State University of New York Press, p. 68.
13. According to Antoine Van Agtmael, among the 25 corporations that are most likely to become the leading multinationals in the near future, ten are Latin American. Van Agtmael quoted in Carlo De Benedetti and Federico Rampini (2008), *Centomila Punture di Spillo*, Milano: Mondadori, p. 9.
14. We borrow this quite intuitive but enlightening consideration from Halliday, *The Middle East in International Relations*, p. 14.
15. Ian Manners and Richard G. Whitman, "Introduction"; Raymond Hinnenbusch (2002), "Introduction: The Analytical Framework," in Raymond Hinnenbusch and Anoushivaran Ehteshami (eds.), *The Foreign Policies of Middle East States*, Boulder CO: Lynne Rienner, pp. 1–27; see also, Walter Carlsnaes (1986), *Ideology and Foreign Policy. Problems of Comparative Conceptualization*, Oxford and New York: Basil Blackwell, p. 81.

16. Richard Snyder, H. W. Bruck, and Burton Sapin (1962), "Decision-making as an Approach to the Study of International Politics," in Richard Snyder, H. W. Bruck, and Burton Sapin (eds.), *Foreign Policy Decision-making. An Approach to the Study of International Politics*, New York: The Free Press of Glencoe, pp.14–185.
17. Hedley Bull (1995), "The Theory of International Politics, 1919–1969," in James Der Derian (ed.), *International Theory. Critical Investigations*, Basingstoke and London: Macmillan, pp. 181–211.
18. Jorge I. Dominguez (2007), "Las Relaciones contemporáneas Estados Unidos-América latina. Entre la ideología y el pragmatismo," *Foreign Affairs en Español*, last accessed March 19, 2008: www.foreignaffairs-esp. org.
19. Gordon Mace and Jean-Philippe Thérien (eds.) (1996), *Foreign Policy and Regionalism in the Americas*, Boulder, CO: Lynne Rienner.
20. Frank Mora and Jeanne Hey (eds.) (2003), *Latin American and Caribbean Foreign Policy*, Lanham, MD: Rowman and Littlefield.

CHAPTER 1

LATIN AMERICAN FOREIGN POLICIES BETWEEN IDEOLOGY AND PRAGMATISM: A FRAMEWORK FOR ANALYSIS

GIAN LUCA GARDINI

Ideology and pragmatism are integral components of foreign policy, in fact, of any political activity in the broader sense. Principled beliefs are indispensable lenses through which to view the world, to assess and make sense of events and issues, and to establish goals and preferences. As a consequence, principled beliefs provide selectors of options for action, to translate ideals and political preferences into policy decisions and implementation. When it comes to translating theory into practice, however, feasibility, consequences of action, and constraints of several types must also be taken into consideration, since they too act as selectors of options. The worlds of aspirations and ideals, realities and calculated interest, are part of human nature; they guide human behavior and are therefore present in foreign policy design and implementation.

The argument defended in this chapter and throughout the book is that ideology and pragmatism in foreign policy are complementary, rather than opposite or irreconcilable, terms. Although there is certainly a tension between ideology and pragmatism, they are interrelated and compatible. They are certainly not mutually exclusive. A policy dominated only by ideas would easily turn into a utopian expression, while one guided solely by pragmatism would risk slipping into short-term opportunism at best, and a long-term lack of direction at worst. Any concrete foreign policy bears elements of both, and it is for the chapters that follow to analyze the possible combinations of the two elements in specific case studies.

The more confined and humble mission here is to provide the instruments to read and dissect the foreign policy of a number of Latin American countries in the light of the observable tension between ideological and pragmatic elements. There is no pretension here to formulate mechanisms or models to demonstrate rigid laws governing the relationship between the two. Instead, the goal of this analytical framework is to explore the possible motives, locate the possible sources, and identify the possible agents of ideology and pragmatism in foreign policy. Therefore, the chapter first provides a working definition of ideological and pragmatic foreign policy, and then focuses on five factors that affect the combination of the two.

IDEOLOGY, PRAGMATISM AND FOREIGN POLICY: CONCEPTS AND DEFINITIONS

The notion of ideology, as with many concepts in political science, is controversial, complex, and debatable. Born as a would-be science of ideas, the term ideology was in fact read by Marx as in opposition to science, thus implying a disparaging and unfair association between science and truth on the one hand, and ideology and falsification on the other. Later political theorists, especially from the liberal and conservative camp, have also adopted a pejorative interpretation of ideology. The stronger the acceptance of empiricism, the more critical the conceptualization of ideology.

Non-Marxist theorists have attributed to ideology a number of defining characteristics, including, more rightly, its "persuasive" and "explanatory" force.[1] In other words, ideology often appears or acts as moral imperative and, at the same time, aims to make the world comprehensible to its followers, as opposed to pragmatism that does not advocate either moral imperative or provide an explanation of the world as it is or ought to be. In this sense, ideology can be said to refer to "systems of thought that orientate politics towards abstract principles and goals and away from practical and historical circumstances."[2] The terms ideology and pragmatism are employed here specifically to capture this difference in emphasis. More specifically, ideology is not understood in a derogatory sense, it is not associated with radical, nondemocratic, or totalitarian political views, and it is not placed in hierarchical competition with political theory or political philosophy.

The dichotomous relationship between ideological views of politics or policies on the one hand, and "pragmatic," value-free approaches to them, on the other, is at best misconceived. Values are key to any understanding of all social activities. In a broad sense, "all coherent political doctrines are ideological, as is our use of political ideas themselves."[3] Not only are revolutionary or radical political doctrines ideological, but so are conservatism and liberalism. To a degree, not even pragmatism itself escapes this logic in that its assumptions and judgments are guided by value-oriented preferences. Indeed ideology does not deserve simplistic marginalization in political analysis as value-biased or misleading. Ideologies are "forms of political thought that provide important direct access to comprehending the formation and nature of political theory,"[4] as well as action and practice, one may add, and hence the ideological character of a political doctrine is its "non-negotiable set of beliefs" that direct its practice.[5] Finally, while ideology "straddles the conventional boundaries between descriptive and normative thought and between theory and practice,"[6] pragmatism clearly privileges practice, negotiation, and the descriptive dimension.

The nexus between ideology and pragmatism on the one hand, and foreign policy actions on the other also deserves scrutiny. Ideology and pragmatism are not direct causes of foreign policy. The preeminent function of ideology is to affect the belief system of individuals in the pursuit of political goals. According to Carlsnaes, "Ideologies are by definition not causal factors in the explanation of foreign policy actions [. . .]", but they are, nevertheless, always directly related to values and perceptions, which are in turn causal factors.[7] A certain type of ideology does not necessarily result in the same type of political outcome. If a causal nexus exists, this is indirect and takes place at three levels, with ideology and pragmatism acting as: (a) an analytical prism to make sense of certain situations, (b) a guide for action prescribing policy solutions, and (c) a legitimization or justification of a certain course of action, responding to preset principles or expected consequences.[8] Ideology and pragmatism converge to shape the determinants of foreign policy and are at the same time a manifestation of it.

Politics and International Relations (IR) literature, with reference to Latin America in particular, has abounded with terms apt to capture the tension and sometimes the incongruence between broadly ideological and pragmatic approaches to foreign policy. There is a widespread sense that consideration of ideals and aspirations on the one hand, and their practicality with regard to existing constraints on the other, constitutes a sort of continuum with various intermediate combinations possible. This is reinforced by a solid methodological and empirical tradition in both political and historical disciplines, regarding the tension between ideology and pragmatism. In terms of method, the debate on pragmatism and its perceived opposite was the subject of a special issue of the academic journal *Millennium* in 2002. This perceived opposite was defined as a "fixation with absolute and exclusive [. . .] solutions."[9] Pragmatism instead should constitute an "alley of inquiry into international relations" that "invokes a methodological pluralism and a disciplinary tolerance grounded in the resolute acknowledgement of fallibilism and contingency."[10] While pragmatism privileges "punctual engagement with practice" and complementarity, its opposite, which in this volume we call ideology, emphasizes theoretical solutions and opposition.[11]

Examples of the use of ideology and pragmatism span across time, academic disciplines and schools, geographic backgrounds, and a variety of topics. One analyst suggested that in the conclusion of the 1942 Anglo-Soviet alliance, both Britain and the Soviet Union were driven by "supremely ideological interests," but that their actions were inspired by "a resolute pragmatism."[12] In a search for legitimizing criteria for humanitarian intervention, one scholar employed the terms *pragmatism* and *solidarism*, the latter understood as the underpinning idea/ideology that would confer legitimacy on international humanitarian intervention.[13] Other scholars had recourse to the terms *ideology* and *prudence* in an attempt to lay the social foundations of realism.[14] These authors also argued that ideology tends to prevail only when few consequences are attached to actions, which is rarely the case in international affairs.

Ideology and pragmatism have also been used to describe current U.S.-Latin American relations. Jorge Dominguez described pragmatism as:

> A state policy that identifies clear purposes and well-defined goals, that is carried out with means and instruments specifically aimed at the achievement of these purposes, with the awareness as much of pursuing verifiable benefits as of the possible costs that may be incurred in the pursuit of these benefits.[15]

Conversely, ideology was understood as a mechanism to catalogue, assess, and value information that is a useful instrument to understanding the world we live in.[16] The most undesirable effects of ideological excess were distinct and separate from ideology itself. These were in fact associated with a third category, dogmatism, which is "a mental scheme elaborated at some point in the past [. . .] that is disconnected from current reality, prevents learning of new ideas, acknowledgement of new information and change or modification of existing policies."[17] However, dogmatism can be considered as an excess or a degeneration of both ideology and pragmatism.

Following the lessons drawn from the existing literature, this brings us to a working definition of pragmatism and ideology in foreign policy. A **pragmatic foreign policy** is a foreign policy based on the principle that the usefulness, workability, and practicality of ideas, policies, and proposals are the criteria of their merit. It stresses the priority of action over doctrine, of experience over fixed principles. Strong emphasis is placed on evaluation of assertions and actions according to their practical consequences. A pragmatic foreign policy may be associated with and characterized by medium-term planning and state, rather than government, policy. An **ideological foreign policy** emphasizes principles and doctrinaire solutions over adaptability and the practical consequences of assertions and actions. Compatibility with established principles is the key criterion with which to assess the merit of foreign policy. Although ideological stances are clearly not necessarily dogmatic, a foreign policy based on ideology prioritizes preconceived positions and remedies over their actual viability and usefulness. An ideological foreign policy may be associated with and characterized by relatively short-term planning and a personalized vision of international relations related to a specific leader or administration rather than to a consistent national interest.

Reiterating the concept that elements of both pragmatism and ideology coexist in any concrete foreign policy, the aim here is to look at where the two elements meet, overlap, and interact, and to analyze their output in terms of foreign policy behavior. Ideology and pragmatism are used as qualities or attributes of foreign policy, comprising its conception, formulation, and implementation. Attention therefore now shifts to those factors that may determine or affect their interrelationship and combination. These include the ends and purposes of a given foreign policy, the means available to achieve them, the role of significant individuals, the process through which foreign policy is designed and then implemented, and the historical and political context.

ENDS AND PURPOSES

The aim of a country's external actions and the specific objectives that it intends to pursue affect the employment of pragmatism and ideology in its international positioning. This is as true for objectives in terms of material gains (access to resources, markets) as it is for immaterial ones (prestige, influence). For example, is a given country trying to radically change an internationally concerted policy or even the system, or is it pursuing more recognition or prominence within that system or issue at stake? Or is it in fact struggling only to achieve greater autonomy or bargaining power? Another key dimension in terms of objectives is the recipient of foreign policy. The language and the style employed, as well as the combination of pragmatism and ideology, may vary according to the interlocutor. Is the objective of a given foreign policy to reach and rally internal constituencies, or to galvanize allies, or is it aimed at reassuring neighbors or international institutions?

Evidence suggests that a country whose aim is to gain greater respectability and prominence within an established club will tend to adopt more pragmatic positions, essentially designed to please or appeal to the members of the club, while emphasizing its own agenda within it. Such is the case, for example, of the rise of Brazil to global power status. Brazilian foreign policy has consistently sought a more prominent role for the country in both regional and global arenas, and hence the purpose has not been to radically change those arenas or their principles, but rather to gain status within them in order to advance the Brazilian agenda. If a country intends to become a global power, as Brazil does, it has to accept responsibilities and duties, and avoid, where possible, confrontation lest it jeopardize its bid. Its diplomacy will stress commonalities and complementarities with as many interlocutors as possible and on as many subjects as possible and the country will have to abide by and promote the rules of the club to which it seeks membership. With power comes responsibility, an adage that Hedley Bull incorporated into the English School of International Relations.[18]

The problem with more pragmatic stances is that sooner or later ideological elements enter the fray and force a choice. Brazil has until now stressed its common interests with the United States, its historical and current ties with Europe, and, most recently, its commonalities with the other BRIC countries, Russia, India, and China. The first BRIC ministerial meeting at Yekaterinburg in May 2008 brought to light the ideological preference for change that the BRIC hold with regard to the international order and international institutions.[19] Whether this is compatible with the more conservative and gradual approach of Washington and Brussels remains to be seen, but what has already emerged is a sense of an uncomfortable balancing act that Brazil has to perform in order to present itself as a champion of the underdogs and the poor, and at the same time, a respected and influential member of the most powerful nations. Brazil's identity as one of the former reinforces its claims to the latter, but this ambivalence cannot last forever.

Conversely, a country whose aim is to reject or subvert a given system or course of action may place more emphasis on ideology and assertive behavior, stressing change and confrontation with the existing order and its agents. This is the case of Venezuelan foreign policy under Hugo Chavez, which has aimed to reform the regional system, to purge it from the excess of capitalism, neoliberalism, and the dependence of peripheral countries on the developed nations. With the aim of a deep rupture with the past and to create greater independence from the powerful countries of the North, ideological discourse and confrontational behavior may well be viable options, since more conciliatory approaches may simply reproduce the patterns of domination and asymmetry that the policy seeks to break.

While a broadly speaking ideological stance may be dominant in such cases, elements of pragmatism are not discarded. Chavez's inflamed and at times offensive rhetoric against the United States and President Bush was meant to mark an ideological boundary between good and evil, desirable and unacceptable, while concrete Venezuelan initiatives such as the regional ventures ALBA, *Petrosur, Banco del Sur,* and *Telesur,* represent a counterhegemonic ideological project. However, in order to achieve its ideological and strategic goals, the Chavez administration has not rejected pragmatic tactics. After ten years of *chavismo,* the United States remains the major buyer of Venezuelan oil and the first commercial partner for Caracas.[20] Oil revenues and trade with the United States are indispensable in sustaining the regime and funding its ideological goals and initiatives.

To the extent to which Bolivarian states and their likes can be considered revolutionary states, their behavior is entirely consistent with the theory, history, and practice of what Fred Halliday terms "the antinomies of revolutionary foreign policy."[21] A revolutionary state often adopts a dual foreign policy stance: support for similar regimes or revolutionary movements abroad, but alongside necessary relations with other states. Tensions and contradictions, such as change vs. continuity, revolution vs. counterrevolution, nationalism vs. internationalism, arise in the revolutionary state's conduct at home and abroad. Behind an emphasis on rupture, "aspiration and constraint enduringly interact," while "calculations born of domestic and international considerations affect the form and degree of the challenge to the system."[22] While ends and objectives may tell us something about the prevalence of ideology or pragmatism in foreign policy, either element can in fact be tactically used to foster the other strategically.

This is precisely the case of countries whose foreign policy goal represents a more pragmatic effort to assert their autonomy and role in a context dominated by others, and to extract gains from more powerful neighbors. President Correa of Ecuador has pursued a diplomatic rapprochement with the Bolivarian countries and distanced himself from Washington to give his country greater freedom of maneuver from dependence on the United States and a dollarized economy. While employing a seemingly Bolivarian ideology and at times hyperbolic rhetoric, Correa has also displayed a clear sense of pragmatism. He declared himself ready to reject the bilateral Free Trade Agreement with the United States, which is not yet into force and whose ratification is still pending at the U.S. Senate, but strongly campaigned in favor of the renewal of the U.S. Andean Trade Promotion and Drug Eradication Act (ATPDEA), which actually grants Ecuador vital access to the U.S. market with preferential conditions. Moreover, Ecuador has so far only joined the Chavez-created regional bloc ALBA as an observer, rather than a full member, thus retaining a degree of space for maneuver between Washington and Caracas.

Objectives understood in terms of the intended audience also play a role in defining the combination of pragmatism and ideology. In 2005, President Lula of Brazil addressed both the World Economic Forum gathering of captains of industry and world leaders, and the World Social Forum gathering of antiglobalization activists. While this is a tribute to Brazil's ability to champion diverging interests and to sit quite comfortably on very diverse tables, the speeches delivered by Lula in the two venues bore significant differences, in tone, substance, and emphasis.[23] Interestingly, however, Hugo Chavez's most aggressive verbal attacks against the United States were delivered at national party rallies, as well as (less successfully) before the UN General assembly in 2006, reflecting that at high profile international venues certain ideological excesses may prompt more irritation than solidarity.[24] Both cases highlight how the nature of recipient audiences affects the rhetorical mix of pragmatism and ideology.

THE AVAILABLE MEANS

The resources available to a country to pursue its foreign policy also determine the mix of pragmatism and ideology. Certainly, traditional elements of power, such as size, natural resources, geography, demography, and military and economic capabilities affect the international presence of a country. Although it is difficult to predict toward which direction—ideology or pragmatism—the available assets may lead, a number of examples may provide interesting indications. More industrialized, developed, and wealthier countries may afford more variety in foreign policy options, while limited resources may lead to ideologically driven positions of alignment or rejection. Indeed, ideology itself may be an invaluable asset to the international profile of an otherwise marginal and resource-poor country.

More developed countries with good resources (geographic, demographic, material, and human) will tend to adopt quite pragmatic international positions. This may be for four reasons: first, the possession of the resources necessary for development and status tend to make the country a more satisfied and conservative power; second, the country's assets allow it to enjoy credibility and influence without making ideology a prominent feature; third, an ideological and assertive posture on a global scale may cause more friction than cooperation; and fourth, extensive interests and reach engage the country on several negotiating tables and issues thus providing greater room for maneuver. This eases the management of reward and concessions, which in turn favors pragmatic and flexible stances over nonnegotiable requests. An extensive network of international political and economic connections also increases the price for deviance or defiance.

Brazil exemplifies these considerations. The country has no appetite for disputes, and since 1985 has consistently sought regional cooperation to reinforce its standing and promote its agenda within Latin America and beyond. Although it has maintained a position of autonomy from the United States throughout most of its history, Brazil has long been perceived in Washington as a favorite partner in Latin America for its political and economic weight. Brazil has rarely resorted to fixed ideological positions and has been able to pursue its ideological agenda ("thirldworldism" or social democracy) through pragmatic diplomacy, by virtue of its size, economic power, strategic location, and most recently "soft" power. Its considerable resources facilitate its presence in many international institutions, allowing it greater pragmatic use of leverage through rewards and sanctions to critics and allies, especially at the regional level. A country with less attributes of power than Brazil would probably not be able to afford such eclecticism.

While those with such resources may display a preference for pragmatism, those without may be tempted by a greater emphasis on ideology. This is due to four possible reasons: first, poor or peripheral countries are in pressing need for immediate solutions to urgent problems and hence may not be in a position to pursue the lengthy negotiations and gradual progress that pragmatism generally entails. Second, a vigorously ideological stance is a rapid and cheap way to increase international visibility and potentially, negotiating power. In this sense ideology acts as a supplement to otherwise limited capabilities. Third, for poorer countries there is little to lose from defying the existing order. On the contrary, confrontation may lead to concerns being registered on the international agenda, raising awareness of previously unrecognized needs, claims, and objectives. Fourth, those most adversely affected by the rules of the international system, will often have an ideological criticism of the system and have a genuine desire for change in the rules of the game.

It is probably not a coincidence that it has been some of the poorest countries that have taken the most ideological positions and bold initiatives in twenty-first-century Latin America. Lacking the means to make their voice heard in international forums, Bolivia and Ecuador, for instance, have embraced aspects of the radical Bolivarian agenda of Hugo Chavez, joining Venezuela due to a genuine desire to create a more equitable regional system. However, it is also in their interest to capture international attention and increase their negotiating power with neighbors and other international actors. Conversely, none of the wealthier and more influential countries in South America have joined the Bolivarian initiatives.

A country lacking substantial power may opt to rely more significantly on the support of international allies, or attempt to play them off each other (often adopting appropriate ideological stances) in order to extract as many gains as possible. Historically, Latin American countries with limited power have had a choice to align with the systemic or subsystemic hegemon or to opt for ideological resistance.[25] In the case of alignment, the link between the style and preferences of the dominant and subservient partners is obvious. In the case of resistance, rejection of the hegemon's ideology may prompt the endorsement of the ideology of a counter hegemon. For example, without Venezuelan ideological and material support, Bolivia would hardly be in a position to stand in its current ideological opposition to the United States. Venezuela itself, without its natural resources may not be able to sustain its ideological stance and initiatives. Similarly, Peru and Uruguay, that seem to acquiesce happily in the Brazilian lead on the continent, have adopted Brasilia's preference for pragmatic and negotiated—rather than ideologically based—solutions. In the absence of significant resources, siding with allies and their predominant foreign policy feature—ideology or pragmatism—is both a rational and a likely position.

However, in the absence of significant resources and assets, international partners and allies can also be exploited to one's own advantage by using a calculated mix of ideology and pragmatism. During the Cold War several Latin American countries played the anti-Communist card and exaggerated the threat of subversion in order to obtain better deals and concessions from the United States. Likewise, historically, Paraguay and Uruguay have oscillated between the influence of Brasilia and Buenos Aires in order to improve their position in the Plata Basin system. More recently, both Paraguay and Uruguay, disillusioned by the lack of expected, tangible benefits from membership of Mercosur, sought closer relations with the United States, employing the rhetoric of dissatisfaction and the threat to switch ideological camps in order to force Argentina and Brazil to offer greater concessions within Mercosur. Precisely because a U.S. free trade area with either country would prejudice the entire Mercosur project, the bargaining power of both small countries increased.

Finally, ideology can be a resource in itself. The attention that Cuba has received in the last fifty years is largely due to its ideological stance. Were it not for that, Cuba's strategic position alone would not have been sufficient to generate so much attention and Cuban foreign policy would have undoubtedly remained off the list of U.S. priorities. However, while weak countries may generally be more attracted to ideological postures than powerful states, there is nothing deterministic in this and it does not entirely explain the mix of ideology and pragmatism. Instead, human agency and the particular qualities of a country's leaders are further, often crucial, variables in explaining foreign policy

AGENCY AND THE HUMAN FACTOR

The beliefs, perceptions, and individual preferences of decision makers have a paramount impact on the mix of ideology and pragmatism informing the external relations of a country, since these individuals formulate and implement foreign policy. The relationship between agency and structure goes two ways, and while structures certainly affect individual perceptions and behaviors, individuals can drastically affect structures and policy outcomes. As Robert Kennedy recalled in his memoirs of the 1962 Cuban missile crisis, President John Kennedy sought advice from some thirty of the most competent and brilliant personalities in the U.S. administration, but if six of them had been president instead of JFK the crisis would have resulted in nuclear war.[26] The purpose of this section is therefore to explore how, through what processes or mechanisms this occurs.

To argue that the international environment fully accounts for a state's behavior implies, implicitly or explicitly, that all states endowed with comparable capabilities react similarly to the same objective external circumstances, an argument that is simply not sustained by historical evidence. Robert Jervis, a pioneer of cognitive approaches to international politics, maintains that individual perceptions may explain a number of aspects of international politics.[27] Indeed, the quality and perceptions of the political leadership may well account for differences in the international behavior of states, which cannot be explained solely in the light of national or international constraints.[28]

Recent studies have demonstrated how the quality of national elites can affect the fate of a nation.[29] One could hardly imagine Venezuela taking such vociferous and bold positions were it not for the ideological orientation emanating from Hugo Chavez's personal convictions. A similar argument can be made for Bolivia and Evo Morales. Lula's charisma and personal background have made him an example both for the international financial sector and antiglobalization protestors, an almost unique status in contemporary world politics. On the other hand, in the case of Chile, socialist leaders such as Ricardo Lagos and Michelle Bachelet have retained the same foreign policy model despite neoliberalism being the legacy of its authoritarian past under General Pinochet.

Goldstein and Keohane have identified three possible pathways to explore how the ideas and beliefs of individual leaders affect foreign policy.[30] First, ideas provide road maps to interpret reality and select a limited set of desired outcomes among the many possible. Second, in the absence of a unique or clearly defined course of action, ideas orientate decision makers' strategic choices. Finally, once ideas are institutionalized in a consolidated set of norms and rules, they define policy in the absence of further innovation. Adopting this theory and applying it to the relationship between ideology and pragmatism, the relationship between individual leaders' predispositions toward ideology or pragmatism may translate into policy, affecting its nature and style.

Two examples clarify this. First, Hugo Chavez's ideas strongly associate the historic role of the United States with the current problems of Latin America. This forms a road map, providing a range of options in terms of reaction to U.S. actions. In the wake of the 2008 Colombian attacks on FARC guerrillas in Ecuadorian territory, Chavez adhered to his ideological position and immediately condemned both Colombia and the United States, despite the lack of concrete evidence of the latter's involvement. Indeed, it may be argued that anti-Americanism has become an embedded guiding norm in Venezuela's foreign policy, due to the ideological position of its president.

Second, following the 2001 crisis in Argentina, President Kirchner aimed to prioritize the recovery of production and employment above any ideological stance on foreign policy. In the absence of immediately clear solutions, Kirchner's pragmatic style informed Argentina's international action, leading to odd but pragmatically calculated choices, such as the acceptance of assistance from Venezuela and the rejection of traditional partners such as the IMF and Italy. This stance became the rule of Argentina's foreign policy until economic stability was regained. While the process of translation of ideas into action followed similar paths in the two cases, in the absence of obvious solutions, Chavez adhered to ideological convictions, whilst Kirchner pragmatically assessed options.

THE FOREIGN POLICY PROCESS

The process through which foreign policy is designed, adopted, and implemented is as important as the output[31] and affects the mix of ideology and pragmatism. The process not only places constraints on the available options and possible actions, but also influences the very way in which people think and act. For example: the presence of a charismatic leader may affect the behavior of advisors; respect for institutional procedures may bring into play additional issues or delay decisions; too much or too little information may prompt decision makers to rely on reassuring ideological behavior; or time pressure may engender "gut feelings" and ideological decisions.[32] Regime type, the openness of the decision-making process, the role and power of different national and international stakeholders, the weight of domestic considerations, and the issues at stake, all deserve scrutiny.

The extensiveness and inclusiveness of the foreign policy-making process may influence the mix of pragmatism and ideology. Processes that are inclusive and open to several voices, including dissent, seem to produce effective, consistent, and well-grounded foreign policy. Highly professionalized decision-making structures, characterized by competence and experience, are more likely to select information efficiently and objectively. Also, the wider the support for a policy, the easier and more consistent its implementation becomes. All of these examples relate to pragmatism and fit the case of Brazil. Brazilian foreign policy is devised and conducted by the president, in close cooperation with the foreign ministry, Itamaraty, a highly professionalized body with a reputation for efficiency, and is relatively open to civil society input. It is no surprise that Brazilian foreign policy has enjoyed a high degree of consistency, pragmatism, and ultimately success.

On the other hand, restricted, inaccessible, and exclusive decision-making processes seem to produce less than desirable effects, and "group think" studies have highlighted distortions that may occur when small, cohesive, and insulated elites take decisions.[33] The group may display an inclination toward emotional responses, uniformity, and a proclivity to support the leader, or preserve the group unity. The selection of information may be biased leading to the consideration only of those options that conform to the dominant or established view. Newcomers to power may suffer from an additional "new group syndrome" as they strive for success, often through change.[34] These findings fit what we have defined here as ideological foreign policy. The symptoms seem to match the cases of Chavez and Morales among others. Both rely on a restricted circle of trusted and like-minded advisors, both came to power as newcomers and nonprofessional politicians and were eager to emphasize and implement political change, and were hungry for high profile success.

Foreign policy is rarely confined to presidential circles. In democratic regimes policy decisions involve several state agencies and may require delicate political negotiations between government and opposition, executive and civil service, or among coalition parties. In the presence of complex state machines, the definition and implementation of foreign policy is the result of *organizational processes*—the interactions between state departments and their own interests, cultures, and agendas—and *bureaucratic politics*—the political bargaining between stakeholders in a given issue.[35] In these instances, rather than decisions as winning positions, policy outcomes are the end product of compromise and incremental change. Thus, bureaucratic and political apparatuses are crucial to an understanding of the motives, sources, and agents of ideology and pragmatism in modern states.

Two examples clarify the dynamics of organizational processes and bureaucratic politics. When Argentine-Brazilian integration was first discussed in the mid-1980s, there was consensus in Brasilia on the principle, but divergence on the practical measures. The Customs Policy Committee within the Ministry of the Economy was in favor of a pragmatic compromise with the Argentines, while the Agency for External Trade initially displayed a more ideologically protectionist stance.[36] The different attitudes stemmed from different organizational cultures and interests and the deal eventually struck with the Argentines was the result of compromise within the Brazilian delegation.[37] Chile's international projection as an international commercial power characterized the foreign policy of the *Concertación* government, whether headed by the Christian Democrats or the Socialists. Such consistency is even more striking if one considers that it dates back to the Pinochet years. Such consistency was possible due to a widely shared (and highly pragmatic) consensus, spanning across the political spectrum and Chilean civil society,[38] regarding the desirable international identity of Chile.

If foreign policy is often the continuation of domestic politics with other means,[39] then the impact of domestic divisions and debates clearly has an impact on the mix of ideology and pragmatism in foreign policy, and may focus domestic attention onto foreign policy issues. For example, ongoing negotiations on migration with the United States attract significant domestic attention in Mexico. Whilst national sensitivity may lead to more emotional and ideological response, the larger the number of stakeholders the more negotiated and pragmatic the policy outcome will usually be, especially on vital international issues.[40]

Moreover, the role of foreign actors may play a dual role in such situations. For example, strong U.S. positions on migration in Mexico or drug trafficking in Colombia or Bolivia, may cause irritation and an ideological resistance based on claims to national autonomy, or they may encourage more contained and pragmatic reactions. While foreign NGOs, governments, media, and commercial interests may influence a country's domestic decisions, foreign actors do not tend to make decisions in sovereign states.[41] Ultimately, therefore, the combination of ideology and pragmatism in foreign policy may be externally influenced, but it is adopted by internal decision makers, who ultimately bear responsibility for the choice.

THE HISTORICAL AND POLITICAL CONTEXT

Events and episodes occur within a historical and political context. Domestically, national character, history, and institutions affect international conduct. Internationally, Neorealists argue that the configuration of the international system has an impact on the interactions between its units,[42] while others maintain that the influence of the system depends on the reading that actors make of it.[43] Nevertheless there is a shared view that the context offers both opportunities and constraints. The structure within which foreign policy takes place may play a significant role in determining the mix of ideology and pragmatism.

On the domestic plane, regime type, institutional arrangements and procedures as well as national character or culture deserve exploration. While the former two elements relate more to the process of foreign policy formation, the focus here is on how national culture, history, and identity shape foreign policy postures. For instance, attitudes toward otherness define a nation, as exemplified by the ambivalent relation of Latin America with the United States. "Natural role conception"[44] can shape perceptions and self-perceptions, thus directing foreign policy attitudes toward more ideological or pragmatic behavior, as witnessed in the cases of the United States and Brazil.[45] Ultimately, however, culture is not in itself a cause of foreign policy behavior. Instead the point is rather who draws what ideas, how and for what purposes or agendas.[46] This takes the discussion back to issues of goals and agency in foreign policy.

A further factor strongly influencing foreign policy, is that of nationalism, on the rise throughout Latin America and which may well affect the combination of ideology and pragmatism in foreign policy. On a global level, nationalism has consistently been accompanied by a more assertive foreign policy, informed by strongly ideological elements and the defense of national sovereignty and national interests. Ideologically, nationalism has been diverse and multifaceted, embodying a "cluster of perspectives," but essentially taking two main forms: either narrow, tribalist, bellicose, and potentially totalitarian, or attached to a sense of emancipation and civic liberation.[47] In contemporary Latin America the latter clearly prevails.

Nonetheless, its consequences for foreign policy are complex. The links between group, identity, culture, and allegiance that underpin nationalist ideology(ies) are being redefined. Latin America's rising assertiveness has in fact at least three dimensions: subnational (indigenous nations and marginalized communities seeking liberation from exclusion or elite domination), national (state sovereignty to counter external pressures), and regional (Latin America as a unity, especially in opposition to the United States and global change). The reconciliation of these dimensions poses challenges for the state itself, the elaboration of its foreign policy, and the regional integration projects supported by states. The prominence and management of these aspects and the tensions they may generate (nationalism vs. regionalism) produce diverse combinations of ideology and pragmatism in foreign policy and most of all in the possible construction of regional unity.

On the international plane, several studies have pointed to a correlation between the structure of the system, the rules for interaction within it, and a predisposition toward ideology or pragmatism. Different rules and working principles characterize different international system configurations. For example, in a balance of power system, as was in place until World War I and possibly today after the end of the U.S. unipolarity, alliances depend on advantage and hence states would tend to give priority to advantages and interests over ideology, at least in term of alliances. In the bipolar system of the Cold War, relations tended to rest more on ideology.[48] The prevalence of pragmatism in today's Latin American foreign policies could be explained by the end of U.S. unipolarity, the growing number of competing powers in the international system, and the increased number of solutions that this offers to all countries.

There is also an additional, related, and complementary explanation. The increase in the number of significant actors entails an increase in the number and nature of interests and thus contested issues on the international agenda. This has an impact on the mix of ideology and pragmatism. The greater the number of issues contested in the international system, the greater the degree of bargaining behavior in foreign policy and the lower the level of ideological intransigence.[49] This further explains the prevailing pragmatism of Latin American foreign policies in today's multipolarity. More influential actors provide not only a variety of ideological options, but also of issues for contestation and hence greater potential for cross-issue alliances. This in turn creates greater interdependence, increasing the costs of confrontation, and raising the attractiveness of international diplomacy.

Accepting this argument, one may ask what happens under conditions of unipolarity. Logic would have it that with only one dominant power in the system, the international agenda is reduced to that of the hegemon. In this case, ideological behavior in foreign policy would reach its peak, promoting wide acceptance of the hegemon's ideology along with greater ideological uniformity (whether imposed or not) and less ideological opposition. This was largely the case in the mid-1990s when post–Cold War euphoria and the generalized acceptance of the U.S. ideology of electoral democracy and free markets permeated the whole of Latin America. In a sense, ideology and pragmatism coincided, since no alternative option seemed to be available. The most pragmatic stance therefore became ideological alignment. Indeed the only Latin American contribution to IR Theory in that period, *realismo periférico*, preached exactly this kind of behavior.[50]

Historical phases of upheaval, fragmentation, or centralization, in other words of system transition, also impact upon foreign policy choices. George Modelski has argued that the international system experiences cycles of change every 120 years, including four phases of global war and emergence of new power(s), world power, delegitimization of world power, and finally deconcentration of power to other actors.[51] Foreign policy predispositions may derive from the specific phase of the cycle.[52] Following this reading, the end of the Cold War and the 1990s represented the apogee of U.S. power, resulting in ideological conformity. Such a reading would also suggest that we are currently between the delegitimization and the deconcentration phase; U.S. power and values are increasingly under question. Ideology and pragmatism coexist, the former challenges and delegitimizes established power, the latter grabs the opportunities decentralization offers.

CONCLUSION

Identifying factors affecting foreign policy is not the same thing as tracing their influence.[53] The acknowledgement that ideological and pragmatic elements shape foreign policy does not equate to understanding how they interact or to establishing under which conditions one may prevail over the other. The variables are so many, so complex, and so interrelated that a convincing explanation can only be sought in specific case studies and limited periods of time. Accordingly, the purpose and task of this analytical framework was to explore the possible motives, locate the possible sources and identify the possible agents of ideology and pragmatism in foreign policy. It is the task of the chapters ahead to comprehend and make sense of the rise of pragmatism and the parallel surge of ideology in the foreign policy of specific countries.

With no pretension of being exhaustive, a number of factors were singled out as determinants of either ideology or pragmatism (or both), depending on their combination with other variables. The objectives of a country's international presence may influence the means employed to attain them, in terms of not only strategy and gains, but also in terms of the different audiences that may be the target of foreign policy discourse and action. The resources available for the conduct of foreign policy may also have an impact upon the form and style policy may take, while the ideas, beliefs, predispositions, and personal and professional skills of influential individuals greatly contribute to the formulation and implementation of foreign policy. Finally, the political and historical context, both domestic and international, offers opportunities and constraints to foreign policy styles and options.

Of course, the tension between pragmatism and ideology underlies other tensions in national and international politics. More often than not, choices regarding ideology and pragmatism are dependent on discourse and practice, as well as domestic and international audiences and issues. Significantly, however, although the influence of domestic politics on international relations remains significant, it would appear that the difference between the two spheres is becoming more blurred, leaving space for "intermestic politics," the intersection between national and international interests, issues, and actors.[54]

In such a complex and interconnected reality, the traditional foreign policy analysis distinction between levels of analysis seems to lose some of its explanatory power and perhaps does not capture the empirical picture satisfactorily. For instance, factors that explain or determine the mix of ideology and pragmatism in foreign policy can no longer simply be artificially categorized into individual, national, or international levels. More flexible categories and analytical concepts, suitable for crosslevel analysis, would appear to us to be more appropriate and useful, and therefore have been proposed in this volume. This may be welcomed or criticized, but its aim is to stimulate debate over whether foreign policy analysis should move toward a more specialized, self-contained, and compartmentalized approach on the one hand, or whether it should pursue a more holistic and pluralistic method and agenda on the other; or indeed if a combination of the two is possible.

NOTES

1. Barbara Goodwin (2003), *Using Political Ideas*, Chichester: Wiley, p. 22.
2. Andrew Heywood (2000), *Key Concepts in Politics*, Basingstoke: Palgrave Macmillan, p. 23.
3. Goodwin, *Using Political Ideas*, p. 17.
4. Michael Freeden (1996), *Ideologies and Political Theory: A Conceptual Approach*, Oxford: Oxford University Press, p. 1.
5. Michael Freeden (2001), "Political Ideologies in Substance and Method," in Michael Freeden (ed.), *Reassessing Political Ideologies*, London and New York: Routledge, pp. 1–12, 7.
6. Heywood, *Key Concepts in Politics*, p. 22.
7. Walter Carlsnaes (1986), *Ideology and Foreign Policy. Problems of Comparative Conceptualization*, Oxford and New York: Basil Blackwell, p. 180.
8. See ibid., p. 168.
9. Harry Bauer and Elisabetta Brighi (July 2002), "Editorial note," *Millennium*, 31:3, p. iii.
10. Ibid., p. iii.
11. Ibid.
12. Ennio Di Nolfo (2000), *Storia delle Relazioni Internazionali, 1918–1999*, Bari: Editori Laterza, pp. 427–28.
13. Alex J. Bellamy (July 2002), "Pragmatic Solidarism and the Dilemmas of Humanitarian Intervention," *Millennium*, 31:3, pp. 473–97.
14. T. V. Paul and J. Hall (eds.) (1999), *International Order and the Future of World Politics*, Cambridge: Cambridge University Press, pp. 69–71.
15. Jorge Dominguez (2007), "Las relaciones contemporáneas Estados Unidos-América Latina. Entre la ideología y el pragmatismo," *Foreign Affairs en Español*, October–December, http://www.foreignaffairs-esp.org, last accessed March 19, 2008.
16. Ibid.
17. Ibid, p. 3
18. See Hedley Bull (1977), *The Anarchical Society: A Study of Order in World Politics*, Basingstoke: Macmillan.
19. On the occasion, Brazilian Foreign Minister Celso Amorim declared: "We are changing the way the world order is organised," quoted in Vladimir Radyuhin (2008), "For a New Order," *Frontline*, 25:12, 7–20 June, http://www.hinduonnet.com/fline/fl2512/stories/20080620251205200.htm, last accessed March 5, 2009.
20. Miguel Angel Centeno (2008), "Left Behind? Latin America in a Globalized World," *The American Interest*, 3:3, pp.12–20.
21. Fred Halliday (1999), *Revolution and World Politics*, Basingstoke: Macmillan, pp. 133–57.
22. Ibid., p. 156.
23. Compare the speeches given by Lula at the World Economic Forum on January 28, 2005 (http://www.weforum.org/en/knowledge/

KN_SESS_SUMM_13926?url=/en/knowledge/KN_SESS_SUMM_ 13926, last accessed March 5, 2009) and at the World Social Forum just two days earlier on January 26, 2005 (http://news.bbc.co.uk/1/hi/ business/4213987.stm, last accessed March 5, 2009).

24. On the back of that experience, during the 2008 Ecuador-Colombia crisis Chavez adopted a stark anti-Colombian stance at home but a much more conciliatory attitude at the international Summit of the Group of Rio.

25. Peter H. Smith (2000), *Talons of the Eagle. Dynamics of US-Latin American Relations*, Oxford and New York: Oxford University Press.

26. Robert F. Kennedy (1999), *Thirteen Days. A Memoir of the Cuban Missile Crisis*, New York: Norton Company, pp. 14–15.

27. Ibid.

28. Fore a more extensive discussion on the topic, see R. Jervis (1976), *Perception and Misperception in International Politics*, Princeton: Princeton University Press; Chih-yu Shih (1992), "Seeking Common Causal Maps: A Cognitive Approach to International Organization," in Martha L. Cottam and Chih-yu Shih (eds.), *Contending Dramas. A Cognitive Approach to International Organizations*, New York, Westport, CT, and London: Praeger, pp. 39–56; Martha L. Cottam (1994), *Images and Intervention. U.S. Policies in Latin America*, Pittsburgh and London: University of Pittsburgh Press.

29. For Latin America, see Michael Reid (2007), *Forgotten Continent, The Battle for Latin America's Soul*, New Haven and London: Yale University Press. For Africa, Martin Meredith (2005), *The State of Africa. A History of Fifty Years of Independence*, London: The Free Press.

30. Judith Goldstein and Robert O. Keohane (1993), "Ideas and Foreign Policy: An Analytical Framework," in Judith Goldstein and Robert O. Keohane (eds.), *Ideas and Foreign Policy. Beliefs, Institutions, and Political Change*, Ithaca, NY, and London: Cornell University Press.

31. Valerie Hudson (2007), *Foreign Policy Analysis. Classic and Contemporary Theory*, Lanham and Plymouth: Rowman and Littlefield, p. 17.

32. Ibid, p. 50.

33. Irving L. Janis (1982), *Groupthink*, Boston: Houghton Mifflin.

34. Erik K. Stern (1997), "Probing the Plausibility of New Group Syndrome: Kennedy and the Bay of Pigs," in Paul 't Hart, Erik K. Stern, and Bengt Sundelius (eds.), *Beyond Groupthink: Political Group Dynamics and Foreign Policy-Making*, Ann Arbor: University of Michigan Press, pp. 153–90.

35. Graham Allison and Philip Zelikow (1999), *Essence of Decision. Explaining the Cuban Missile Crisis*, New York: Longman.

36. José Tavares de Araujo, Head of the Customs Policy Committee in 1986, interview with the author, Brasilia May 19, 2003; Roberto Fendt, Head of the External Trade Agency in 1986, interview with the author, Rio de Janeiro, June 11, 2003.

37. Gian Luca Gardini (2005), "The Hidden Diplomatic History of Argentine-Brazilian Bilateral Integration: Implications for Historiography

and Theory," *The Canadian Journal of Latin American and Caribbean Studies*, 30:60, pp. 63–92.

38. Simon Collier and William F. Sater (2004), *A History of Chile, 1808–2002*, Cambridge: Cambridge University Press.

39. Hudson, *Foreign Policy Analysis*, p. 125.

40. Ibid.

41. Robert Putnam (1988), "Diplomacy and Domestic Politics: The Logic of Two-Level Games," *International Organization*, 42:3, pp. 427–60.

42. Kenneth Waltz (1979), *Theory of International Politics*, Reading: Addison Wesley.

43. Alexander Wendt (1992), "Anarchy Is What States Make of It: The Social Construction of Power Politics," *International Organization*, 46:2, pp. 391–425.

44. Kal J. Holsti (1970), "National Role Conceptions in the Study of Foreign Policy," *International Studies Quarterly*, 14, pp. 233–309.

45. For the United States, see Smith, *Talons of the Eagle*. For Brazil, see Celso Lafer (2002), *La Identidad Internacional de Brasil*, Buenos Aires: Fondo de Cultura Economica.

46. Hudson, *Foreign Policy Analysis*, p. 121.

47. Andrew Vincent (2001), "Power and Vacuity. Nationalist Ideology in the Twentieth Century," in Michael Freeden (ed.), *Reassessing Political Ideologies*, pp. 132–53, 133.

48. Morton Kaplan (1957), *System and Process in International Politics*, New York: Wiley; Morton Kaplan (1972), "Variants on Six Models of the International System," in James Rosenau (ed.), *International Politics and Foreign Policy*, Glencoe: Free Press of Glencoe, pp. 291–303.

49. Maurice East, Stephen Salmore, and Charles Hermann (eds.) (1978), *Why Nations Act*, Beverly Hills: Sage.

50. Carlos Escudé (1997), *Foreign Policy Theory in Menem's Argentina*, Gainesville: University of Florida Press.

51. George Modelski (1981), "Long Cycles, Kondratieffs, and Alternating Innovations," in Charles Kegley and P. McGowan (eds.), *The Political Economy of Foreign Policy Behaviour*, Beverly Hills: Sage, pp. 63–83.

52. Ibid.

53. James Rosenau (1966), "Pre-Theories and Theories of Foreign Policy," in Barry Farrell (ed.), *Approaches in Comparative and International Politics*, Evanston: Northwestern University Press.

54. Russell Crandall (2008), *The United States and Latin America after the Cold War*, Cambridge: Cambridge University Press.

CHAPTER 2

PRAGMATISM, IDEOLOGY, AND TRADITION IN CHILEAN FOREIGN POLICY SINCE 1990*

JOAQUÍN FERMANDOIS

INTRODUCTION: MAIN HISTORICAL TRAITS

Chile has been widely recognized as having adopted a pragmatist approach to foreign relations since the return of democracy in March 1990. This appreciation is based on the "economization" of its foreign policy, since one of the main traits of the international orientation of the country has been the acceptation of "globalization," understood as economic dynamism beyond borders. In the atmosphere of the 1990s, this orientation converged with the policies and ideology of the United States and other industrialized economies, in terms of further opening its economy, pursuing free-trade agreements, and in participating in international accords on a "post-international system." This policy reached one of its goals in the first decade of the twenty-first century, with the signing of multiple free-trade treaties, although by then, the regional economic consensus was already waning.

Throughout the history of Chilean foreign policy two traits are clear. One of them is the legacy of nineteenth century territorial conflicts with neighboring countries, with which Chile is still dealing. As essentially interstate disputes, they have demanded a "realist" approach, couched in legal discourse. The second trait, especially visible from the 1920s onward, consists of the development of a foreign policy within the framework of the Inter-American system, including Latin American cooperation and integration. However, this approach has always been based on the understanding that the fundamental interests of the country are at least convergent with those of the international and regional systems.

Identification with the West was a dominant feature of the Cold War years, at least until 1970, but what the "West" meant was interpreted in different ways, depending on the focus of different political discourses. The Chilean left, a key actor in the political system, identified the West with "capitalism" and "imperialism," and thus the Popular Unity government of Salvador Allende (1970–1973) set out a foreign policy that was strategically directed against the "imperialism" of the United States, and sought improved relations with other anti-imperialist allies, such as Cuba. This was clearly an ideological approach, yet tactically the foreign policy of Popular Unity was highly pragmatic in its relations with the rest of Latin America, including with right-wing military regimes in Argentina and Brazil and, especially, with Western Europe.[1]

The military regime of Augusto Pinochet (1973–1990) was characterized by a fervent anti-Communist sentiment, which provided the setting for its foreign policy. Yet this was not a decision taken solely by Pinochet. The Popular Unity government had been viewed with tolerance if not outright sympathy in many Latin American and Western European countries (as well as by the liberal academic public in the United States), and its violent overthrow and the subsequent establishment of an indefinite military dictatorship, received worldwide condemnation. Anti-Communism provided a sustaining ideology for the regime, as well as an ideological platform for regional and U.S. support. Despite this, by the mid-1980s, the military regime was suffering a degree of international isolation unprecedented in the history of twentieth century Latin American states.[2]

Pinochet's foreign policy was ideological in its anti-Communism, reflecting the ideological nature of the regime itself. The regime, however, was not simply anti-Communist, and indeed oversaw a period of economic modernization and insertion into the world market economy, which in itself offered an ideological (as well as pragmatic) position in terms of economic development. Despite uneven growth, by the end of the 1980s, the "Chilean model" was considered an economic success and became a forerunner of the neoliberal economic reforms of the so-called Washington consensus in the 1990s.

This combination of pragmatism and ideology was not only maintained but was reinforced by the center-left Concertación governments in its two decades of power. While there was a degree of change in foreign policy reflecting domestic pressures, Chile remains dedicated to a highly pragmatic foreign policy that reflects an ideological framework of adherence to liberal democracy, the international framework of law and free-market economics.

SOURCES OF FOREIGN POLICY
IN THE NEW DEMOCRACY

What can we consider were the "sources" of the new Chilean foreign relations since 1990?[3] First, the transition to democracy led to a critique of the Pinochet regime, and especially the role of human rights violations against its opponents. This was related to the second source, the consensus around a definition of democracy. The end of the Cold War had been preceded in Chile by a consensus between Right and Left on issues of both human rights and democracy, as the Left dropped more radical or revolutionary interpretations of both in the 1980s and instead adopted a more social democratic position, with which the Right felt it could coexist.

A third source is directly intertwined with the latter. Accompanying the convergence between Right and Left on the political system, and the legitimacy of liberal democracy, was a rejection of the polarized politics of the Cold War (even before the collapse of the Soviet Union). Following the 1988 plebiscite in which Pinochet was defeated, and the ensuing negotiations between government and opposition, the electoral victory of the Concertación led to a broad consensus on common principles in politics and the economy.

A fourth source of the foreign policy of the Concertación years was of course the end of the Cold War and the new international pressure for the coupling of electoral democracy with market economics. As a result, there was both an internal and external consensus, or at least common ground, in terms of the rules of the game. In this context, the reversal of previous diplomatic isolation was a relatively easy objective to achieve.

A fifth source, a consequence of the end of the Cold War, was the changing political scenario in Latin America related to "re-democratization" (of which Chile was the last case). In this environment, Chile was keen to become a model of transition (as well as end its historical isolation), and hence pursued centrist, "normal" policies that combined (almost interchangeably) ideology and pragmatism.

Finally, a sixth and final source of the new foreign policy was the experience of its political class, which sought a strong influence in terms of agency. The period of the dictatorship was not static or inactive in terms of political debate and analysis. From the late 1970s to the late 1980s there had been a rich exchange of ideas with new international intellectual currents, resulting in an "internationalized" political class, especially in terms of the Centre and Left, many of whom had experience of exile and very different worldviews. Concertación saw in European social democracy a path away from the polarized ideological confrontation that had characterized domestic Chilean politics in the 1960s and 1970s, and a model around which to construct a broad consensus on a "Western model" for Chilean politics and society.

CONCERTACIÓN'S GOALS AND PRACTICE IN THE 1990S

The foreign policy program of the Concertación, written in 1988–1989, showed a clear language of "democratic internationalism," as well as underlining the interests of the country and the goal of reducing foreign "dependence."[4] This produced a situation wherein a very pragmatic policy could be envisioned, without formally negating a principled or ideological orientation. Breaking the international isolation that the country suffered under the Pinochet regime, and promoting democracy and human rights protection, within a Latin America orientation, were indeed the main electoral promises of Patricio Aylwin.

The inauguration of the democratically elected President Aylwin on March 11, 1990, dissolved in one stroke the international isolation that Chile had suffered under Pinochet. In the following two decades, two phases—each roughly a decade long—are visible in terms of foreign policy. The first phase, from 1990 to 1999, included the first two governments of the Concertación (Patricio Aylwin [1990–1994] and Eduardo Frei [1994–2000]). In this phase there appeared to be no contradiction between a pragmatic and an ideological approach to foreign relations. The second phase from 2000 to 2010 (comprising the governments of Ricardo Lagos [2000–2006] and Michelle Bachelet [2006–2010]) was characterized by a more problematic relationship between pragmatic and ideological approaches, especially in terms of relations with the United States. However, despite some conflict of interests, there has been a remarkable continuity in terms of the continuing convergence of ideology and pragmatism.

The government of Eduardo Frei emphasized a pragmatic approach. His first foreign minister, Carlos Figueroa, talked of the importance of "diplomacy for development,"[5] and that Chile had ceased to be a "beggar Nation,"[6] while in his first message, President Frei placed Chile's foreign policy priority as "the deepening of international relations."[7] Of course, there was also an accompanying ideological element to foreign policy; the Frei government emphasized the importance of developing democratic stability in Latin America,[8] stating in the Río de Janeiro Summit of 1996, that "democracy and human rights are now indivisible in the world of today, and that they are set above national self-determination."[9]

This dual approach was relatively easy to sustain during most of the 1990s, but with the detention of General Pinochet in London in October 1998, Chilean foreign relations were placed in an awkward, unexpected, and ironic situation. Faced with almost universal international criticism, Foreign Minister Insulza expressed the government's dilemma as follows:

> Whether we like it or not, this is a matter of national sovereignty. It is especially painful when the individual concerned is Pinochet, but if we surrender the legislative, governmental and judicial powers of the democratic State of Chile, we are abdicating our duties as a sovereignty State.[10]

This essentially pragmatic approach was very efficient in many fields of foreign relations. At the beginning of the 1990s, most if not all Latin American countries attempted, in one way or another, to implement neoliberal economic reforms, thus dispelling the image of Chilean economic policy as exceptional and even eccentric. Indeed, in 1990 Chile received an early invitation from the administration of George Bush Sr. to be the first Latin American nation to join the planned "free trade zone from Alaska to the Patagonia" in the framework of the Initiative of the Americas. As this developed into the Free Trade Area of the Americas (FTAA), Chile maintained its support for a general free-trade agreement despite regional criticism (especially from Brazil). On the other hand, however, Chile showed markedly less enthusiasm for the newly created MERCOSUR economic alliance, led by Brazil and Argentina, a decision widely interpreted as a rejection of a "Latin American approach" to economic integration. In June 1996 Chile joined MERCOSUR as an "associate" partner, allowing Chile to enjoy certain rights in the union including participation in the political structure. This was essentially a pragmatic move, which allowed Chile to participate in an important regional organization, but without compromising its trade policies or its economic independence.[11]

NEITHER PRAGMATIC NOR IDEOLOGICAL: HISTORICAL LEGACIES AND NEIGHBORING COUNTRIES

In this first phase of Concertación, and for the first time in the twentieth century, Chilean investment began to flow into the region, beginning, notably (given historical tensions) with Argentina and Peru. Given the particular complexity of Chile's relations with its neighbors, "pragmatic" or "modern" solutions to outstanding problems were promoted as the solution to "out of date conflicts." Such a pragmatic approach depended on consensual support within Chile, which was to a large extent achieved. Indeed, from a neoliberal persuasion, many Chilean investors believed (and still believe) that investment and business opportunities will create enough bridges with Peru and Bolivia so as to overcome seemingly insurmountable political differences (although as yet this has not occurred).

Nonetheless, Chilean investment in neighboring countries has been a significant new development, given historical tensions. Of course, this was facilitated by the rapid development and growth of the Chilean economy in the late 1980s and early 1990s as well as by the free-market economic reforms undertaken in neighboring countries in the 1990s and a more favorable (democratic) political climate. In the case of Peru, the advent of the Fujimori administration facilitated negotiations that (despite obstacles) led to an agreement in December 1999 on the implementation of the Treaty of Peace signed in 1929, after the war of 1879.

However, there was one exception to the successes of this pragmatic foreign policy, which was seemingly devoid of the traditional political competition and mistrust. Fujimori's *autogolpe* in 1992 led to strong and principled condemnation by Chile, probably led by Aylwin himself, resulting in almost frozen relations between the two countries. Of course, the 1991 Democratic Clause of the Organization of American States (OAS) should have led to the suspension of Peru on the grounds of an unconstitutional change of government, but the authoritarian traits of the regime had not yet become evident and there was a degree of support for Fujimori's war with Sendero Luminoso, which led to a gradual resumption of relations.

Relations with Argentina under Carlos Menem (1989–1999) were clearer in terms of pragmatism and benefits. Indeed, the decade was one characterized by probably the closest relationship between the two countries since the "May Pacts" of 1902, which had laid to rest fears of war between them. Even the arbitration of a border dispute, Laguna del Desierto, in 1994, which many felt was unfair toward Chile, was calmly received, while even the armed forces undertook an unprecedented steps toward collaboration. The "special relationship," in part based on Menem's shared preference for "open door" trade policies, reached a peak in 1996, with the agreement of Argentina to supply gas to Chile (although ironically later this became a source of tension) and led to a significant increase in Chilean investment in the Argentinian economy that continues today.

Relations with its other neighbor, Bolivia, improved in the 1990s following the OAS decision that Bolivian claims should be settled bilaterally, as argued by Chile. Progress was made possible by a Chilean position that discarded ideology in favor of a pragmatic solution between the two countries. Finally, relations with Cuba offer a further insight into the balance of ideology and pragmatism in foreign policy in the 1990s. Under Pinochet, of course, there had been no diplomatic relations for ideological reasons. Despite the fact that other Latin American states had restored relations with Cuba, Aylwin opted for a gradualist policy that led to the postponement of the reopening of full diplomatic relations until 1995. The slow progress was above all a pragmatic consideration of the power relations of domestic forces and the strength of anti-Cuban feeling among the Chilean Right.

OPEN REGIONALISM

From the outset of the transition, Chile sought to follow a dynamic policy of "open regionalism.[12] In a sense the expression was an oxymoron. On the one hand, Chile expressed interest in MERCOSUR, as part of a policy of greater integration into world markets. On the other, however, Chilean officials were keen to underline that integration was a long process (pointing to the example of European integration, which began with six members in 1957)[13] and that Chile would follow a similarly gradualist policy toward integration in Latin America. Thus, Chile showed interest in integration, while simultaneously actively seeking to sign a free-trade agreement with the United States. Although Chilean efforts to join the North American Free Trade Agreement (NAFTA) were eventually unsuccessful, it did manage to sign a free-trade agreement with Canada in 1996, perhaps as a first step toward future integration.

On a global level, Chile successfully joined APEC in 1994, although this had been initiated by the military government in an attempt to find trade partners who were interested in trade, but not especially concerned about the regime's human rights record. This relationship developed over the following years, as Japan, China, Korea, and even Indonesia, acquired a new importance for Chilean trade and political relations.[14] President Frei visited Indonesia before the fall of Suharto, without any official of the Chilean government offering any criticism on the subject of human rights violations; and the same silence was evident in relations with China, reflecting that the "ideological" politics of human rights was clearly restricted to Latin America.

This was an essentially pragmatic policy, devoid of any strong ideological component, in line with the concept of the promotion of democracy and the market economy. In another sense, the two first Concertación administrations were acutely aware of their potential vulnerability in two aspects. First, the Government still felt itself vulnerable to the power of the armed forces, especially in terms of the figure of General Pinochet, Commander in Chief of the Army until 1998. Any disruption, it was feared, could lead to unrest. Second, the free-market political economy inherited by Concertación was working well in terms of its highest recorded economic growth and was almost universally acclaimed. As Chile sought to become a developed nation, foreign policy was guided by a strong sense of pragmatism, which conveniently converged within the broad ideological guidelines of the Washington Consensus.

THE TURN OF THE CENTURY AND THE "LATIN AMERICAN CRISIS"

By 2000 political change within Chile was accelerating. The process began with the arrest of General Pinochet in London in 1998. The two year process led to the political defeat of Pinochet inside Chile, the defeat of *pinochetismo* in the public political arena, the judgment and jailing of hundreds of former officers accused of human rights violations, and the disappearance of what had previously been labeled (and eulogized) as the "Pinochet model."[15] The clear message was that Chile wished to adopt a common Latin American post-dictatorship policy, no longer encumbered by the dictator's legacy.

On a regional level, 1999 witnessed the beginning of dramatic political change in the form of an institutional crisis and the rejection of neoliberalism. First, the election of Hugo Chávez in Venezuela inaugurated a form of "neopopulism" in Latin America as a political persuasion and, later, as a more aggressive foreign policy. Argentina, Bolivia, Peru, Ecuador, Nicaragua, Honduras (until 2009), and more recently, El Salvador, followed the path either of institutional crisis, or of democratically elected center-left governments that rejected the Washington Consensus and sought to deepen their model of democracy. In Peru, a moderate, market friendly social democracy emerged as the main political force, while in Argentina, the 2001 crisis was followed by the Kirchner years with a strong rhetoric of "continental nationalism" (with overtones of anti-imperialism). Ecuador's rapprochement with Peru denied Chile a tactical ally in its border conflicts with the latter, while in Bolivia, the rise of Evo Morales threatened to reignite tensions over Bolivian nationalist claims for access to the sea (although relations until the present have proven to be surprisingly good).

The main challenge to Chile, in both a pragmatic and ideological sense came from Hugo Chávez's "Bolivarian Revolution." In terms of ideology, Chávez offered a serious challenge to the established left in

Chile, which had accepted a more centrist position of adherence to the institutions and procedures of liberal democracy as well as, to an extent, the value of the market economy as a regulatory force.[16] There is no doubt that the political orientation of Concertación would be considered reformist or at worst neoliberal by those supporting Chávez, while the politics of free markets and free-trade agreements is in complete opposition to the vision proposed by the Bolivarian Alliance for the Peoples of Our America (ALBA). In the pragmatic sense, the challenge of neo-populism has undermined Chilean aims of promoting regional free-trade agreements, and certainly undermined the concept of Chile as the model of political and economic development.

The administration of Ricardo Lagos was inaugurated in March 2000, in the midst of the political changes sweeping across the continent. His response, as evident in his inaugural speech, represented the reverse of the new trends in Latin American and a continuation of moderate social democracy in an international context:

> The beginning of my administration coincides with the beginning of a new century, and a new millennium. We are the first administration of this twenty first century, a century that heralds many changes and adjustments to the new reality of globalization [. . .] A century in which the countries of the world will have to try to find a new international order, one which is more just, more egalitarian, more sustainable. A century, in which the classical concept of sovereignty at home will give way to new ways of shared sovereignty on a whole range of global issues of the universal domain.[17]

These words sum up the ideological interpretation of socialism held by Ricardo Lagos in the international field. A believer in the concept of the so-called Third Way of Tony Blair, of moderate Western socialism, Lagos sought a foreign policy that combined a "Latin American policy" with a more Western-orientated policy. Within this, there was of course an inevitable reference to a "Latin Americanism," which in some ways was not insincere, and promised to give "priority to our relations with Latin America, especially with the MERCOSUR countries."[18] However, this was far from the Latin Americanism proposed by Chávez.

In the first years, there was some hope of maintaining regional trends. The fall of Fujimori in Peru brought the likeminded President Alejandro Toledo to power. In Argentina, Fernando de la Rúa, and, in Brazil, Fernando Henrique Cardoso promised to follow a path generally akin to the Third Way, a modern market-oriented social democracy, with social and environmental content. Lagos even got on well with President

Luiz Inacio da Silva (Lula) who likewise appeared to be sympathetic to a pragmatic Third Way policy.

There was also a high degree of consistency in other areas of foreign policy. In terms of free trade, Chile successfully sought free-trade agreements with the United States and the European Union, both signed in 2003, and in November 2004, Chile hosted the APEC forum. Foreign policy success helped increase Lagos' domestic popularity, which increased in the last three years of his administration. Indeed, even if the presidential elections of 2005 were close, the opposition were severely weakened by both the economic recovery and the positive international image of the president himself.

To what extent, then, should this policy of this center-left coalition be seen as pure "pragmatism?" It was certainly a term in fashion at the time. Nevertheless, it was highly consistent with the ideological convergence that took place in Chile—and beyond—in the late 1980s, between the intellectual left and the forces of market economics. In the APEC summit in 2004, held in Chile, Ricardo Lagos asked, "Who would have imagined 15 years ago, that the Presidents of the United States, Russia, and China would meet in Chile?"[19] His son and close adviser, Ricardo Lagos-Weber, answered, "The only asset that Chile enjoys is credibility and intelligence."[20]

FREE TRADE AND IRAQ

The free-trade agreement signed with the United States in 2003 came close to failure in an episode that is highly illustrative of the conflict between idealism and pragmatism. Criticized for its neglect of Latin America, the Bush administration supported the free-trade agreement with Chile in order to show its interest in the region and, importantly, to identify itself with a relatively progressive, social democratic government in the Southern Cone during the post–September 11 crisis.[21] Chile would be a perfect favored ally for the Bush administration. For the Chilean government under Ricardo Lagos, the idea of a successful "international strategy" was fundamental in breaking the paralysis on the domestic political front.

This dramatically changed with the U.S. invasion of Iraq in 2003. Chile was a nonpermanent member of the Security Council when the United States demanded Chilean support for its intervention. It was an unpleasant moment for the Chilean government, faced with implicit threats, not least to the coveted free-trade agreement, which, as Condoleezza Rice clearly stated to a Chilean official, would be in danger if Chile did not support the U.S. position.[22] While wishing to remain an ally of the United States, the Lagos administration strongly believed that to support the United States would undermine a longstanding tradition of legality in Chilean foreign policy, as well as going against the wishes of the majority of Chilean citizens.

Chile had supported the United States in the UN over its intervention in Afghanistan in 2001, but this case was clearly different.[23] In accordance with a traditional belief in the legal foundations of the international system, reflected in the Chilean attitude to both World Wars, Chile did not see the legal motives for authorizing the war. At the last moment, Lagos tried to postpone the decision, with a counterproposal to the Security Council, for a new inspection by a new UN team. Although this may just have been a smokescreen in order not to appear too hostile to the United States, the White House disdainfully rebuffed the idea. Buoyed by the public moral indignation in the United States toward countries that did not support U.S. policy toward Iraq, the White House played with the idea of dropping the free-trade agreement, a measure that would have been harsh and counterproductive against an erstwhile ally. After some weeks of silence, Chilean fears were laid to rest when the White House gave the green light to the agreement, even if the ceremony itself was very low key.

Did the Chilean government follow an ideological script in the case of the Iraq war? This would have implied that La Moneda was prepared to sacrifice the free-trade agreement in favor of an ethical principle—and this may well have been the case. On the pragmatic side, however, even if Lagos had wished to support the U.S. intervention, it would have been almost highly damaging and political risky to do so, given the strength of opposition of the vast majority of the Chilean public, not to mention that of Concertación itself. In ideological terms then, the political culture of Chile—strong political beliefs and a traditional adherence to international law—led to a rejection of any unconditional support for the U.S. invasion. In pragmatic terms, support for the U.S. could well have alienated domestic as well as regional support for the Lagos administration.

CHILE'S RESPONSE UNDER LAGOS AND BACHELET

The challenge posed by neopopulism has been especially difficult for Chilean foreign policy. Given that a main goal of foreign policy since 1990 has been to privilege relations with the region and build a genuine Latin American foreign policy, this may seem perplexing, but is due to a number of reasons.[24] First, the underlying ideology of Bolivarianism lies in direct conflict with the ideology of the Chilean model. Chile's economy, political system, and indeed, political culture has taken a very different path from that proposed by Bolivarianism, and there is little common ground. Opposition to Bolivarianism is thus both pragmatic—it would be impossible, and indeed undesirable given the level of economic success since the mid-1980s for the Chilean model to consider embracing Bolivarianism—and ideological, in that Bolivarianism challenges the very tenets of the Chilean free-market model.[25]

Second, Chile has encountered difficult relations with several governments of the so-called Pink Wave. Relations with the Kirchners have been strained at times, due in part to the neopopulist rhetoric emerging from the Casa Rosada, while in the case of Bolivia, the rhetorical nationalism of Evo Morales has threatened to reignite tensions over Bolivia's lack of access to the sea. Failures in negotiations since 2000 have been directly related to the popular mobilizations led by, among others, Evo Morales, which led to the fall of two elected presidents with whom Chile felt it could negotiate. Indeed, one of the causes of these mobilizations was the perception in Bolivia that too many concessions were being made to Chile. With Evo Morales in power, it is possible that this issue, which has deep nationalist roots in Bolivia,[26] could lead to renewed tensions, especially should Morales' domestic support begin to fall.

The traditional Chilean reaction to any dispute has been based on concepts of legality and respect for international law and international treaties, a stance that is perceived as a matter of national interest and hence above party politics. This is an eminently pragmatic policy in some senses, based on a perceived historical legacy, but it is also related to deeply ideological concepts with roots in national identity and an adherence to a certain political culture. While opposition politicians and parties may promise to implement different policies to deal with outstanding issues in a different way, once in power, they find little space or support for a viable alternative.

Thus relations with Peru follow similar lines. The legacy of the War of the Pacific (1879–1883) is still very much alive in both countries, but to a far greater degree in Peru. With the fall of Fujimori in 2000, a new government led by Alejandro Toledo, a presumed political ally of Ricardo Lagos, promised better relations with Santiago, but made little concrete progress. This indicates the extent to which relations are still influenced by a longstanding distrust based on the legacy of the nineteenth century conflict. Indeed, Peru has revived the issue of maritime borders with Chile since 2000, with the result that a border dispute that Santiago had long believed settled, has now been taken to the International Court in Hague. As in the case of Bolivia (and the two questions are related), Chilean foreign policy is based on respect for past treaties, past practice, and international law.

Such is the adherence to this stance that not even the government of Michelle Bachelet was able to improve relations with the region or with neighbors.[27] Despite the fact that Argentina and Peru are the major recipients of Chilean external direct investment, valued in total at about US$20 billion, relations are far from pragmatic and still find themselves trapped in the very particular culture of historically strained bilateral relations.

There are shades of difference between the diplomatic efforts of Lagos and Bachelet. Lagos was well known on the international stage and followed an international career after being president. Michelle Bachelet had a more symbolic international presence, and was known more for her story and her personal struggle than for her impact on international relations.[28] Domestically, while Lagos fully embraced the social democratic model and the Third Way, Bachelet was forced to attenuate her more radical views in order to accommodate the "Chilean consensus" on the value of market economics.

Nor was there a great difference between the two in terms of foreign policy. The main political model for Bachelet was the European Union, but she has maintained close links with the United States, both with the Bush administration and especially with Barack Obama who praised her handling of the economy in 2009.[29] She stressed the importance of the social content of democracy, and was not afraid to speak out on human rights issues, especially regarding violations committed by authoritarian, anti-Communist dictatorships and military regimes, in direct reference to General Pinochet in Chile. On the question of Cuba, she downplayed earlier criticism of a lack of democracy, instead focusing on the injustice of the U.S. embargo, while on her much-publicized visit to the island in February 2009, she did not mention the issue of Cuban dissidents, but did hold an interview with an ailing Fidel Castro.

Latin American integration remains an issue on the Chilean agenda, but differs greatly from the regional integration proposed by Chávez. The fact that Chile's free-market orientation has been the target of a new anti-neoliberal discourse among center-left governments throughout the region provides an obstacle to greater integration. Yet the alternative of following the center-left reforms introduced elsewhere in Latin America is unthinkable in Chile; the consensus over the Chilean model of social democracy combined with market economics and social policies designed to help the most vulnerable, on the one hand, and a foreign policy with its emphasis on protecting the national interest, on the other, remains stronger than ever. Thus, while the Chilean Left, including Bachelet, may push for a more Latin American-centered foreign policy, this should be seen through Chilean eyes as part of a broad Chilean consensus that sees political and economic integration as firmly in the Chilean national interest.[30] This consensus is summed up in the words of President Bachelet:

> We cannot permit that the international crisis destroys the gains of democracy in Latin America. The only way to ensure this is to strengthen [economic] growth, and to guarantee that the gains of growth reach the people, a challenge that can only be met with stronger social policies, and with a powerful and efficient State [. . .] As I have said, this vision supposes a break not only with individualism, but also with populism.[31]

Chilean foreign policy thus still corresponds with the basic tenets of the Third Way. It displays an orientation that differs from both neoliberalism and from populism and is coherent (in ideological terms) with the social democratic worldview of Concertación. It is also coherent with the concept of a historical political consensus on the promotion of the national interest within a legal and democratic framework.

THE CENTRE-RIGHT GOVERNMENT OF PIÑERA

The presidential election of December 2009 and the run-off vote of January 17, 2010, brought to an end the dominance of the Concertación, and gave rise to the government of the center-right coalition, headed by President Sebastián Piñera. While in some ways this represented the end of an era, in terms of foreign policy it is more probable that it will lead to the continuation of the general trend set by the Concertación governments, yet with a greater ideological element. At the head of the Foreign Ministry was appointed the CEO of a large company, in the hope that his negotiating skills would be advantageous in increasing Chilean trade and investment in neighboring countries and Latin America as a whole. Whether this is a pragmatic, ideological, or a technocratic approach is open to question.

After Iraq and the main free-trade agreement signed with the United States and with the European Union, relations with the wider world really are less problematic for Chile. The key issue remains relations with its neighbors. The Piñera government improved relations with Peru, in spite of the case taken to the International Court of Justice over the maritime border, and used this as proof of a new more professional approach to foreign policy. In the same vein, Chile supported the candidacy of former Argentina President Néstor Kirchner, as Secretary General of UNASUR, in spite of muted criticism of some politicians in the center-right coalition. This was a pragmatic decision for a country that has always feared the possibility of isolation.

There has been a notable (ideological) difference in the approach of the new government to the two "hot" issues in Latin American international relations, Cuba and Venezuela. In the first months, the Piñera Government was vocal in its support for political dissent in Cuba, but did not want it leading to open confrontation with Havana. Even if direct confrontation with Hugo Chávez was avoided, center-right members of Congress have been very vocal in their support for the Venezuelan opposition, supported by some members of the Concertación revealing divisions inside the center-left coalition over the issues of Cuba and Venezuela. The government also insisted that the OAS should enhance the definition of "defense of democracy" to include governments that assume excessive executive powers. Behind the scenes, Chilean diplomats continue to promote the recognition of the new Honduran Government by the UNASUR countries. These are political maneuvers with a notable ideological component.

However, the president and the foreign minister have been very careful to avoid any direct confrontation with Venezuela or ALBA countries. In any case, because of the maritime dispute with Peru, Chile must seek some level of cooperation with Rafael Correa of Ecuador. In reference to the intractable issue of a "gateway to the sea" for Bolivia, Piñera had even played football with Evo Morales. All of this is of course highly pragmatic and is almost a mandatory course given the uncertainties in the region.

CONCLUSION

Historically, Chilean foreign policy has been defined by the combination of an adherence to international law, agreements, and treaties; a pragmatic, "realist" approach to relations with other Latin American nations; and a close affinity with Western models of democracy and economic development. This has continued since the beginning of the transition, as Chilean foreign policy has reflected domestic concerns to ensure a stable, progressive, and nonviolent transition to democracy and continued economic growth and development. Both of these highly pragmatic policy objectives took place, of course, within the framework of a hemispheric ideological convergence in the 1990s over the merits of the combination of liberal democracy and free-market economies, encapsulated in the Washington Consensus.

In this sense, Chile's post-dictatorship foreign policy has been highly pragmatic in terms of pursuing national economic interests, through free-trade agreements and increased foreign direct investment in neighboring countries as well as, in terms of politics, through efforts to ensure democratic stability throughout the region. Pragmatism converged perfectly with the dominant ideology of the 1990s; neoliberal reforms may have been initially associated with Pinochet, but the continuation of free-market economics throughout the transition (albeit with social welfare policies) was clearly seen to be in the national interest first and foremost, and conveniently in line also with the dominant ideology of the time (thus aiding Chilean efforts to increase overseas trade and investment). Indeed, both ideologues and pragmatists have viewed Chile as a model of transition and economic development for others in Latin America to attempt to follow.

The rise of the Pink Tide in Latin America, and its opposition to the dominant ideology of the 1990s, in terms of the perceived limits of both market economics and electoral democracy, represented a challenge for Chile's center-left ruling Concertación and will continue to do so for the new center-right administration. This has provoked a degree of change in foreign policy, with greater emphasis on the defense of human rights and improved relations within the region. Yet Chile ultimately remains dedicated to a pragmatic foreign policy that best reflects its own economic and political interests, and which has, with only a few exceptions, remained within the ideological framework of adherence to liberal democracy, the international framework of law and, more recently, free-market economics. Despite changing times, Chile has remained surprisingly faithful to a long-term commitment to an ideology of legality, development, and pragmatism.

NOTES

1. Joaquín Fermandois, *Chile y el mundo 1970–1973. La política exterior del gobierno de la Unidad Popular y el sistema internacional* (Santiago: Ediciones Universidad Católica de Chile, 1985). For a different view, see Jorge Vera Castillo, ed., *La política exterior chilena durante el gobierno del Presidente Salvador Allende 1970–1973* (Santiago: IERIC, 1987). For a general assessment of the concept of "ideology," see Alan Cassels, *Ideology and International Relations in the Modern World* (New York, London: Routledge, 1996), pp. 1–8.

2. For the most complete interpretation, see Heraldo Muñoz, *Las relaciones exteriores del gobierno militar chileno* (Santiago: Ornitorrinco, 1986).

3. For a general view, see Manfred Wilhelmy and Roberto Durán, "Los principales rasgos de la política exterior chilena entre 1973 y el 2000," *Revista de Ciencia Política* 23, 2 (2003); and Joaquín Fermandois, *Mundo y fin de mundo. Chile en la política mundial 1900–2004* (Santiago: Ediciones Universidad Católica de Chile, 2005), Chapter 16.

4. Concertación de Partidos por la Democracia, *Programa de Gobierno* (Santiago, 1989). For an analysis of the program, see Renán Fuentealba, "Un nuevo estilo diplomático para el nuevo Gobierno Democrático," *Diplomacia*, No. 54–55 (October 1990–March 1991), p. 28.

5. *El Mercurio*, March 15, 1994.
6. *El Mercurio*, June 25, 1994.
7. *El Mercurio*, May 22, 1994.
8. *El Mercurio*, April 6, 1994.
9. *La Epoca*, September 9, 1996.
10. *La Segunda*, November 10, 1998.
11. Joaquín Fermandois and María José Henríquez, "¿Contradicción o díada? Política exterior chilena ante MERCOSUR," *Estudios Internacionales* XXXVIII, 148 (January–March 2005).
12. Alberto van Klaveren, "América Latina: hacia un regionalismo abierto," in Alberto van Klaveren, ed., *América Latina en el mundo* (Santiago: Los Andes, Pehuén, 1997).
13. José Miguel Insulza, *Ensayos sobre política exterior de Chile* (Santiago: Los Andes, 1998), pp. 69–74.
14. Pilar Armanet, Pilar Alamos, and Luz O'Shea, *Las relaciones de Chile con los organismos multilaterales de la Cuenca del Pacífico* (Santiago: Instituto de Estudios Internacionales, 1996). Manfred Wilhelmy, "Los empresarios chilenos frente a la región Asia-Pacífico," *Estudios Internacionales* XXXVI, 144, enero-marzo de 2004.
15. As a reference, see Angelo Codevilla, "Is Pinochet the Model?" *Foreign Affaire* 72, 5 (November/December 1993).
16. The initial reaction of the government of Lagos to the failed coup against Chávez in 2002 was ambiguous. The ambassador was later dismissed. See *La Nación*, April 13, 2002.
17. March 29, 2000, www.presidencia.cl.
18. Ricardo Lagos, Mensaje a la Nación, 21 de mayo de 2001, www.presidencia.cl. (accessed in 2004).
19. *El Mercurio*, November 22, 2004.
20. *El Mercurio*, November 21, 2004.
21. Joaquín Fermandois, "Peace at Home, Turbulences Abroad: The Foreign Policy of the Lagos Administration," Silvia Borzutzky and Lois Hecht Oppenheim, eds., *After Pinochet. The Chilean Road to Democracy and the Market* (Gainesville: The University of Florida Press, 2006).
22. Heraldo Muñoz, *Una guerra solitaria. La historia secreta de EE.UU. en Irak, la polémica en la ONU y el papel de Chile* (Santiago: Mondadori, 2005), p. 19.
23. Joaquín Fermandois, "Chile y la guerra de Irak del 2003," *Bicentenario* 7, 1 (2008).
24. José Rodríguez Elizondo, *Las crisis vecinales del gobierno de Lagos* (Santiago: Debate, 2006).
25. *Encuesta Nacional Bicentenario*, 2006 and 2008. Pontificia Universidad Católica de Chile; y diario *El Mercurio*. This poll generally reflects a self-assured position of Chile in the region.
26. José Rodríguez Elizondo, *De Charaña a La Haya. Chile, entre la aspiración marítima de Bolivia y la demanda marítima de Perú* (Santiago: La Tercera, Mondadori, 2009).

27. For an analysis of the situation at the beginning of her administration, see César Ross, "Chile: los desafíos de la política exterior de Michelle Bachelet," *Foreign Affairs*, en español, abril–junio 2006.

28. Bachelet was the daughter of a general who was an ally of Allende, and who died while imprisoned in 1974; a victim of torture under Pinochet and a former exile in the DDR, she became the first female president of Chile.

29. *El Mercurio*, June 24, and June 25, 2009. Interestingly, there was no report of her visit on *NYT* online.

30. Instituto de Estudios Internacionales, Universidad de Chile; Instituto de Ciencia Política, Pontificia Universidad Católica de Chile, *Chile, las Américas y el mundo. Opinión pública y política exterior* (Santiago, 2008). This study stresses that the Chilean public considers current relations with other Latin American countries in a positive light.

31. http://expreso.co.cr/notiicias/?p=1744. Visited, June 2009.

CHAPTER 3

BRAZILIAN FOREIGN POLICY: CAUSAL BELIEFS IN FORMULATION AND PRAGMATISM IN PRACTICE

MIRIAM GOMES SARAIVA

INTRODUCTION

In general terms, Brazilian foreign policy has been marked by continuity. Behind this continuity lie a number of long-held beliefs that have influenced its evolution: the importance of autonomy, universalist action, and destiny, the idea that the country will one day come to occupy a place of greater distinction in international politics ("the destiny of grandeur"). These beliefs can be clearly identified as long-term aims and are rooted in a structured diplomatic corporation.[1] The means available to achieve these objectives, as will be seen, are not constant, but rather vary according to the specific historical and political context.

The strong tendency toward centralization in the formulation of Brazilian foreign-policy in Itamaraty (the Brazilian Foreign Office) contributed to more stable policies and behavior based on longer-term principles. Indeed, some authors use the organizational behavior model in order to analyze the history and behavior of Brazilian diplomacy.[2] This concentration makes foreign policy less vulnerable to the direct interference of domestic policy.

These beliefs, however, do not necessarily provide a basis for actions based on ideology. On the contrary, in the Brazilian case in general, they orient the organization of behavior, which is in turn inspired by clearly realistic premises of a pragmatic nature. As Pinheiro highlights, within the framework of realism, Brazilian behavior at times assumes a Hobbesian character as a matter of priority, in which a relative increase in power is sought vis-à-vis others, while at other times preference is given to realism of a Grotian nature, emphasizing initiatives that bring absolute gains but may also bring benefits to other states.[3] Brazil has frequently adopted multifaceted ways of behavior in terms of international policy, seeking to simultaneously benefit from the possibilities of the international system, and also assume a position of leadership, especially of Southern hemisphere countries.

Nonetheless, change is found alongside continuity. There are alternatives regarding the strategy to be adopted based on the tension between a preference for more autonomous action, on the one hand, and the role of leadership of initiatives concerning Southern hemisphere nations, on the other. Both are defined in terms of the international context, the strategy of national development, and certain calculations of foreign-policy experts that vary according to their political vision and their perception of what constitutes the national interest, the international situation, and other more specific variables. In this case, elements of realist pragmatism are found but are occasionally combined with elements of an ideological nature on the part of those formulating policy.

In leadership terms, during the administrations of Fernando Henrique Cardoso (1995–2002) and Luiz Inacio Lula da Silva (2003–2010), the above-mentioned principles and the weighting given to pragmatism were consistent, but operated in different contexts and scenarios. However, in general terms, the particular worldview of Lula allowed the features of what is here understood by ideology to be more evident.

The aim of this chapter is to analyze Brazilian foreign policy under the administrations of Fernando Henrique Cardoso and Lula da Silva. Two specific variables are taken into account: on the one hand, the degrees of continuity and change between the two administrations and, on the other, the greater or lesser presence of elements inherent in ideology and pragmatism in the formulation and implementation of foreign policy. The first part of the chapter examines traditional beliefs underlying foreign policy (and indeed aspects of domestic policy), which represent what can be termed a "Brazilian ideology." The second part analyzes different understandings of, and approaches to, foreign policy in Brazil over the past ten years. The third section examines the characteristics of foreign policy implemented under the Cardoso and Lula governments, especially with regard to relations with South America, while the conclusion examines trends in continuity and change over this period in terms of ideology and pragmatism.

UNDERLYING BELIEFS OF
BRAZILIAN FOREIGN POLICY

The influence of beliefs in Brazilian foreign policy is highly relevant to the debate on pragmatism and ideology. According to Vigevani, Ramanzini Jr., Favaron, and Correia (2008),[4] Brazil's position on many issues should be seen in light of constitutive factors of foreign policy, rooted in the very nature of Brazilian society and state: namely, autonomy and universalism. Universalism involves a willingness to maintain relations with all countries, regardless of geographical location, type of regime, or economic concerns, as well as an independence of action in relation to global powers. Autonomy is defined as the freedom of manoeuvre that a country has in its relations with other states and in its participation in international politics, and is reflected in the historical tendency of Brazilian foreign policy to avoid agreements that may come to limit future alternatives.

Underlying the ideas of universalism and autonomy is a historical belief within Brazilian society and among foreign-policy makers of Brazil's destiny. Indeed, since the beginning of the twentieth century, allusions in speeches and publications to the grandeur of Brazil's future are common, contributing to the belief that Brazil should occupy a "special place" on the international scene in politico-strategic terms. At the beginning of the twentieth century, the foreign minister Barão do Rio Branco highlighted the "similarities" between Brazil and the United States in terms of territory, ethnicity, cultural diversity, as well as its geopolitical position, all of which made it the natural "counterpart" of the United States in Latin America.[5] In 1926 and in 1945, Brazilian diplomacy made a bid for a permanent seat on the League of Nations/United Nations Security Council, while in the early 1970s, the ex-foreign minister Araújo Castro stated that "few countries in the world have Brazil's potential for diplomatic reach" and "no country can escape its destiny and, for good or ill, Brazil is condemned to grandeur."[6] Indeed, this issue has returned to the foreign-policy agenda in the new millennium.

Based on these beliefs in its own role and destiny, Brazilian diplomacy has structured its behavior emphasizing policy initiatives with a view to increasing its power on the international scene. As a result, during the 1970s, Brazilian foreign policy became known as "Responsible and Ecumenical Pragmatism," a policy that condensed the above-mentioned ideas of autonomy, universalism, and a destiny of grandeur.

DIVERGENCE IN POLITICAL PERCEPTIONS
AND STRATEGIES SINCE THE 1990S

The predominance for many years of a paradigm based on the beliefs of autonomy and universalism in Itamaraty gave rise to a convergence and consistency of thinking in Brazilian diplomacy, as well as the presence of important traits of continuity in foreign policy.

However, the arrival of Collor de Mello to the presidency in 1990, brought a new liberal-oriented policy, advocated by a minority in Itamaraty, to the forefront of foreign-policy decision making. This proposed that Brazilian diplomacy should leave aside the normative principles outlined above and instead privilege relations with "First World" countries in order to "join the club." This would involve abandoning the discourse of solidarity with developing countries in favor of stronger economic relations with the developed economies. Nevertheless, even during the Collor government, the translation of these ideas into practice abroad was limited. While the attempt to impose such a change in foreign policy did not translate into practice and did not survive much beyond the impeachment of the president,[7] it did give rise to a crisis of paradigm within Itamaraty, leading to a division within the Brazilian Foreign Office into two main lines of thinking—the autonomist and the pragmatic institutionalist.[8] Each influences—and struggles for influence in—foreign-policy making today with different views regarding the beliefs outlined earlier.

On the one hand, the pragmatic institutionalist current holds a more favorable view of economic liberalization, although without rejecting the policy of industrialization (import substitution industrialization—ISI) adopted in the developmentalist period. In political terms, pragmatic institutionalists, without renouncing the causal beliefs of Brazilian foreign policy such as autonomy, universalism, and a destiny of grandeur, place greater emphasis on Brazil's support of international structures and institutions as a pragmatic way to advance the national agenda. They defend the idea of Brazil's international insertion based on "autonomy through integration," according to which global values must be defended by all. Leadership in South America is sought and pursued discretely.[9]

On the other hand, the autonomist current hold a more traditional, nationalist, and developmentalist view, defending a model of development based on the expansion of the infrastructure sectors and an assertive industrial projection abroad. In terms of foreign policy, autonomists defend a more assertive projection of Brazil abroad in terms of leadership in North/South issues, Brazilian participation in the United Nations Security Council, and Brazilian leadership in South America.

Priority is given to cooperation with Southern countries, not through notions of solidarity, but to advance Brazil's regional leadership and hence global standing.

Lastly, a more ideologically oriented group, with roots in academic and political groups, emerged during the Lula administration, establishing an important dialogue with Itamaraty and exercising some influence over foreign-policy decisions (above all in relation to South American issues). This group prioritizes regional integration with South American countries and, more specifically, within Mercosur, but through the deepening of the process in political, social, and economic terms.[10] For integration to be successful, compatibility is needed between values and real common advantages, as well as a degree of common identity.

THE MAIN FEATURES OF FOREIGN POLICY IN THE CARDOSO AND LULA GOVERNMENTS

The emergence of competing orientations led to the emergence of different characteristics under the Cardoso and Lula da Silva governments, and hence a break with the consistency of the past. While the most permanent principles underlying foreign policy were maintained, policy was adapted to different contexts and situations.[11]

(I) 1995–2002: AUTONOMY THROUGH INTEGRATION

According to Cardoso's Chancellor, Luiz Felipe Lampreia:

> We are a great country, with traditions of growth and a long history of participation, very often as a protagonist, in the construction of international and regional relations. We are committed to international partnerships which increase our presence in the world. . . . We are a "global trader" and a "global player". . . . The pre-eminence on the international scene of values dear to the Brazilian people, such as democracy, individual liberties and respect for human rights and the evidence that . . . the world is committed to a process of growth in civilization . . .[12]

The strengthening of the pragmatic institutionalist line during the first mandate of the Cardoso government resulted in the adoption of the concept of "shared sovereignty," which differed from the classical concept of sovereignty. This view perceived the world as marked by a "concert" of nations with the same discourse defending universal values. One of the conditions of maintaining this "concert" would be a greater adaptability of the U.S. global leadership to both the demands of the emerging powers, and the demands of medium-sized and small nations.[13] This scenario would open spaces for Brazil—in search of mechanisms to enlarge its capability for international action—to adopt a position that meant neither alignment with the United States nor a free-rider posture. This position would be oriented, first, by the perception of the existence in the new scenario of variable alignments, and second, by the adhesion to leading international regimes. It also meant a modification of the concept of autonomy with the new idea of "autonomy through integration" replacing previously established concepts of sovereignty, understood as distancing or self-sufficiency.[14]

The pragmatic institutionalists identified the institutionalization of international relations as favorable to Brazilian economic development, since the rules of the international game would be followed by all countries, including the richest. Brazil's position vis-à-vis the richest countries should be simultaneously one of convergence in terms of values and one of criticism of the distortions and inequalities of the existing international order.[15] Within this context, Brazil sought an active role in multilateral forums, as a global player, bidding within the UN for a permanent seat on the Security Council. In the area of international security, Brazil chose to support those international regimes that were already in place.

At the same time, the government sought to play the role of "global trader," with participation in different arenas of trade negotiations, the World Trade Organization (WTO) being the privileged forum, since it favored Brazilian interests in terms of its dispute settlement mechanism.[16] In relation to the European Union (EU), in 1995 Brazil promoted the Interregional Framework Cooperation Agreement between the EU and Mercosur that encompassed free trade, economic cooperation, and political dialogue. However, despite common interests in terms of political dialogue and common positions in international forums, strong disagreements in terms of commerce hindered further progress.

With regard to political relations with other Southern countries, the rise of pragmatic institutionalists slowed progress as priority was given to trade. In 1996, the Pretoria Agreement was signed and trade negotiations were begun between Mercosur and South Africa, culminating in a framework agreement signed in 2000. In addition, at the beginning of the decade, China became the third largest importer of Brazilian exports. Relations with Portugal and with the countries of the Community of Portuguese Language Countries were also stimulated. Within the framework of universalism, emphasis on interactions with new partners was important.

In the Americas, Brazilian pragmatism was dominant over ideology in policy formulation. Brazil clashed with the United States over issues of the organization of international trade and of protectionism in industrialized countries, as well as on issues relating to hemispheric integration. While the U.S. government was eager to conclude the Free Trade Area of the Americas (FTAA), the Brazilian government preferred to delay the process, emphasizing subregional initiatives such as Mercosur. However, following the low-profile line of the Itamar Franco administration, Brazilian diplomacy under Cardoso adopted what it labeled a "de-dramatization" of U.S.-Brazilian relations, lowering the Brazilian profile, and seeking to dispel the image of a Third-World opponent of the United States.[17]

In relation to neighboring countries, Brazilian diplomacy did not alter its traditional and realist view of national sovereignty. On the contrary, it was careful to avoid the possibility of integration leading to any shared sovereignty in relation to its behavior with other foreign partners. Indeed, the idea of autonomy was in fact reinforced. According to Pinheiro,[18] in the case of Brazil's relations with neighboring countries, this desire for autonomy "uses the [Grotian[19]] conception to satisfy its search for power." Thus, Brazil's quest for its own sphere of influence regionally and for a protagonistic role on the international stage came to the fore.

During Cardoso's second mandate, South American countries came to be seen more clearly as important partners with a view to strengthening Brazil's role as a global player, in the belief that the consolidation of the integration process would strengthen Brazil's bargaining position in multilateral forums as a regional leader. Diplomacy then began a revision of traditional Brazilian behavior in the region based on the principle of nonintervention. It sought to build its leadership in the region on the twin bases of security and democratic stability, establishing strong links with neighboring countries and acting as a mediator in crisis situations when called upon to do so. Acceptance of the idea of democracy as a universal value contributed to the establishment of a consensus around the links between democracy, regional integration, and perspectives of national development.[20] In this way, without giving up principles of nonintervention, it sought to include in its agenda the defense of democracy, and to act accordingly in cases of crisis.

As a parallel strategy, construction of a South American Community of Nations began, with the first meeting of South American countries taking place in Brasília in 2000, where the main ideas discussed were economic integration and the infrastructure of the region, and support for democratic consolidation. With access to the energy resources of neighboring countries a priority, Brazil sought to promote infrastructural integration projects, which opened the way for the formation of the Initiative for the Integration of the Regional Infrastructure of South America (IIRSA). On the domestic political front, however, there was resistance to

Brazil's involvement with initiatives that could divert domestic resources to regional integration projects.

The pragmatic institutionalists saw Mercosur as a means of increasing the country's economic power, thus prioritizing trade integration. It was seen as important to preserve open regionalism so as not to prejudice possible relations with other partners, and the institutionalization of the block was not seen as necessary or even desirable. Moreover, the most favored vision identified partnerships with industrialized countries as an important element in stimulating Brazilian foreign trade and Mercosur as a space in which to reduce the potentially damaging impact of overseas economic opening. Despite frictions, Mercosur as a bloc conducted the negotiations toward the formation of the FTAA and was able to develop the dialogue previously established with the EU. Politically, Mercosur was seen as a means of reinforcing Brazil's hand, giving it a greater importance on the international stage.

The harmonization of relations with Argentina was an important achievement for the universalist current of Brazilian foreign policy. On a regional level, there were efforts to seek common positions with Argentina in relation to issues that, until then, had not been agreed upon, as part of a process of joint initiatives. The main cases involved common positions in the Rio Group and the Organization of American States (OAS). Within Mercosur, Brazilian and Argentine support for democracy was best reflected in response to the political crisis experienced by the Paraguayan government in 1996, which resulted in the democratic clause in Mercosur.

By the end of the Cardoso's administration, a number of steps had been taken to increase Brazil's influence and standing on the international scene. Yet autonomists criticized the pragmatic institutionalist preference for moderation and action within the institutional framework of the international order rather than adherence to the beliefs in autonomy, universalism, and destiny of grandeur as the best way to guarantee the success of long-term objectives.

(II) LULA, REGIONAL LEADERSHIP AND INTERNATIONAL ACTIVISM

The arrival of Luiz Ignacio da Silva Lula to the Brazilian Presidency rein-vigorated the autonomist line of thought in international politics. The rise of the autonomists diminished the conviction that Brazil's interests were best guaranteed through international institutions, and instead advocated a more active approach in favor of the interests of both Brazil and other Southern countries.[21] Lula's administration thus saw a shift toward the primacy of beliefs in autonomy, universalism, and, above all, in the view of increasing Brazil's presence in international politics.

Regional leadership and ascension toward a role as a global power was a clear aim of Brazilian diplomacy in this period.

As a first step, the priority of Brazil's candidature to permanent membership of the UN Security Council was reinforced. As credentials for its candidature, Brazil chose to defend more distributive aspects of international trade, and campaigned to tackle problems of hunger and poverty that would affect international stability (the fight against terrorism was not assumed to be a priority). However, the obstacles presented by the reform project in the UN General Assembly of 2005 slowed the pace of this campaign.

In terms of trade, the government adopted an active policy to deal with politico-strategic issues. It undertook a proactive policy in search of markets, which resulted in an increase of exports and the Brazilian economic surplus, as well as an active role in defense of Brazilian interests in negotiations held in the WTO through joint action with other developing countries. In his acceptance speech, President Lula stated that:

> In relation to the FTAA, in negotiations between Mercosur, the European Union and the World Trade Organization, Brazil will combat protectionism, fight for the elimination of subsidies and will undertake to obtain trade rules which are more just and appropriate to our condition as a developing country.[22]

To this end, the G-20, composed of Southern nations including India, China, and South Africa, became an important forum for Brazilian diplomacy, linking progress in WTO negotiations to the inclusion of issues such as agricultural subsidies in the discussion agenda.

Cooperation framework agreements were signed between Mercosur and India, and with SACU (South African Customs Union) as well as with the United States in terms of formative negotiations on the FTAA. However, in the case of the FTAA, Itamaraty introduced a series of proposed modifications that aimed to block and delay its implementation, resulting in the failure of talks in 2005. This led to an emphasis on establishing an integrative but dominant stance with South American countries, including a series of talks between Mercosur and the EU. However, when these foundered, the Brazilian government signed a strategic bilateral partnership agreement with the EU in a clear show of autonomy in relation to Mercosur, with the aim of increasing the country's international profile and presence.

The rise of the more autonomist line in Itamaraty gave new impetus to South-South cooperation, based on the belief that there were not only shared characteristics but also shared interests in reordering the international system. Thus, in addition to the agreements signed with the G-20, the IBSA Dialogue Forum (India, Brazil, and South Africa) was set up, with a view to discussing issues relating to the international order, the UN, and technology (and maintaining strongly the idea of nonintervention in partners' domestic issues). While Brazil maintains autonomy in such initiatives in relation to Mercosur, it clearly enjoys the benefits of its regional influence and power to enlarge its international projection.

During Lula's second term, Itamaraty sought to take advantage of the opportunities available through its membership of BRIC (Brazil, Russia, India, and China), the G-7, and other forums such as the Group of 20. Activism aimed at achieving a greater international presence increased significantly. The increasingly accepted identification of Brazil as a "bridge" between developed and underdeveloped nations, a concept that had been talked about since the 1970s, would give the country a powerful position in international relations.

In terms of the United States, Brazil sought to maintain its position of nonalignment and autonomy, maintaining a firm distance from U.S. policy in the region. Although Brazil's more autonomous and reformist participation in international politics has created new areas of friction between the two countries, Brazil has also attempted to maintain a low-profile policy, actively seeking to avoid conflict and confrontation with the United States.

However, its policy toward South America is markedly opposite with Itamaraty seeing regional integration under Brazilian leadership as a political priority, as well as the most effective way to promote Brazil's objectives to become a world power. To this end, Lula attempted to improve the strategy of the Cardoso administration, and without renouncing the principles of nonintervention, to develop regional leadership and a role as a broker of regional consensus, linking regional integration processes to national development.

According to the Chancellor Celso Amorim:

> Brazil has always based its agenda on non-intervention in other states' domestic affairs. . . . But non-intervention cannot mean lack of interest. In other words, the precept of non-intervention must be seen in the light of another precept, based on solidarity: that of non-indifference.[23]

Such a policy included a more vigorous promotion of the South American Community of Nations (SACN) as a priority in regional policy, leading to its creation in 2004 before evolving into the Union of South American Nations (UNASUR) in 2008. A further example was Brazil's leading role in the UN Peacekeeping Forces in Haiti, which can be seen as an attempt to consolidate Brazilian leadership in the region and increase its importance in the international arena, even though this violates traditional principles of noninterventionism.

Brazilian initiatives were, however, not without tensions. With the rise of nationalist sentiments, some neighboring countries sought to challenge Brazil's regional power and position, demanding economic concessions. Lula was forced to adopt a low-profile position (much criticized by the Brazilian press) and accede to the nationalization of hydrocarbons implemented by the Bolivian government, with Petrobras, the Brazilian oil company shouldering the expense. Likewise, despite pressures from Itamaraty and the Brazilian right, Lula and Celso Amorim have sought to maintain a dialogue with Paraguay over the latter's demand for renegotiation of the 1973 Itaipú hydroelectric dam Treaty, which strongly favors Brazilian interests. Without acceding to all demands, some significant concessions regarding decision making, transparency, and completion of works on the Paraguayan side were made in 2009, although these were not ratified by the Brazilian Congress. Moreover, the Brazilian government has to an extent assumed the role of providing technical and economic support in the region, despite internal resistance, with, for example, the Brazilian Development Bank (BNDES) offering to finance infrastructure works in other South American countries (albeit only if carried out by Brazilian companies). From this point of view, which is strongly influenced ideologically by the Workers' Party (PT), Brazilian diplomacy supports the initiatives of anti-liberal, left-leaning governments of the region, and proposes some kind of diffuse solidarity with countries of the continent, with Brazil willing to bear the majority costs of regional integration.

This new, more ideological, posture was supported by autonomists in the belief that integration would offer greater access to foreign markets and hence greater opportunities for the development of Brazilian industry with its competitive advantages in terms of internal production systems. It was also supported and influenced by progressives, from within the PT, as expressed by the President's foreign advisor, Marco Aurélio Garcia:

> Brazil has a greater sense of solidarity towards its neighbors. We do not want the country to be an island of prosperity in the midst of a world of poverty. We do have to help them. This is a pragmatic vision. We have trade surpluses with all of them.[24]

This does not mean that the progressive view of the PT does not clash with autonomist visions at times. Indeed, foreign policy toward Mercosur during this period was marked by very different visions from the two orientations within the government. The progressives strongly favored the political and social deepening of the integration process and both the Olivos Protocol and the setting up of the Mercosur Parliament as a step toward greater institutionalization were a direct result of progressive thinking. On the other hand, the autonomist view sees the broadening of South American integration under Brazilian leadership as a priority, and hence adopted a greater focus on UNASUR, while Mercosur is seen more as an instrument to strengthen Brazil's regional position, as well as a mechanism to open the way for a regional free-trade area.

Despite patterns of continuity, foreign policy under Lula has shown signs of change and flexibility. The objective of regional leadership has been central to policy, and despite the predominance of the autonomist view, policy was influenced favorably by progressives, pushing for a deepening of regional relations and international solidarity. The coexistence of autonomist and progressive orientations reflected a difficult but innovative balance between ideological beliefs and pragmatism.

CONCLUSION

The comparison of foreign policies adopted by the two administrations confirms a high level of continuity in the general features of Brazilian behavior based on the causal beliefs of universalism, autonomy, and a greater destiny. These beliefs approximate to what can be understood as ideology, creating a backdrop that guides behavioral patterns in foreign policy. However, it also reveals a pragmatic flexibility in the comparative weightage awarded to these beliefs in terms of implementation of foreign policy.

Without doubt the autonomist line, stronger during the Lula government, rested greater importance on beliefs, seeking both the reinforcement of autonomy and the search for a stronger projection of the country as a rising power on the international scene. In this way, the combination of strategic pragmatism and ideological considerations favored a discrete, but definite, reinforcement of autonomist orientation, combined at times with a progressive current, over the institutionalist currents favored by Cardoso. Within this combination, in which the beliefs offer an ideological strategy-orienting framework, both administrations ultimately favored a more pragmatic foreign policy.

This combination of ideology and pragmatism can be found in foreign policy from the beginning of the twentieth century. Variations over time reflected the domestic political options of the government in question, the correlation of forces within Itamaraty and the international context. Furthermore, the changing international milieu, in the form of a more multipolar, fragmented international scene, and the election of left-leaning governments in South America, strongly influenced Brazilian foreign policy. Despite the variation experienced and in different measures, one can say that, both in the Cardoso term and in the Lula government, pragmatism prevailed over ideology.

This orientation is not just the result of a political choice, but has been constructed within the autonomist line since the beginning of the 1990s and represents a specific—and highly pragmatic—form of adapting beliefs to new configurations and challenges in the international order. Political change resulting from the presidential elections in 2010 may again favor a move toward institutionalism as under Cardoso, but the overall orientation toward activism and Brazil's rapid international ascension as an autonomous global power will almost certainly be retained.

NOTES

1. In the Brazilian case, it is important to work with the idea of "beliefs" in addition to ideological features of foreign behavior. Ideologies, by definition, take as their starting point the agent's option, while beliefs are rooted in a worldview that appears to the agent not as optional, but as a reality. Here, the definition of beliefs is based on Goldstein and Keohane (1993), which points to three types of beliefs: worldviews (which create identities), principled beliefs (normative ideas), and causal beliefs (capable of generating cause and effect).

2. This is the model of organizational behavior proposed by Allison, G., and P. Zelikow. 1999. *Essence of Decision: Explaining the Cuban Missile Crisis.* New York: Longman; and used by Silva, Márcia Maro. 2008. "Itamaraty's Role in the Process of Recognition of the Independence of Angola and of the MPLA Government." Doctoral thesis. Flacso/Buenos Aires.

3. See Pinheiro, L. 2000. "Traídos pelo Desejo: um ensaio sobre a teoria e a prática da política externa brasileira contemporânea," *Contexto Internacional* 22(2), pp. 305–36.

4. Vigevani, T., H. Ramazini Jr., G. Favaron, R. A. Correia. 2008. "O papel da integração regional para o Brasil: universalismo, soberania e percepção das elites," *Revista Brasileira de Política Internacional* Ano 51, n. 1, pp. 5–27.

5. Cited by Silva, A. de M. 1995. "O Brasil no continente e no mundo: atores e imagens na política externa brasileira contemporânea," *Estudos Históricos* 15, pp. 95–118.

6. Castro, J. A. de A. 1972. "O congelamento do Poder Mundial," *Revista Brasileira de Estudos Políticos*, n. 33, pp. 7–30, 9, 30. Araújo Castro was foreign secretary in 1963, Brazilian ambassador to the UN at the end of the 1960s, and ambassador to the United States in the 1970s. (Castro 1972, p. 9, 30).

7. In countries where diplomatic bureaucracy is more fragile, foreign policy is more conditioned by brusque changes in politics, thus taking on a more erratic aspect. In Brazil's case, Itamaraty's power favors continuity.

8.   Pinheiro 2000.
9.   Ibid.
10. See Deutsch, K. 1982. Análise das Relações Internacionais. Brasília: Editora UnB.
11. See Vigevani, T; M. F. Oliveira; R. Cintra. 2003. "A política externa do governo Cardoso: um exercício de autonomia pela integração," Tempo Social, n. 20, pp. 31–61.
12. Lampreia, L. F. 1995. "Discurso de posse," Resenha de Política Exterior do Brasil, n. 76. Brasília, Ministério de Relações Exteriores, pp. 17–27, 20.
13. See Fonseca Jr., G. 1999. "Anotações sobre as condições do sistema internacional no limiar do século XIX: a distribuição dos pólos de poder e a inserção internacional do Brasil," in: Dupas and Vigevani (eds.), O Brasil e as novas dimensões da segurança internacional. São Paulo: Alfa-Omega/ Fapesp. pp. 17–42. Fonseca was Brazilian ambassador to the UN during part of the Cardoso government.
14. Lampreia, L. F. 1998. "A política exterior de Fernando Henrique Cardoso," Revista Brasileira de Política Internacional 41(2), pp. 5–17.
15. See Vigevani, T, M. F Oliveira, R. Cintra. 2003. "A política externa do governo Cardoso: um exercício de autonomia pela integração," Tempo Social, n. 20, pp. 31–61.
16. See ibid.
17. See Hirst, M., and Pinheiro, L. 1995. "A política externa do Brasil em dois tempos," Revista Brasileira de Política Internacional 38(1), pp. 5–23.
18. Pinheiro, L. 2000. "Traídos pelo Desejo: um ensaio sobre a teoria e a prática da política externa brasileira contemporânea," Contexto Internacional 22(2), pp. 305–36, 323.
19. "Grotian" is this author's clarification.
20. See Villa, R. D. 2004. "Brasil: política externa e a agenda democrática na América do Sul," paper presented in 4to. Encontro Nacional da ABCP, Jul. 21–24, Rio de Janeiro.
21. See Lima, M. R. S. de. 1990. "A economia política da política externa brasileira: uma proposta de análise," Contexto Internacional 6. n. 12, pp. 17.
22. da Silva, Lula. 2003. "Discurso de posse," Resenha de Política Exterior do Brasil, n. 92. Brasília, Ministério de Relações Exteriores, pp. 13–20, 17.
23. Celso Amorim, 2005, quoted by Oliveira, M. F. de. 2005. Elites econômicas e política externa no Brasil contemporâneo. São Paulo: IEEI (draft). Author's translation, pp. 21–22.
24. Interview with Marco Aurélio Garcia made and quoted by Dieguez, Consuelo. 2009. "O Formulador Emotivo," Piauí, n. 30, March, pp. 20–24.

Dancing between Superpowers: Ideology, Pragmatism, and Drift in Paraguayan Foreign Policy*

Peter Lambert

Introduction

Since the 1950s, Paraguayan foreign policy has been shaped by four key factors. First, the country's long tradition of personalist, authoritarian rule has led to a predominance of the executive—and hence agency—in all areas of government. Second, related to this, Paraguay has suffered from the lack of development of foreign-policy institutions. Instead, a highly politicized state bureaucracy dominated by the Colorado Party has evolved, which has been characterized by clientelism, incompetence, and inefficiency, more an instrument of political patronage and control than a modern, professional arm of government. Third, Paraguay's low level of socioeconomic development, poor infrastructure, and historic isolation has restricted its opportunities and room for maneuver in foreign policy. This is related to the fourth factor, which is that Paraguay's geopolitical position as a small, landlocked state, bordered by regional powers (Brazil and Argentina) has meant that political development has been influenced to an unusually high degree by the impact of external power relations, which have constrained and limited—but not dictated—foreign-policy options.

Jeanne Hey (2003) has argued that less-developed countries with weak foreign-policy bureaucracies provide greater opportunities for strong individual leaders to dominate foreign-policy formulation.[1] In Paraguay, foreign policy has been defined by a marked presidentialism, with domestic priorities of the executive and the Party consistently taking precedence over national interests. The result has been a foreign policy over the past 20 years that has for the most part been incoherent and inconsistent, responding to the rapidly shifting demands of domestic policy with long term national interests subordinate to short term domestic political priorities. Although, both ideology and pragmatism have been used to cloak policy narratives, for much of the transition to democracy (1989–2008), foreign policy was reactive and opportunistic, characterized by neglect, drift, and drag.

In part, this was due to the strong legacy of Paraguay's authoritarian past, apparent in "the lack of checks and balances in the powers of the state, high levels of impunity and corruption, the extensive practice of clientelism, the inability of political parties to promote debate and reach consensus, and the highly limited participation or control of the government by civil society,"[2] all of which have had a direct impact on foreign policy, undermining the development of consistent aims and objectives in the national interest. Given this, the chapter will begin with a necessary but brief analysis of foreign policy under the Stroessner dictatorship (1954–1989), which established the style, workings, priorities, and structural frameworks of foreign policy that to a great extent still operate in Paraguay. The chapter then traces the decline of foreign policy through the transition period in the 1990s, from a pragmatic instrument of the first democratic government (1989–1993) to its subservience to domestic polices and subsequent neglect in a decade dominated by Colorado Party governments that were weak, unstable, and lacked legitimacy.

The chapter will then focus on the two administrations of the new millennium, those of Nicanor Duarte Frutos (2003–2008) and Fernando Lugo (2008–present). While Duarte was the presidential candidate of the same Colorado Party that had been in power since 1947, he was initially at least seen as a progressive reformist. With an ideological and pragmatic discourse of strengthening foreign policy, he sought to eliminate the drift of the previous administrations, link foreign policy to concrete developmental and trade issues of national interest, and take a proactive role in exploiting the greater opportunities available in terms of international relations in a more globalized environment. Finally, the chapter will examine the first year of the administration of Fernando Lugo, who ended 61 years of Colorado rule and came to power on a platform of far-reaching socioeconomic reform. Combining pragmatism with an ideological discourse, Lugo has sought to make a sharp break with the past and develop a more coherent, dynamic, and proactive foreign policy that seeks to balance ideology, principles, and pragmatism.

HISTORICAL OVERVIEW

Although the dictatorship of General Alfredo Stroessner was based on a complex set of mechanisms of social and political control,[3] his adept use of foreign policy to garner international and domestic support for his regime was a key explanatory factor for regime longevity. Stroessner designed policy in response to the needs of his regime rather than those of the nation, as simply another mechanism of control. As a result, the Ministry of Foreign Affairs, and the rest of the public sector, was used not to develop or implement policy, but to deepen patronage and clientelism, representing a source of jobs and wealth for loyal political support, with appointments and promotion based on political expediency rather than professional criteria.

Stroessner's foreign policy responded to the Cold War, the key defining international conflict of the period. In the crucial period of regime consolidation (1954–1960), lacking regional support, the dictator sought to take advantage of international polarization and developed an incipient relationship with the United States. By adopting a firm anti-Communist stance, epitomized in the adoption of the U.S. National Security Doctrine,[4] and offering unwavering and unconditional support to U.S. foreign-policy initiatives, Stroessner gained access not only to material benefits such as economic aid, technical assistance, military aid, trade concessions, grants, and loans, but also diplomatic support and regime legitimacy, all of which proved critical to the survival of the regime. Indeed, during the period 1954–1961, the total U.S. aid plus loans reached an average of $6 million per year, or almost a third of the total Paraguayan state budget.[5] With the United States happy to overlook issues such as human rights violations and arms and drugs trafficking, a strong alliance developed, at least until 1976, and the advent of the Carter regime. As Frank Mora argues, "It is hard to imagine how the Stroessner regime . . . could have survived and consolidated without the political, economic and military support provided by Washington."[6]

On a regional level, Stroessner sought to exploit tensions between Argentina and Brazil, by shifting the traditional "pendular policy" toward the anti-Communist Brazil, also a close U.S. regional ally. Closer financial, trade, and military links with Brazil effectively broke the trade reliance on Buenos Aires, through which 90 percent of Paraguayan exports passed in the 1950s, while offering Stroessner huge benefits in terms of regional support and vital military and economic aid.[7] This included essential infrastructure loans, trade concessions, trade access to the port of Paranaguá, as well as the joint construction of the Itaipú hydroelectric dam in 1973, which, despite its controversial terms in favor of Brazil, sparked a construction-led boom in Paraguay.

Parallel to closer relationships with the United States and Brazil, Paraguay developed a policy of what Fernando Masi has termed "benign isolation,"[8] the maintenance of a low international profile, with relations with select (anti-Communist or neutral) states, such as Taiwan, South Africa, South Korea, and Japan. Opportunistic and highly pragmatic, This policy allowed Paraguay to minimize international attention and condemnation, while obtaining significant foreign investment and trade benefits and technical and financial assistance, all of which benefited the regime.

To a great extent, Stroessner manipulated the opportunities provided by international configurations, opportunistically using anti-Communism as a surrogate ideology for the highly pragmatic purpose of gaining international support to strengthen an authoritarian regime and justify internal repression. Foreign policy was essentially another mechanism used to consolidate, legitimize, and then strengthen the dictatorship, reflecting personal rather than national priorities and objectives.[9] As a result, there was neither a coherent foreign policy responsive to national development needs, nor any development of the institutions necessary to develop one, in the form of a strong professionalized, independent, and modern Ministry of Foreign Affairs.[10] The spread of democracy in the region in the 1980s and the shift in U.S. policy toward a focus on democratization, human rights, and drug-trafficking, revealed the limits of an inflexible foreign-policy orientation, as Paraguay became increasingly isolated.

RODRÍGUEZ, PRESIDENTIALISM, AND THE TRANSITION TO DEMOCRACY

Stroessner was overthrown in February 1989 in a "palace putsch" organized by the traditionalist faction of the Colorado Party that had been a pillar of his regime since 1954, and led by his erstwhile military ally, General Andrés Rodríguez. Although democratization was among the stated aims of the conspirators, the primary objective was the reunification of the Colorado Party and the armed forces.[11] Indeed the process was supported by many of the same political and military interests that had previously supported the dictatorship and that set out to control the pace, timing, and nature of the transition. As a result, the subsequent transition process was highly controlled from above, limited in terms of substantive reforms, and characterized by a high degree of structural continuity. Such continuity was also evident in many aspects of foreign policy, even if the rhetoric was significantly different.[12]

Given his close former allegiance to the dictatorship, his lack of democratic credentials, and his fear of internal opposition, General Rodríguez adopted a highly active, personal, and presidentialist diplomacy with the objective of breaking the "malign isolation" to which Paraguay had been subjected in the 1980s. He was thus active in signing a series of treaties and accords (including the Pact of San José and membership of the Río Group and Mercosur), attaining a higher international presence and visibility, to enhance and ensure his regime's legitimacy and hence security. The policy also included improved relations with the Untied States, which once again began to play a central role in regime consolidation and stability, chiefly through its ambassador Timothy Towell. Closer relations also led to benefits in trade, aid, and investment, including the restoration of General System of Preferences (GSP), trade concessions, and military assistance. In return, the United States obtained significant leverage in Paraguayan domestic affairs, which would last throughout the decade.[13]

The period of 1989–1993 of course was one of intense international change, including the collapse of Communism in the Soviet Union and Eastern Europe, the end of the Cold War, the emergence of the Washington Consensus on free markets and electoral democracy, and regionally, the creation of Mercosur. As Latin American and indeed world economies opened to the forces of globalization in terms of free markets and freer movements of goods and services, Paraguay found itself exposed and in a weak competitive position. While it had huge energy resources, these were vastly underused. Its economy remained based on traditional agricultural exports and characterized by weak communications, poor infrastructure, minimal industrialization, and little professional capacity. Unable to respond adequately to the rapid changes in international and regional politics, Rodríguez's foreign policy was swept (or dragged) along by external changes and forces.[14]

Nowhere was this more evident than in the most momentous event of the Rodríguez administration, namely the signing of the Mercosur Treaty (1991). Paraguay was slow to enter into talks, was excluded from the initial discussions, and missed the opportunity to negotiate important concessions before the official signing. Indeed, Paraguay was dragged, pulled, and pressured into Mercosur relatively late in the day, with accelerated membership negotiated mainly by Uruguay, in whose interest it was to have another small member state. Although membership had huge implications for Paraguay, there was no thorough consultation process, no thorough study of the advantages or possible disadvantages and minimal negotiation of the conditions under which Paraguay might enter the Treaty. Instead, it was an executive decision to promote the international profile and stability of the administration, the president, and the Colorado Party.

Although cloaked in an ideological rhetoric of free markets and democracy, regional integration, and solidarity, Rodríguez's foreign policy was essentially pragmatic. As a former ally of Stroessner, allegedly deeply involved in corruption, his overriding concern was to seek international support in terms of aid and investment, and most crucially, in order to bestow international legitimacy on his regime. External support was crucial to boost his own standing, authority, and legitimacy within the factionalized Colorado Party and within society as a whole. In this sense, foreign policy became the main pillar of the domestic legitimacy and hence survival of the Rodríguez administration. It also reflected a high degree of continuity; presidentialist in style, reactive in approach, it continued the practice of using foreign policy for executive rather than national interests. As a result, Rodríguez failed to confront key issues such as renegotiation of the Itaipú Treaty or more favorable conditions for Paraguay's entry into Mercosur. Nor did he implement any reform of the highly inefficient, weak, and politicized foreign-policy bureaucracy inherited from the dictatorship.[15]

BETWEEN 1993 AND 2003: CRISIS AND DRIFT

The transition to democracy in the 1990s was dominated by the Colorado Party, which remained undefeated in presidential elections. However, Colorado Party dominance thinly concealed almost constant political and economic crises in what was a tumultuous decade. Weak and ineffective leadership, continuous and highly damaging internal party power struggles, serious bouts of political instability in 1996, 1999, and 2001, rampant corruption, and the rise of the populist maverick General Lino Oviedo, all threatened to undermine and overturn the transition process. Indeed, in the infamous *marzo paraguayo* of 1999, sparked by the assassination of vice-president Jose María Argaña, the attempted coup d'état of Lino Oviedo came close to success and was only thwarted by significant civilian resistance in Asunción.[16]

Underpinning political instability was severe economic mismanagement and incompetence, characterized by constant economic recession and stagnation between 1996 and 2003, leaving Paraguay on the edge of bankruptcy. This was accompanied by a growth in poverty and inequality, with per capita income falling below $1000 in 2002, and a rise in social conflict. Confronting seemingly constant crises and lacking strength or popular legitimacy, the embattled administrations of Juan Carlos Wasmosy (1993–1998), Raúl Cubas (1998–1999), and Luís Gonzalez Macchi (1999–2003) placed their priority on regime survival. With no strong, independent foreign-policy institutions and little interest in Congress or civil society, foreign policy was reduced to a mechanism to generate international support in confronting domestic crises.

Indeed, the reins of foreign policy were effectively handed to regional neighbors and the United States, which moved from simply offering legitimacy to the incumbent regime (as under Rodríguez) to actively assisting and defending it against internal threat. In 1996, it was firm support and pressure from the United States and Mercosur members that allowed President Wasmosy to stand up to and eventually survive an attempted coup d'etat by Lino Oviedo.[17] As a result, the United States played an increasing role in Paraguayan domestic affairs, not only promoting issues of U.S. national interest (such as counternarcotics, copyright violation, arms smuggling, and contraband), but also engaging in internal Paraguayan policy, to the extent that throughout the decade "the United States could shape any, perhaps all, political outcomes in Paraguay."[18]

The combination of a weak, inefficient, corrupt, and discredited executive, the lack of a strong, professionalized bureaucracy to design or implement policy, and a highly presidentialist foreign policy in terms of structure and practice, produced a vacuum in terms of international relations. To an even greater extent than under Rodríguez, key issues such as renegotiations on the Itaipú dam Treaty, negotiations over the financial impact of Mercosur policy on Paraguay's economy,[19] and the growth of drug-trafficking and money laundering were not so much subjected to party political or presidential objectives as simply left neglected, unresolved, and off the political agenda. This was exacerbated by the spread of instability to the realm of the Ministry of Foreign Relations—with eight foreign ministers (under three different presidents) between 1998 and 2001. Foreign policy became increasingly subject to drag and drift, improvisation and inaction, and the questions of ideology and pragmatism became irrelevant as Paraguay became simply "a nation without a foreign policy."[20]

NICANOR DUARTE FRUTOS AND THE (TEMPORARY) ADOPTION OF PRAGMATISM

The victory of the Colorado Party candidate Nicanor Duarte Frutos in the presidential elections of April 2003 promised a break with the past. Although Duarte was from the same Colorado Party in power since

1947, he presented himself as a reformist with an initial discourse based on anti-neoliberalism, social and economic reform, and anticorruption. Offering the first strong leadership of the transition and with a coherent discourse—combining pragmatism with ideology—based on Latin American integration and solidarity, human rights and nonintervention, he seemed to fit the new inclusive and social narrative in Mercosur driven by presidents Lula, Kirchner, and Vázquez.

Duarte swiftly put an end to the foreign-policy drift that had characterized the previous administrations and put forward a new policy that intended to break with the alignments of the dictatorship and respond to the opportunities arising from Mercosur and beyond. Appointing a dynamic foreign minister, Leila Rachid (2003–2006), he pursued a new narrative, positively embracing the new discourse emerging at presidential level throughout Latin America, stressing, human rights, nonintervention, environment, and solidarity. While seeking closer links with a wide range of Latin American countries, including Cuba and Venezuela, on a regional level, he promoted greater economic integration through investment in a process of agro-industrialization (using energy from Itaipú), agricultural diversification, and increased exports to Mercosur.[21]

Initial policy statements—notable for their apparent ideological content—indicated a closer relationship with Mercosur in preference to the United States; Paraguay opposed U.S. intervention in Iraq, refused to back down on its support for the International Criminal Court established by the Treaty of Rome,[22] and struck highly favorable deals with Cuba over teachers and with Venezuela over diesel imports. It also added its voice to opposition to agricultural subsidies in the United States and the European Union and refused to sign the FTAA. Duarte also resisted pressure from the United States to send Paraguayan troops to Iraq and even refused to meet Otto Reich, the assistant secretary of state for Western Hemisphere Affairs, on a visit in 2004.

The integrationist narrative did produce some positive results. In 2005, Mercosur members approved the long-awaited Structural Development Funds (Fondos para la Convergencia Estructural de Mercosur—FOCEM) in a first step toward reducing economic asymmetries between country members.[23] Closer links were established with Bolivia in terms of agreements on trade, infrastructure, and defense, and with Venezuela through agreements on diesel with PDVSA, the Venezuelan state oil corporation. In March 2007, Paraguay received the first $48 million from Mercosur to improve infrastructure, while Brazil and Argentina promised to study compensation for the alleged loss of income for Paraguay from the Itaipú and Yacyretá dams respectively, and Brazil signed several agreements for infrastructure funding.

However, the lack of institutional cohesion, weak enforcement of agreed rules, vast structural and political asymmetries, and disappointing economic benefits led to mounting criticism of Mercosur, and the growing perception that, in the absence of established supranational institutions, Paraguay had "no commercial, cultural, diplomatic or political weight" in the bloc.[24] This in turn led to disenchantment with Mercosur within the private sector, the media, and the unions, reflected in an increasingly nationalist discourse criticizing Mercosur and specifically Brazil.[25] This was exacerbated by the lack of progress made since 1991 regarding a number of Paraguayan demands in terms of development aid, compensation for the collapse of its informal triangular trade, and renegotiation of the unfavorable treaties and loan conditions of the hydroelectric projects at Itaipú and Yacyretá, leading to criticisms that Mercosur was "at best not helping and at worst blocking Paraguayan development."[26]

Such lack of progress pushed Duarte to respond to U.S. overtures and explore increased bilateral relations with the United States in a new twist to Paraguay's traditional "pendular policy." An accompanying shift in rhetoric accompanied the move toward the United States as Duarte dropped his references to regional solidarity and cooperation in favor of security and governance. For the United States, improved relations with Paraguay may well have been spurred by its perceived lack of regional allies and a desire to divide Mercosur, which some saw as a potentially threatening trade bloc, especially given the centre-left orientation of its governments and the possibility of imminent Venezuelan membership. However, officially, U.S. concerns focused on Paraguay's lack of effective sovereignty along the Brazilian border and fear of terrorism and drugs in such "non-governed spaces" especially in the Tri-Border area around Ciudad del Este. Relations warmed rapidly; in 2005, Duarte became the first Paraguayan president to have been received in the White House, an event that was followed by the unprecedented visit of Donald Rumsfeld, secretary of state, during which he expressed concern over regional instability, clearly alluding to growing Venezuelan military, economic, and political cooperation with Bolivia. This was followed by a high-profile visit of vice-president Luis Castiglioni to the United States in 2006.

The results were a package of trade and aid agreements from 2005, including increased presence and investment of USAID, continued cooperation on the counterterrorism and anti–money-laundering activities in the Tri-Border area, and Paraguay's inclusion in the Millennium Challenge Corporation (MCC) Threshold Country Program (TCP) in May 2006, which brought $37 million of investment in various areas. In 2005 the possibility was raised of a free-trade agreement, which would have represented a serious violation—and indeed rejection—of the

Mercosur Treaty. Even more controversial, principally in symbolic terms, was the widely condemned agreement of Paraguay to permit 13 U.S. military missions on national territory in 2005–2006. Although, such operations had been held previously (indeed there were 46 operations between 2002 and 2006), the conditions that were agreed (including diplomatic immunity for U.S. troops while on exercise in Paraguay in terms of equipment and liability),[27] and the widespread fears of the establishment of a U.S. military base at Mariscal Estigarribia in the Chaco led to widespread condemnation, especially from within Mercosur.[28]

Despite a more proactive foreign policy between 2003 and 2005, which sought to combine pragmatism and a shifting ideological narrative,[29] by 2006 Duarte began to focus almost exclusively on domestic and Colorado Party concerns regarding succession. Having failed to gain congressional approval to prolong his mandate beyond the statutory one term by reforming the Constitution, he focused on guaranteeing the victory of his favored candidate in the Colorado primaries and then the presidential elections of 2008. Established Colorado practices replaced the national interest in foreign policy, as the first FOCEM funds that arrived in 2007 (earmarked for social projects), were used to strengthen clientelism (social housing and road resurfacing in contested constituencies) among the Colorado Party loyalists.[30] Furthermore, with reforms abandoned, there was "practically no advance in terms of professionalization of personnel and human resources" within the Ministry of Foreign Affairs.[31] As Duarte became increasingly embroiled in domestic issues, and with no independent ministry, foreign policy became paralyzed, reverting to its former stagnation and drift and reflecting its structural and institutional weakness.

TOWARD A NEW FOREIGN POLICY: ETHICS, PRAGMATISM, AND IDEOLOGY

The 2008 presidential elections stood out for a number of reasons: first, they resulted in the victory of an ex-bishop, Fernando Lugo; second, they ended 61 years of continuous Colorado Party rule; and third, they marked the first ever peaceful transfer of power between political parties in Paraguayan history. What made this even more striking was the highly ideological electoral platform of Fernando Lugo who promised far-reaching social reforms aimed at reducing Paraguay's high levels of poverty and inequality. To finance these reforms, Lugo included as part of his electoral platform the renegotiation of the Treaty of Itaipú with Brazil in order to obtain "a fair price" for Paraguay's electricity, based on market values. From the outset therefore, foreign policy was to be key to the success of Lugo's mandate.

The appointment of Alejandro Hamed Franco as minister of foreign relations (2008–2009) and his successor Héctor Lacognata (2009–present) put into motion a fundamental shift away from drift, dependency, and reaction, and toward a "redefinition" of the role and aims of foreign policy. In the context of Paraguay's historical dependency and vulnerability, Hamed Franco identified three guiding principles for foreign policy: recovery and defense of national sovereignty, independence of decision making, and the recovery of strategic resources.[32] Accompanied by long-overdue institutional reforms, these principles would go far in explaining many of the policies and conflicts of the first two years of Lugo's administration in terms of foreign policy.

From the outset, renegotiation of the Itaipú Treaty was presented as crucial to the success of Lugo's domestic policy. The hydroelectric dam is jointly owned by Paraguay and Brazil and is the largest in the world. Signed in secret between the two military governments in 1973, the terms that remain in force until 2023 are deeply unfavorable to Paraguay. Paraguay is entitled to 50 percent of the energy produced but uses less than 20 percent of its share (or 10 percent of the total). Under the terms of the treaty, however, it is unable to sell the remaining energy to third parties. Instead, it must cede the unused energy to Electrobras, the Brazilian state electricity corporation, at cost rather than market price, with minimal compensation. Electrobras then resells the energy in Brazil at a huge profit. As such, the current inequitable terms of the Treaty are hugely beneficial and of great importance to Brazil (to which Itaipú provides about 20 percent of its total energy) while "scandalously unfair to Paraguay," which effectively subsidizes cheap energy for Brazil.[33]

The issue of Itaipú—widely seen in Paraguay as a political issue regarding an enclave of Brazilian power[34]—was portrayed by Lugo within the framework of national sovereignty and control over natural resources, as well as dependency, asymmetry, and injustice. However, as well as an ideological dimension, it also had a clear pragmatic element; renegotiation would produce a higher income from Itaipú, which would fund the social reforms and poverty alleviation projects that were central to Lugo's program.

What was initially seen as a radical position on Itaipú during the presidential election campaign, rapidly snowballed into a national consensus on the imperative of renegotiation. Having initially refused to even consider renegotiation, Brazil gradually relented on holding talks, perhaps encouraged by Paraguay's veiled threat to resort to the International Court of Justice in The Hague within one year should diplomatic avenues prove unworkable. Following the establishment of the Bilateral Technical Negotiating Commission in September 2008 to examine and respond to Paraguay's demands, in July 2009, presidents Lula and Lugo signed a 31-point *aide memoire* that represented a potential breakthrough for Paraguay. Under the agreement, Brazil confirmed concessions already offered, including parity in management (as established in the 1973 Treaty), a full audit to be carried out by the Paraguayan Comptroller General, and the completion of outstanding works on the Paraguayan side (including the key issues of a sectional substation and transmission line to Asunción). It also made further concessions, including, most importantly, an increase in annual compensation payment received by Paraguay for the sale of excess electricity from US$120 million to US$360 million. On the other hand, the agreement did not include any reduction of the disputed Paraguayan share of the dam's US$19 billion debt to the Brazilian treasury, nor recognition of Paraguay's claim that "just compensation" should be in the region of US$900 million per year, nor any compromise on Paraguay's right to sell excess electricity to third countries until 2023—although it will gradually be allowed to sell surplus energy on the Brazilian market.[35]

Although the agreement was immediately approved in Paraguay, by mid-2010 it was still awaiting approval by the Brazilian Senate. There is little support for the measure in Itamaraty or the Brazilian Right, and with elections approaching in late 2010 it became increasingly unlikely that the Lula administration would push the measure through the Senate, given the potential electoral risk involved. Moreover, President Dilma Rousseff, elected in November 2010 has made it clear that this is not a priority for her administration. However, whether or not it is approved, the agreement does reveal a number of important elements in terms of foreign relations: first, agency was key to the deal, with Brazilian willingness to compromise widely attributed to the personal chemistry between the two presidents and the personal desire of Lula to help boost Lugo's flagging domestic support; second, despite the rhetoric of justice, sovereignty, and regional solidarity, the deal was essentially pragmatic, both from the Paraguayan (a significant and desperately needed potential growth in income stream) and the Brazilian side (concerns over political instability and lack of security in the Eastern Border Region); third, its lack of implantation reflected the vast asymmetries of power between the neighbors and the lack of leverage that Paraguay, very much as the junior partner, enjoys.

The second major foreign policy issue with Brazil concerns the Eastern Border Region. Brazil has been increasingly concerned about increasing evidence of a lack of Paraguayan state presence in certain areas, increasing cross-border lawlessness, and the growth of narcotics smuggling in the region. This insecurity and lack of state presence is also related to

issues of soya production and *brasiguayos*, Brazilian immigrants—now
numbering about 500,000, or 10 percent of the population—who have
been settling and buying vast tracts of land in the Eastern Border Region
since the 1970s. Over the past ten years, Paraguay has undergone a boom
in soya production, and is now the fourth largest exporter with almost
3 million hectares under cultivation, with production and exports dominated by *brasiguayos*. Despite the vast profits involved, soya producers
pay no direct taxes, use cheap labor, and contribute disproportionately
to widespread environmental destruction and landlessness. This has
resulted in growing resentment and increasingly violent land occupations
backed by peasant organizations, especially in the departments of San
Pedro del Norte and Alto Paraná. Efforts by President Duarte to force
soya producers into the tax system and to enter dialogue regarding land
reform were blocked by *tractorazo* protests by Brazilian landowners who,
with high-level backing from Brazil, rapidly emerged as one of the most
powerful—and conservative—lobby groups in the country.[36]

Reflecting the strength of nationalist interests, Brazil sought to
strengthen Paraguayan state presence in the region, but also to offer protection to the rights and livelihoods of Brazilians in Paraguay and show
its neighbor that it would not tolerate threats to its citizens. In October
2008, the Brazilian armed forces carried out a series of military exercises
along the border with Paraguay. Since this followed soon after legislation
creating SINAMOB, a national mobilization system designed to protect
companies and citizens outside Brazil prepared jointly by Itamaraty and
the armed forces, it was widely interpreted in Paraguay as an inappropriate warning from a bullying regional superpower not to pursue nationalist
policies that could adversely affect the interests of *brasiguayo* landowners
or harm Brazil's benefits from Itaipú. This in turn has fueled support for
the more independent, ideological, and highly pragmatic stance taken
by Lugo in terms of foreign policy. The issues of Itaipú, *brasiguayos*, soya
production, and lack of security reflect parallel, often colliding ideological and pragmatic issues. From a Paraguayan perspective, they may be
intrinsically related to ideological concerns over sovereignty, justice, and
equality; however, on a pragmatic level, Paraguay cannot run the risk of
potential conflict with a powerful neighbor on whom it is dependent
for approximately 20 percent of its exports and 30 percent of its foreign
investment.[37]

In other areas too, the Lugo administration sought to adopt pragmatic
policies to broaden international relations, in which ideology or at least
principles, played a central role. Responding to political changes and a
certain shared ideological affinity, Lugo formed closer links with Latin
America, especially with those countries in ALBA. In April 2009, Lugo

and Evo Morales signed a historic and definitive agreement settling a border dispute that had led to the Chaco War (1932–1935), while pointedly declaring the hope that natural resources could now "be developed and used by both countries without any foreign intervention."[38] Lugo also sought to reinvigorate URUPABOL, the forum for negotiation and joint action between Bolivia, Paraguay, and Uruguay.

It was over Venezuela's entry into Mercosur that Lugo found his foreign-policy vision clashing with the realities of a foreign-policy framework historically dominated by domestic and party interests. In 2009 the Brazilian Senate voted to accept Venezuela's full membership to Mercosur, leaving Paraguay the only Mercosur member still to approve the measure. Despite strong support from Lugo, Hamed Franco, and his successor Héctor Lacognata, the Paraguayan Senate remained fiercely opposed, both on ideological grounds (opposition to the content of "21st Century Socialism") and party political grounds (the wish to undermine the president whenever possible). Initial attempts to push the bill through in June 2009 were withdrawn due to the scale of congressional opposition and a relentless media campaign, spearheaded by Paraguay's leading daily newspaper, *ABC Color*, which strongly denounced Lugo's alleged objective of introducing 21st Century Socialism into Paraguay, in a campaign reminiscent of the anti-Communist diatribes in the press under Stroessner. By mid 2010, with no apparent sign of agreement with the Senate, Lugo was under considerable pressure from Brazil (allegedly linking promises of progress on Itaipú with approval of Venezuela's membership) and Venezuela (in renegotiations regarding the spiraling debt of Petropar, the state owned oil company, with PDVSA) to force the bill through. Once again, internal domestic politics shaped and limited Paraguay's foreign-policy objectives.

Despite domestic criticism from the Paraguayan right, such a proactive policy in Latin America was also highly pragmatic: agreements on energy (oil), technology, agriculture, education, health, and food with Venezuela were on terms highly favorable to Paraguay; support for Venezuelan entry into Mercosur, was not merely an ideological act of solidarity, but a pragmatic attempt to broaden and deepen Mercosur and adjust the balance of power away from Brazil; agreements with Cuba brought much-needed teaching expertise; the development of close relations with Brazil—despite so many sources of tension—led to potential concessions on Itaipú; and reinvigoration of UPRABOL sought to give a stronger voice to smaller countries at a time of increased regional integration.

Likewise, the strengthening of economic ties with a broad array of developing countries in North Africa, the Middle East, the Gulf States, and Southeast Asia had a strong ideological component (solidarity with other developing countries) but held pragmatic advantages, not only in attempting to break Paraguay's historical isolation and low profile, but in bringing favorable investment and trade. These initiatives were accompanied by the establishment of relations with Russia and Scandinavia, and overtures made to China, currently the main source of Paraguayan imports but with whom Paraguay has no diplomatic relations. [39]

Lugo also sought to modify relations with the United States. In September 2009 he revoked plans for U.S. troops to hold joint military exercises and development projects in Paraguay. Although couched in ideological terms, this was a highly pragmatic gesture given the strong regional opposition from countries such as Argentina, Brazil, Venezuela, Bolivia, and Ecuador to the expansion of U.S. military bases in the region. Pragmatism in the form of good relations with the United States was however restored when Lugo visited the White House the following month during the last days of the Bush administration. In a further effort to appease U.S. concerns regarding security, insurgency, drug-trafficking, and contraband, Lugo not only agreed to full cooperation with the Drug Enforcement Administration (DEA), but also to the signing of various deals on internal security with Colombia, the main U.S. ally in the region, in 2009.

Finally, in a reflection of what can be seen as the beginning of the true transition (the fall of the Colorado Party from power in 2008), a long-overdue process of professionalization was promoted in the Ministry of Foreign Affairs. With most appointments and promotions traditionally reflecting Colorado Party affiliation and political interests, the system was overhauled and a merit-based system was introduced as from 2008. The aim was clearly to create an independent, modern, and professional ministry that would be able to formulate and implement policies pertaining to the national, rather than merely Party, interest. By 2010 the Ministry of Foreign Affairs was widely seen as a model of state reform in terms of progress toward greater transparency and professionalization.

In its first two years, the administration of Lugo succeeded in breaking a tradition of a reactive, low profile, and noninstitutionalized foreign policy, which reflected domestic (and Colorado Party) interests, was executive in nature, and which was characterized by opportunism at best and drift at worst. In its place, it rapidly developed a proactive, high-profile foreign policy, which contained an ideological discourse based on solidarity and national sovereignty. However, given the realities of isolation, underdevelopment, and weakness it was also a highly pragmatic policy designed to "open new spaces" in foreign policy to use the words of Hamed Franco,[40] raise the international profile of Paraguay, and attract much-needed trade and investment on favorable terms. In this sense, pragmatism and ideology went hand in hand to a remarkable degree.

CONCLUSIONS

James Rosenau has argued that small states, especially underdeveloped ones, are more susceptible to pressures of external forces and changes in the international system. Historically, Paraguay has been constrained by the structure of international relations and, as with other small states, disproportionately vulnerable to international configurations.[41] Yet within this, as we have seen, agency is clearly of paramount importance. During the Cold War, Stroessner adopted an opportunistic and pragmatic policy to gain support based on anti-Communism for his authoritarian regime. Rodríguez responded rapidly to international pressures in favor of free markets and democratization with a highly pragmatic policy in order to enhance his legitimacy and hence sustain his administration. Duarte (initially) and Lugo, far more effectively, responded pragmatically, and in the case of the latter ideologically, to the trend toward greater regional integration, based on solidarity, sovereignty, and control of natural resources. International configurations have not predetermined policy, but they have provided significant limitations and opportunities, and while policy under Colorado administrations has been predominantly reactive, Lugo has shown that there is space for a more proactive policy.

Paraguay, as with many small states, has tended to be more susceptible to agency, in the form of a presidentialist foreign policy designed for a domestic audience and domestic objectives, but with the added factor of policy designed to support both dictatorship (1954–1989) and Colorado Party interests (1954–2008), both under authoritarian and democratic systems. A consequence of this has been the underdevelopment of a modern, professional, bureaucratic body able to design or implement a coherent foreign policy in the national interest. The dangers inherent in such a model are obvious, especially if the presidency is weak or lacks domestic legitimacy—as in Paraguay during much of the 1990s—when both pragmatism and ideology become irrelevant, and foreign policy became characterized by neglect, inactivity, and, above all, drift. The Paraguayan case clearly shows that domestic political structures, interests, and limitations go far in defining not only the orientation of foreign policy, but also its implantation, effectiveness, and success.

Within this panorama, pragmatism and ideology have been present in an interactive and changing relationship. Stroessner's foreign policy was pragmatic in sustaining his regime, and opportunistic, in promoting an anti-Communist ideological stance—at least until international changes rendered it outdated and isolated in the 1980s. Likewise Rodríguez sought to absorb ideological currents (democracy and free markets) in a pragmatic and successful attempt to gain support for his administration. Whether these polices were ideological (as claimed by their protagonists) or merely opportunistic is certainly open to debate, but they contrast with the period of prolonged political crisis between 1996 and 2003 when foreign policy become characterized by prolonged drift.

Despite the pervasiveness of the legacy of authoritarianism and Colorado Party rule and hence strong elements of continuity, the attempts to develop a new foreign policy since 2003, and especially under Lugo, reflect that there is significant space for change, and for a combination of pragmatism and ideology, or at least principle, to create a more coherent foreign policy in the national, rather than purely regime, interest. The current promotion of a principled and ideologically informed stance on a raft of issues including poverty, inequality, and dependency is not only unique among administrations in the past 50 years, but reflects and informs the development of a new foreign policy. Such efforts indicate that in the current globalized environment, in which new spaces and opportunities for bilateral, regional, and global relations have emerged, considerations based on principle, ideology, and pragmatism can be complementary and form part of a dynamic foreign policy pursued in the national interest—even in poor and previously isolated countries.

NOTES

1. Hey, J. (2003) "Redefining our Understanding of Small State Foreign Policy," in Hey, J. A. K. (ed) *Small States in World Politics*, Boulder, CO, Lynne Rienner, pp. 185–95.
2. Masi, F. (2008) "Inserción Económica de Paraguay en el Mundo: Notas para el debate electoral," Asunción: CADEP, p. 1.
3. See Arditi, B. (1992) *Adios a Stroessner: la Reconstrucción Política en el Paraguay*, Asunción, RP Ediciones and Lambert, P. (1997) "Assessing the Transition," in Lambert, P. and Nickson R. A. (1997) *The Transition to Democracy in Paraguay*, London: Macmillan, pp. 200–13.
4. The NSD emphasized the use of security and armed forces to counter both internal and external Communist threats. It was implemented in Paraguay both as a means to suppress opposition and ensure U.S. political and economic support.
5. Nickson, R. A. (1993) *Historical Dictionary of Paraguay.* Metuchen, NJ: Scarecrow Press, p. 607.
6. Mora, F. O., and Cooney, J. W. (2007) *Paraguay and the United States: Distant Allies*, University of Georgia Press, London, p. 142.
7. Mora F. O. (2003) "Paraguay: From the Stronato to the Democratic Transition," in Hey, J. (ed.) *Small States in World Politics*, Boulder, Co: Lynne Rienner, p. 30.

8. Masi, F. (1991) "Relaciones internacionales del Paraguay con Stroessner y sin Stroessner," Working Paper No. 3, Instituto Paraguayo para la Integración de América Latina, Asunción.

9. Lambert, P. (1997) "Ideology and Opportunism in the Regime of Alfredo Stroessner," in Fowler, W. *Ideologues and Ideologies in Latin America*, Westport, CT: Greenwood, pp. 125–38.

10. Simon, J. L. (1990ª) "Una Política Exterior de Automarginamiento: el Paraguay en la Crisis Terminal del Autoritarismo de Stroessner y América Latin en la Década de los Ochenta," in Simón, J. L. (ed.) *Política Exterior y Relaciones Internacionales del Paraguay Contemporáneo*, Asunción: Centro Paraguayo de Estudios Sociologicos, pp. 323–68.

11. Nickson, R. A. (1989) "The Overthrow of the Stroessner Regime: Re-establishing the Status Quo?" *Bulletin of Latin American Research* Vol. 8, No.2, pp. 185–209.

12. Lambert, P. (1997) "Assessing the Transition," in Lambert, P., and Nickson, R. A. (eds.) *The Transition to Democracy in Paraguay*, London: Macmillan, pp. 200–13.

13. Mora and Cooney (2007).

14. Masi, F. (1997) "Foreign Policy," in Lambert, P., and Nickson, R. A., *The Transition to Democracy in Paraguay*, London: Palgrave, pp. 174–84.

15. Simón, J. L. (1995) "Los Déficits de la Actual Política Exterior Paraguaya frente a los Avances de las Democracias Vecinas," en J. L. Simón (ed.) *Política Exterior y Democracia en el Paraguay y sus Vecinos*, Asunción: Fundación Hans Seidel.

16. Abente, D. (1999) "'People Power' in Paraguay," *Journal of Democracy*, Volume 10, Number 3, July 1999, pp. 93–100.

17. This led to the signing of the Ushuaia Protocol, a clause that effectively barred membership to Mercosur for nondemocratic regimes. See Peña, F. (1997) "Integration and Democracy: The Experience of Mercosur," *Economic Reform Today*, No. 3, pp. 8–12; and Valenzuela, A. (1997) "Paraguay: The Coup that Didn't Happen," *Journal of Democracy*, Volume 8, Number 1, January 1997, pp. 43–55.

18. Mora and Cooney (2007), p. 252.

19. Most critically, this included the destruction of Paraguay's comparative economic advantage in triangular trade (or re-exportation) to Brazil and Argentina, due to the lowering of internal tariffs.

20. Mora (2003), p. 27.

21. Masi (2008).

22. Paraguay was one of 139 nations to sign the Treaty of Rome, which set up the International Criminal Court (ICC) in 1998. Fearing that its troops in combat or on exercises would be vulnerable to the Court, the United States opposed the Treaty and pressured (poorer) countries to ratify bilateral immunity pacts with the United States, under threat of withholding aid. Paraguay was one of about 50 governments that refused to cede to U.S. demands.

23. FOCEM is funded by contributions from the Mercosur members to an annual amount of $100 million, of which 70 percent is from Brazil, 27 percent from Argentina, 2 percent from Uruguay, and 1 percent from Paraguay. Under the 10-year scheme, which began in 2007, Paraguay would contribute 1 percent of the total but receive 48 percent of funds.

24. Rodríguez, J. C. (2006) "La Nueva Politica pendular de Paraguay: Entre el Mercosur y el ALCA," *Nueva Sociedad*, No. 203, pp. 10–14, 12. Other issues raised by Paraguay (and indeed, Uruguay) were the reduction of structural trade differentials and political asymmetries, the strengthening and development of supranational institutions, and the implementation of existing laws and mechanisms. Furthermore, Brazil was accused of distortions of regulatory distortions, including restrictions on access to certain markets, discretional use of fiscal incentives and credits, and other forms of state aid and investment. See Masi (2008).

25. Miranda, A. (2006) "Tropas Norteamericanas en Paraguay: Reto para Brasil," Unpublished paper, p. 14.

26. Rodríguez (2006), p. 10. See also Lambert, P. (2004) "Paraguay in MERCOSUR: Why Bother?" in Dominguez, F., and Guedes de Oliveveira, M. (eds.), *Mercosur: Between integration and Democracy*, Oxford: Peter Lang, 2004, pp. 157–79.

27. The Paraguayan Congress approved Law 2594 on May 5, 2005, allowing U.S. troops to enjoy diplomatic immunity, including exemption from inspection of imported and exported goods, exemption from taxes and from any claims of liability for damage or death.

28. U.S. interest in establishing a military presence in Paraguay would appear obvious. Paraguay is strategically situated between Bolivia, Brazil, and Argentina, has significant water and energy resources, and with a weak state has been unable to control arms smuggling, drug trafficking, and other illegal activities, including alleged but unproven terrorist networks in the Tri-Border Area. The presence of increasingly organized peasant movements and alleged U.S. involvement in counterinsurgency training did little to dampen the fears of Mercosur members. See Zibechi, R. (2006) "Paraguay: Platform for Hemispheric Hegemony," IRC Americas program Special Report; and Dangl, B. (2006) "The U.S. Military Descends on Paraguay," *The Nation,* http://www.thenation.com/doc/20060717/dangl. Accessed July 17, 2008.

29. Interview by author with Elvio Venegas, Vice-minister of Foreign Affairs, July 26, 2007.

30. Masi (2008), p. 35.

31. Interview by author with foreign policy analyst, Fernando Masi, July 26, 2007.

32. See Ministerio de Relaciones Exteriores (2008) "Informe de los Primeros Cien Días de Gestión," Ministerio de RREE, Asunción.

33. Nickson, R. A. (2008) "Paraguay: Fernando Lugo vs the Colorado machine," *Open Democracy*, http://www.opendemocracy.net/article/

democracy_power/politics_protest/paraguay_fernando_lugo. Accessed March 4, 2008.

34. Interview by author with Paraguayan Vice-minister of Foreign Affairs, Jorge Lara Castro, June 16, 2009

35. See Nickson, R. A. (2010) "Revising the Past: The Paraguayan Energy Sector in Perspective," http://www2.lse.ac.uk/IDEAS/publications/reports/pdf/SU005/nickson.pdf. Accessed May 16, 2010.

36. For a good analysis of the issue of soya, see Nickson, R. A. (2008) "Paraguay's historic election," *Open Democracy*, April, 22, 2008; and Zibechi, R. (2008) "Paraguay entre Lula y la soya," in *La Jornada*, Mexico DF, November 7, 2008.

37. Masi (2008), p. 38.

38. http://news.bbc.co.uk/1/hi/world/americas/8022017.stm. 28/04/2009. Accessed July 16, 2009.

39. Since the dictatorship of Stroessner, Paraguay has retained very close ties with Taiwan. It is a major recipient of Taiwanese international aid and investment, and is the only Latin American nation that does not have diplomatic relations with China.

40. Interview by the author with Alejandro Hamed Franco, Paraguayan Minister of Foreign Affairs, June 16, 2009.

41. Rosenau, J. (1966) "Pre-Theories and Theories of Foreign Policy," in Farell, B. (ed.) *Approaches to Comparative and International Politics*, Illinois: Northwestern University, pp. 27–93.

CHAPTER 5

ARGENTINE FOREIGN POLICY UNDER THE KIRCHNERS: IDEOLOGICAL, PRAGMATIC, OR SIMPLY PERONIST?

ANDRÉS MALAMUD

INTRODUCTION

Argentina under the Kirchners has become a puzzle for foreign observers. Neither as heterodox as Chávez and Morales nor as orthodox as Lula and Bachelet, the presidential couple are nonetheless vocal members of the contemporary shift to the left in Latin America. Are their policies to be understood as informed by an ideological program or rather as a pragmatic approach wrapped in high-toned rhetoric? Foreign policy is an area relatively prone to the divergence of words from deeds, given its aloofness from public scrutiny and the little direct impact it has on citizens' daily lives—especially in countries that are of lesser international importance. Yet, a third interpretation is possible: foreign policy may not be internally coherent, either ideologically or pragmatically, but rather expresses domestic struggles, reflex actions, and even personal moods. Thus, foreign-policy subordination to short-term domestic concerns (*cortoplacismo interno*) could explain a great deal of the Argentine puzzle.

To attempt a periodization of contemporary Argentine foreign policy requires more imagination than method. Indeed, over the last eighty years the policies flowing out of the Casa Rosada have been at least as many as the presidents themselves. Although in most countries foreign policy tends to be less politicized than domestic policies, and thus more durable, this has not been the case in Argentina. Foreign-policy changes have occurred in the wake of both regime change and administration change—even if the incumbent party did not change—but also under the mandate of the same president. The most conspicuous case was the rapprochement of de facto president Leopoldo Galtieri with Fidel Castro and Yasser Arafat in the context of the Falklands/Malvinas War, after six years of courting of the Western powers. However puzzling this may appear, the Peronist pendulum is even more striking. In ten years, a Peronist administration may evolve from autarkic and militant anti-Americanism to actively seeking American investment in strategic national resources such as oil (as Perón's did between 1946 and 1955) or the other way round (as when overtly pro-American, pro-market reformer Carlos Menem, 1989–1999, was succeeded by such staunch critics of neoliberalism as Néstor Kirchner, 2003–2007, and Cristina Fernández de Kirchner since 2007). To pin down what is behind such volatility it is more important to understand Argentine politics than policies. This is tantamount to saying that foreign policy has been mostly determined by domestic rather than international factors.

Upon a background of barely professionalized state bureaucracy and leader-centered party politics, Argentine presidents have traditionally enjoyed a wide room for maneuver—especially in times of crisis. The Kirchners used this latitude to put foreign policy to the service of two goals: solving fiscal urgencies and gathering electoral support. The former dealt with substance and sought foreign partners, whereas the latter revolved mainly around form and targeted domestic audiences. Remarkably, both were frequently self-defeated by a tactless leadership style, which became the cornerstone of the country's foreign policy under the Kirchners' administrations.

This chapter scrutinizes Argentina's foreign policy vis-à-vis four key foreign actors, namely Brazil (and South American regional blocs), Venezuela, the United States, and the International Monetary Fund, in order to gauge the extent to which it can be explained by recourse to ideology, pragmatism, or rather domestic hiccups.

This chapter shows that the main objectives of the Kirchners' foreign policy have been to garner electoral support at home and to obtain financial assistance abroad. The former has been pursued through ideological and combative rhetoric, the latter through pragmatic international alliances. In order to make means meet ends, collective agency has been as significant as individual agency: the historical flexibility of the Peronist party, compounded by the leadership skills of Néstor Kirchner, made it possible to dissociate words from deeds and to play discursive brinkmanship, while abiding by all relevant international norms. This move was helped by the limited professionalization of the foreign service and the subordinate role played by ministers under the Argentine constitutional provisions, which leave foreign-policy decisions exclusively in presidential hands. Finally, the emergency situation created by the economic collapse of 2001 gave legitimacy to the Kirchners' claim to change and to their appeal of leading Argentina in a new direction.

OVERVIEW OF THE KIRCHNER ADMINISTRATIONS

Between 1930 and 1983, Argentina experienced half a century of political instability and economic decline. Political instability manifested itself in six overt coups d'état and at least as many *coups de palace*. In that period, only three out of twenty-three presidents completed their pre-established mandate: Agustín Justo, Juan Perón, and Jorge Videla. The fact that all three were military officers—although not all came to power through a military coup d'etat—suggests how difficult it was for civilians to stay in office. In 1983, however, a new democratic regime was successfully inaugurated, which would remain unbroken until the present. Yet, political instability continued by other means.

In the twenty-six years that followed, the Justicialist Party (PJ or Peronism) governed for nearly eighteen years while the Radical Civic Union (UCR or Radicals)—alone or in coalition—ruled for about eight. The performance of both parties differed significantly: while the PJ was able to complete all of its constitutional mandates (1989–1995, 1995–1999, and 2003–2007), the Radicals failed to complete any of theirs (1983–1989 and 1999–2003). Because of this, Calvo and Murillo speak of the "new iron law of Argentine politics," whereby "non-Peronists are able to win presidential elections but are unable to govern until the end of their terms in office."[1]

When Néstor Kirchner, the Justicialist governor of the small province of Santa Cruz, arrived to the presidency in May 2003, he faced two important issues. First, Argentina was still recovering from the 2001 collapse that had left the country broken and its political system in shambles. Second, he had won the election with a scant 22 percent of the vote, the lowest percentage ever, and was unable to legitimize his victory through a runoff as the front-runner, Carlos Menem, had already stood down fearing a landslide defeat. Kirchner's mandate seemed to begin under inauspicious circumstances and in turbulent times. However, soon after taking office, he surprised everybody by standing up to vested powers, including the military, the Supreme Court, the business associations, and even his own protector, Eduardo Duhalde, who had decisively promoted Kirchner's candidacy while serving as interim president.

Following four years of soaring economic growth and strong political dominance, Cristina Fernández was elected to replace his husband in 2007. Although there were expectations that she would be more institutionally minded, instilling diplomatic softness where rudeness had predominated, it did not happen. Instead, relations with the United States were embittered by an awkward incident involving illicit Venezuelan money, and a harsh domestic conflict arose only three months later when the farming associations took to the streets in protest against a tax reform.

Unlike Brazil, whose foreign policy throughout the twentieth century was known for its coherence and remarkable continuity,[2] Argentina's foreign policy underwent three different periods over the same century. First, from 1880 until the interwar period, it followed three main orientations: "Europeanism, opposition to the United States, and isolation from the rest of Latin America."[3] Second, following the Second World War, the paradigm entailed nonalignment vis-à-vis the United States, support for Latin American integration without doing much to construct it, opposition to the establishment of supranational organizations that would curtail Argentine autonomy and development, implementation of a development strategy oriented toward import substitution, the introduction of reforms to the international financial and economic institutions in the interests of developing countries, and diversification in terms of trade links irrespective of ideology.[4]

Third, in the aftermath of the Cold War, Peronist president Carlos Menem introduced a radical departure from the existing policy orientation. So-called automatic alignment or pragmatic acquiescence was premised on a number of related factors, including the subordination of foreign policy to the political and strategic interests of the United States, the definition of national interests in economic terms, acceptance and support for the basic rules of the free market (and possibly neoliberal) international economic and financial order, and economic integration.[5] The arrival of the Kirchners gave a new twist to an already twisted history.

As Margheritis explains, "Apparently contradictory and inconsistent foreign policy behavior shaped Argentina's reputation as an erratic and relatively unpredictable international actor—the adjectives going, in fact, from pariah to wayward to unreliable partner."[6] This foreign behavior has included different kinds and degrees of turns, ranging from small adjustments to dramatic policy shifts. Remarkably, such a pattern has been due to policy inconsistencies not only between political parties but also within them. The most striking volte-faces are exhibited by the PJ, a political organization rooted in the popular classes and oriented toward power, but almost completely bereft of a coherent ideology.

The PJ is a party created from above. Its founder was Juan Perón, a military officer who, holding a key executive office, attempted to build a popular base of support to promote his political goals. Consequently, the party doctrine, language, and organization were pervaded by a hierarchical temperament. Hierarchy meant a predisposition toward command and obedience, but it did not imply any substantive content. Hence, the internal fluidity of Peronism facilitated sharp and often contradictory programmatic shifts such as those undertaken by Menem in the 1990s and Kirchner in the 2000s. This was due to the tendency of the Peronist bosses to follow office-holding leaders: as the authority of the party bodies is rarely taken seriously, "control of the state means control of the party."[7] The province and patronage-based nature of Argentine political careers further potentiates this effect;[8] as would soon become apparent, party flexibility would allow for a rapid reversal to a nationalist, populist, and antineoliberal program.

In order to evaluate Argentine foreign relations under the Kirchners it is reasonable to focus on the key allies and enemies as defined by the administration. Whereas Brazil/Mercosur and Venezuela stand out among the former, the United States and international financial institutions, such as the IMF, are prominent among the latter. In all cases, however, hidden nuances and mixed policies have usually been as significant as, and sometimes more significant than, official rhetoric.

FOUR KEY FOREIGN-POLICY ISSUES UNDER THE KIRCHNERS

RELATIONS WITH BRAZIL AND MERCOSUR

Once a pragmatic approach to regional integration, Mercosur has gradually become more ideologically loaded as its effectiveness dwindled over time.[9] Although the Argentine government has continued to support the project at the discursive level, its substantive strategies have been much less constructive and were guided by material interests rather than ideological motivations. Those material interests are rooted in domestic considerations and have promoted protectionist policies as a response to social pressures or fiscal needs; international calculations were less influential in Argentina than they were in Brazil.[10] Thus, whereas ideology-based rhetoric called for integration, interest-based policy hindered it. While it comes as no surprise that concrete policies were oriented toward economic gains, less obvious is that the rhetoric also served a pragmatic purpose, as it was directed toward securing electoral returns. The plea for regionalism is popular in Latin America, explaining the Kirchners' rhetorical support regardless of their lack of effective action.

Nowhere is foot-dragging more evident than in the negligence with which Mercosur member states have implemented, or rather failed to implement, the decisions made to upgrade their common institutions. To start with, the organization lacks a budget; with the exception of a small fund established in 2005 to appease Paraguay and Uruguay, all expenses are supported in equal parts by every country. Second, there is no supranational authority, even less a regional executive office such as the European Commission. Third, there is no effective system of dispute settlement: although an ad hoc mechanism was created in 1991 and a permanent tribunal replaced it in 2006, both mechanisms combined have issued only twelve rulings in eighteen years—as a reference, the European Court of Justice issues around 500 rulings a year, and even at the age of Mercosur it used to issue between 30 and 80 per year. And yet, the most blatant case of noncompliance concerns the decision to set up a permanent parliament. According to the foundational protocol signed in 2005, a decision regarding demographic representation had to be taken by the end of 2007, and direct elections were to be held before the end of 2010; as of 2010, the decision had not been taken and direct elections had been held only in Paraguay, with all evidence suggesting that no other country would follow suit in due time. Massive implementation gaps and inoperative institutions reveal the pragmatic nature of Mercosur, as its advocates wave the flag of regional integration—as long as it is popular—while systematically shirking on regional commitments. In this, to be fair, it should be said that Argentina's strategy is no different from that of the other member countries'.

Brazil is Argentina's main trade partner and key regional ally. Argentine leaders and diplomats alike see this partnership as based on an equal footing. Therefore, any time Brazil hints at affirming itself as either a regional leader or a global power, Argentine foreign-policy moves closer to the United States—or other circumstantial allies such as, more recently, Venezuela—in order to restore the regional balance.[11] This ambivalence, or pendular game, recedes in good times and surges during economic hardship, independent of the party in government. In the 1990s, Carlos Menem was one of the Mercosur founders while simultaneously aligning his country with U.S. foreign strategies. Likewise, in the 2000s, Néstor and Cristina Kirchner cultivated an excellent relationship with the Lula administration, while simultaneously striking a close alliance with the Venezuelan president Hugo Chávez.

Argentina has consistently opposed one of the Brazil's most-cherished foreign-policy goals: to obtain a permanent seat in the United Nations Security Council. In 2004 a high level committee submitted to the UN Secretary-General a proposal that called for the admission of new permanent members, after which four countries jockeyed to obtain the seats: Brazil, Germany, India, and Japan (G-4). Notably, however, a larger group was formed to oppose the proposal and advanced instead the introduction of semipermanent membership. First called the Coffee Group and later renamed Uniting for Consensus, this group brought together the regional rivals of the G-4, including Argentina, Italy, South Korea, and Pakistan and effectively prevented the aspiring Security Council members from selling their bid on behalf of their respective regions.[12] Though not a surprise, the fact that the Brazilian main regional partner was, at the same time, one of its staunchest opponents was a heavy blow to its image as regional leader. Overall, Argentina holds similar political ambitions to Brazil and nurtures recurrent economic grievances toward it, which have given place to protectionist spasms and hindered further integration.

The domestic sources of Argentine regional policy are even clearer vis-à-vis Uruguay, as the so-called pulp mill conflict reveals. The conflict, which concerned the construction of a paper-processing plant by a Finnish company near Fray Bentos, a small Uruguayan town, severely strained relations between the two countries. Lying some 30 kilometers from the Argentine city of Gualeguaychú, a popular tourist resort area on the bank of the Uruguay River, the installation is of significant economic importance to Uruguay, representing the largest foreign investment ever. In April 2005, resident and environmental groups blocked one of the three international bridges that connect the two countries, protesting against the installation of the pulp mills. The protest gained political and diplomatic significance as senior Argentine political figures began to support the protest against the presumed environmental damage that would be produced by the mill's operations and the alleged violation of an agreement regulating the use of the river. During the last days of his presidency, Kirchner backed the protests on environmental grounds. The fact that his administration had done nothing to treat the highly polluted river that surrounds Buenos Aires, on whose shores millions of people live, speaks to the authentic reasons behind the official position: not to alienate potential voters or provoke demonstrations. If the causes were domestic, the consequences were international: in October 2008, after Kirchner had been succeeded by his wife, Uruguay announced that it would veto his candidacy to become the first permanent secretary-general of the newly formed Union of South American Nations (UNASUR). The new mill, which had begun to operate in November 2007, became the subject of a protracted and increasingly hostile dispute that was arbitrated by the International Court of Justice in The Hague. The appeal of both countries to the Court testified to the feebleness of the Mercosur dispute-settlement institutions as much as to the unfulfilled promises of South American integration. In 2010, after the Court had issued a balanced verdict and José Mujica had succeeded Tabaré Vazquez as Uruguayan president, the Uruguayan veto was lifted and Néstor Kirchner was finally elected as the first Secretary-General of UNASUR. A few days later the blockade of the bridge was ended.

RELATIONS WITH VENEZUELA

Foreign relations between Venezuela and Argentina became closer after Néstor Kirchner took office. Lacking much-needed foreign credit, the newly elected President turned to the oil-rich Bolivarian Republic for help, the only country that would buy Argentine state bonds, while the rest of the world still viewed with distrust the ability of the new government to overcome the default on its debt. Taking advantage of oil revenues, President Chávez seized the opportunity to forge a strategic alliance. Venezuela went on to become Argentina's most significant financial supporter. As of early 2007, for example, it had purchased US$4,250 million in Argentine debt bonds. At the behest of the Argentine government, Venezuela provided US$135 million to leading Argentine dairy producer SanCor to ward off a takeover by the American financier George Soros. The total loan, as in other cases, is being repaid with SanCor exports of milk powder to Venezuela. Chávez's foreign aid has not only helped to bail out Argentina, improving its finances and standing among creditors, but it also helped Kirchner to develop his economic program. However, this seems not to be the only way Chávez provided financial support to his friends. In August 2007, during the Argentine election campaign, Venezuelan businessman Antonini Wilson flew to Buenos Aires on a chartered flight with Venezuelan and Argentine oil officials and attempted to bring in a suitcase with about US$800,000.[13] The detection and confiscation of the money at customs control triggered an international scandal.

During the Néstor Kirchner administration, Argentina signed more international agreements with Venezuela (62) than with any other country. After Venezuela came Chile (41), Bolivia (39), Brazil (22), Ecuador (19), and Paraguay (17), with just 10 with the Untied States. What is more, Cristina Kirchner signed roughly the same amount of treaties with Venezuela (61) in the first year and a half of her administration,[14] which eloquently reflects the level of affinity and interaction between the Bolivarian and the Peronist administrations.

Relations with Venezuela were characterized by incoming financial assistance and outgoing political support. Plausibly, family resemblances between Bolivarianism and Peronism fostered reciprocal understanding, but they did not determine foreign alignments or policy outcomes. It was mutual benefit rather than ideological proximity that brought both countries ever closer, although—unlike other South American countries such as Bolivia or Ecuador—Argentina never came to be seen as a follower, even less a client state, of Caracas.

RELATIONS WITH THE UNITED STATES

Acting on moves previously hinted at by his predecessor, Eduardo Duhalde, President Néstor Kirchner suspended the policy of automatic alignment with the United States and moved it closer to other Latin American countries. Argentina withdrew its support for the resolution of the UN Commission on Human Rights that criticized the human rights situation in Cuba, and in the 2006 United Nations Security Council election for a nonpermanent seat, Argentina supported the candidacy of Venezuela over Guatemala, the candidate favored by the United States. In November 2005, at the Fourth Summit of the Americas in Mar del Plata, most of the discussion was focused on the Free Trade Agreement of the Americas (FTAA), and marked a clear split between the countries of Mercosur, plus Venezuela, and the supporters of the FTAA, led by the United States, Mexico, and Canada. Such tensions notwithstanding, the United States and Argentina got along on the two topics that were at the top of their respective agendas: international security, especially regarding Iranian support for terrorist attacks, for the Untied States and support in negotiations with international institutions and debtors' clubs for Argentina.[15]

The Néstor Kirchner administration led reinvigorated attempts to prosecute Iranian figures for their alleged role in the July 1994 bombing of the main Jewish community center in Buenos Aires, issuing arrest warrants for several Iranian officials. Among them were former president Ali Akbar Hashemi Rafsanjani, accused of ordering the attack that killed 85 people and injured more than 200. When one of his key domestic allies—former street activist Luis D'Elia—suggested that U.S. and Israeli pressure was fueling Argentina's pursuit of Iran, he was promptly forced to resign from his government post.[16] This was, perhaps, the only issue in which Buenos Aires was closer to Washington than to Caracas, but it was a crucial one for the United States. Cristina Fernández de Kirchner continued her husband's policy: during the speech she gave at the United Nations General Assembly in September 2009, she had harsh words for

Iran, accusing it of complicity in the 1994 attack and restating Argentine demands for the extradition of Iranians wanted by Interpol for the bombing.

In terms of debt relief, the Kirchner administration sought and found American support from the early months of its mandate. Within a month of his inauguration, President Kirchner had received the secretary of state Colin Powell and the economy minister Roberto Lavagna had met with the U.S. deputy secretary at the Treasury Department, John Taylor.[17] Argentina was facing deadlines to pay up millions of dollars with international lenders in the following months, and the IMF's head, Horst Köhler, was a harsh opponent of any concession on the part of the creditors. U.S. pressure was key in convincing him to offer Argentina more flexible financial requirements. In true Peronist fashion, pragmatism affirmed its primacy over ideology and the administration got its way.

If relations with the only world superpower were stormy but functional during Néstor Kirchner's term, they were widely expected to improve as Cristina's inauguration came closer. However, unforeseen events undermined hopes of an improved relationship; during the first days of her presidency, Argentina's relations with the United States deteriorated as a result of the *maletinazo* (suitcase scandal), which had occurred a few months previously. A Venezuelan-American citizen, Guido Alejandro Antonini Wilson, had tried to enter Argentina in August 2007 carrying US$800,000 in cash in his suitcase, without declaring it to customs, having traveled on a flight chartered by the Argentine government. In December, a United States assistant attorney made allegations before a Florida court that such money consisted of illegal contributions for Cristina Kirchner's presidential campaign. Some of the allegations were proven and several individuals received a prison sentence after a widely reported trial. The Kirchners, as well as Venezuelan president Chávez, called the allegations "a trashing operation"[18] and accused the United States of a conspiracy orchestrated to divide Latin American nations. On December 19, 2007, the Argentine government restricted the U.S. ambassador's activities and limited his meetings to Foreign Ministry officials, a treatment generally reserved for hostile countries. However, on January 31, in a special meeting with Cristina Kirchner, the U.S. ambassador in Argentina declared that the allegations "were never made by the United States government,"[19] thus cooling down the dispute.

In sum, the Kirchners' relations with the United States were mixed and variable but not bad overall. They were marked by a degree of tacit reciprocity, in the form of low-profile Argentine support for the "War on Terror" in exchange for U.S. support in foreign-debt renegotiation, but also by the Argentine rejection of the Free Trade Area of the

Americas (FTAA) negotiations and the occasional scandals that punctuated this period. With an eye on their domestic audiences, the Kirchners retained their rhetorical gestures. Yet, aware of their country's financial fragility and of the shared interest of the United States in bringing the Iranian-sponsored terrorists to justice, they were able to step back from open hostility and maintain bilateral relations.

RELATIONS WITH THE INTERNATIONAL MONETARY FUND

Argentina's relation with the International Monetary Fund has been stormy and superficially contradictory under the Kirchners. Both presidents voiced harsh criticisms of the IMF for its responsibility for the 2001 economic collapse, and strove to reduce its influence on the Argentine economy. They did this not by refusing to serve the national debt, but by doing exactly the opposite. In December 2005, Néstor Kirchner ordered the treasury to repay Argentina's nearly US$10 billion debt to the IMF, a significant gesture in moving Argentina away from external conditionalities. Once again, strong rhetoric against a target portrayed as the Argentine people's greatest enemy was accompanied by concrete actions that were not hostile but of mutual convenience. Commentators related this to the behavior of the Argentine national bird, the *tero*, which sings in one place but keeps its eggs in another, with the aim of diverting the attention of potential predators—or, in this case, electors. Such a pattern is a Peronist trademark.

By celebrating its regained freedom from the IMF while fully canceling its debt, the country that had arguably given more grief than anyone else to the world's lender of last resort—and also the one in which the IMF had made its most costly mistakes—gained applause at home and in Washington.[20] Argentina's decision was followed by other countries in the region, notably Brazil and Uruguay.

When the global financial crisis erupted in 2008, Cristina Kirchner declared that it would have little impact on the Argentine economy. However, Argentina was hit by the crisis, and the cycle of several years of high-rate growth turned slightly negative in 2009, which led in October 2009 to a further volte-face by the administration. During a visit to Istanbul, the economy minister Amado Boudou declared to the Argentine national press agency that the head of the IMF, Dominique Strauss-Kahn, was correctly "interpreting the sign of the times," and further remarked that Argentina was "on its way back into international credit markets."[21] The official argument was that the IMF was rectifying previous mistakes and moving back to the position maintained by Argentina; yet, the underlying reason of the policy reversal was that

Argentina's economic surplus had been dried out by the crisis at the same time as Venezuela had run out of cash for financing large countries. Consequently, the Kirchners decided that the need for funds justified inviting the IMF back to visit Argentina. Once more, financial pragmatism prevailed over ideological stance; skillful rhetoric accomplished the mission to hide the fact from view.

CONCLUSIONS

As with any public policy, foreign policy is rooted in the broader realm of domestic politics. Hence, its main goal is for the ruling officers to stay in power.[22] In times of war or severe international turmoil, continuity in power depends on ostensibly external factors. In times of peace, however, domestic factors are paramount and foreign policy recedes to the background, thus becoming just another means to gather and retain internal support—or to achieve external resources that serve such goals. If this rationale holds true, it does so even more when it involves Peronism, a mass movement whose essential feature is not a substantive agenda but its fondness for power.

During the Kirchner administrations, ideological claims have been discursively pushed forward but not implemented at a later stage. The Kirchners had two main goals: abroad, to ensure the continuing access to financial supply for the public sector; and domestically, to broaden their base of political legitimacy and electoral support. In a nutshell, it all comes down to money and votes. Other objectives related to foreign policy, such as securing energy supplies, improving relations with non-financing partners, expanding foreign markets, gaining international repute, or consolidating economic integration, were either downplayed or utterly neglected.[23] The Kirchners developed a pragmatic behavior in order to accomplish the previously mentioned goals: their policies were oriented toward the first one, money; and their rhetoric was aimed at the second, votes. As they eventually ran out of both around Cristina's middle-term, this strategy could be labeled—with the benefit of hindsight—as short-term pragmatism. They made recourse to two means that only apparently contradicted each other: a combative rhetoric and a few crucial alliances with foreign actors.

Brazil and Mercosur were top priorities according to the public position of both Kirchner administrations. However, gradually but determinedly, Argentina substituted Venezuela for the United States as a preferred balance vis-à-vis Brazil. Likewise, regional integration gained a great deal of discursive support at the same time as it receded on the ground. By mid-2010, Mercosur had stalled and there was no prospect of any relaunch or for it to be superseded by a successful alternative. UNASUR, for its part, only functions as a discussion forum. As diplomatic relations are still tense between Bolivia and Chile and between Colombia and Ecuador, and ties between Colombia and Venezuela worsen over time, the UNASUR founding treaty has been ratified by less signatory countries than it requires. The dominance of rhetoric over action seems to be a regional feature.

Venezuela has become Argentina's most publicized foreign partner under the Kirchners. However, this fact can only partially be explained by recourse to ideology. Indeed, there were two practical reasons for the Kirchners to get closer to Chávez: they sought external legitimacy to garner support from progressive parties and civil society organizations at home, plus they badly needed financial assistance in the context of exclusion from world financial markets. If the former presents the slight possibility of ideological influence, the latter was definitely pragmatic.

Regarding Argentina-U.S. relations, they underwent ups and downs at the rhythm of a handful of scandals and associated rhetorical excesses—which were mostly dependent on Argentine domestic processes. However, issues of mutual interests were workable in areas of maximum concern for each country: security with regard to the United States, and debt relief with regard to Argentina. The Kirchners never courted Iran—as Lula and Chávez did—and the United States never withdrew support to Argentina when it had to negotiate with third countries or international financial organizations.

Finally, the Kirchners never got tired of repeating the classical Latin American mantra about the IMF being the main actor to blame for the nation's economic misfortunes. Yet, not only was Argentina one of the main countries to pay off its debt with the IMF, but it sold a rekindled relationship in 2009 as a triumph over the "old" IMF and of a "new" financial architecture of global governance. Seemingly, necessity trumped ideology but not rhetoric.

Néstor Kirchner's foreign policy was marked by his personal imprint. However, elements of continuity with his predecessor are visible. If the "substance and style of his foreign policy ought to be seen in light of the priority he gave to domestic policy matters,"[24] his predecessor Duhalde also made crucial decisions "thinking more of the internal electoral process than of his country's relations with the United States."[25] In contrast, it can be argued that the administration of Cristina Kirchner has allowed a slightly greater space for ideological concerns. The fact that her performance has declined, as economic indicators, image polls, and electoral results unequivocally show, might suggest that pragmatism pays better than ideology.

The Kirchners' foreign policy can be uncontroversially depicted as personalist, based on short-term planning, and principally pragmatic rather than ideological. Shortsightedness was due to a focus on domestic objectives, to which foreign policy was all but an instrument. Unlike Brazil, whose self-perception as a predestined great power and whose professionalized diplomatic bureaucracy has conferred its foreign policy with a long-term coherence, Argentina's ruling class has never reached a consensus or instilled a significant level of professionalism in handling its relations with the outer world. If Brazilian foreign principles have been universalism, autonomy, and grandeur,[26] Argentina's have often been particularism, oscillation between isolation and subservience, and self-importance rooted in a glorious past rather than any promising future. Notably, such volatility has not only taken place across different party administrations but especially across (and within) Peronist administrations, reflecting Perón's own dramatic policy changes. In sixty years of Peronist foreign policies, the only element of continuity has been its subordination to internal goals, whether financial or electoral, and rejection of an ideological program or a permanent definition of the national interest. For the Peronist leadership, foreign policy has been just domestic politics by other means.

NOTES

1. Calvo, E., and Murillo, M. V. (2005) "A New Iron Law of Argentine Politics? Partisanship, Clientelism and Governability in Contemporary Argentina," in Levitsky, S., and Murillo, M. V. (eds.) *Argentine Democracy: The Politics of Institutional Weakness*, University Park: Penn State Press, p. 226.
2. Lampreia, L. P. (1998) "A política externa do governo FHC: continuidade e renovação," in *Revista Brasileira de Política Internacional*, 41(2): 5–17.
3. Russell, R., and Tokatlian, J. G. (2006) "Will Foreign Allies Help? Argentina's Relations with Brazil and the United States," in Epstein, E., and Pion-Berlin, D. (eds.) *Broken Promises? The Argentine Crisis and Argentine Democracy*, Lanham: Rowman and Littlefield, p. 247.
4. Ibid., p. 266.
5. Ibid., p. 267.
6. Margheritis, A. (2010) *Argentina's Foreign Policy: Domestic Politics and Democracy Promotion in the Americas*, Boulder, CO: Lynne Rienner, p. 1.
7. Levitsky, S. (2003) *Transforming Labor-Based Parties in Latin America. Argentine Peronism in Comparative Perspective*, Cambridge: Cambridge University Press, p. 161.

8. Jones, M. P., Saiegh, S., Spiller, P. T., and Tommasi, M. (2002) "Amateur Legislators, Professional Politicians: The Consequences of Party Centered Electoral Rules in Federal Systems," in *American Journal of Political Science,* 46(3): 656–69.

9. Malamud, A. (2005) "Mercosur Turns 15: Between Rising Talk and Declining Achievement," in *Cambridge Review of International Affairs,* 18(3): 421–36.

10. Gómez-Mera, L. (2005) "Explaining Mercosur's Survival: Strategic Sources of Argentine-Brazilian Convergence," in *Journal of Latin American Studies* 37: 109–40.

11. Russell, R., and Tokatlian, J. G. (2003) *El Lugar de Brasil en la Política Exterior Argentina,* Buenos Aires: Fondo de Cultura Económica; Malamud, A. (2009) "Leadership without Followers: The Contested Case for Brazilian Power Status," in de Rezende Martins, E. C., and Gomes Saraiva, M. (eds.): *Brasil, União Europeia, América do Sul: Anos 2010–2020.* Brasilia: Fundação Konrad Adenauer, pp. 126–48.

12. Arraes, V. (2007) "O Brasil e a ONU, de 1990 a nossos dias: das grandes conferências às grandes pretensões," in Altemani, Henrique , and Carlos Lessa, António (eds.): *Relações internacionais do Brasil Temas e agendas,* volume 2. São Paulo: Editora Saraiva, pp. 27–40

13. Yanuzzi, M. (2008) "Venezuela: The Chávez Effect. Between Ideological Affinity and Economic Convenience," *ReVista. Harvard Review of Latin America,* Fall. http://www.drclas.harvard.edu/revista/articles/view/1126. Retrieved June 19, 2009.

14. CENM (2009) "La relación especial argentino-venezolana," May 26, http://www.nuevamayoria.com/index.php?option=com_content&task=view&id=1459&Itemid=39. Retrieved June 19, 2009.

15. Sullivan, M. P. (2006) "Argentina: Political and Economic Conditions and U.S. Relations," *Report for Congress,* October 12, http://www.fas.org/sgp/crs/row/RS21113.pdf. Retrieved April 13, 2010.

16. "Argentina Pursues Iran in '94 Blast As Neighbors Court Ahmadinejad," Monte Reel, *Washington Post Foreign Service,* Sunday, January 14, 2007, http://www.washingtonpost.com/wp-dyn/content/article/2007/01/13/AR2007011301253.html.

17. Rodríguez Yebra, M., "Kirchner Reorients Foreign Policy," *La Nación,* Buenos Aires, Argentina, June 15, 2003 (reprinted in World Press Review 50(9), September. http://www.worldpress.org/Americas/1416.cfm#down. Retrieved November 24, 2009.

18. "Slush and Garbage. Argentina, Venezuela and America," *The Economist* (2008). http://www.economist.com/world/la/displaystory.cfm?story_id=10438525. Retrieved January 5, 2008.

19. "Declaración del Embajador de EE.UU., Earl Anthony Wayne, luego de reunirse con la Presidenta Cristina Fernández de Kirchner," U.S. Embassy in Buenos Aires' press release, http://spanish.argentina.usembassy.gov/rel244.html. Retrieved November 24, 2009.

20. "Nestor unbound; The IMF and Argentina," *The Economist* (2005). http://www.highbeam.com/doc/1G1-139962114.html. Retrieved June 19, 2009.

21. "Boudou in Istanbul: 'Argentina is on its way back into the credit markets'," *Telam*, October 5, 2009. http://english.telam.com.ar/index. php?option=com_content&view=article&id=5562:boudou-in-istanbul-argentina-is-on-its-way-back-into-the-credit-markets&catid=37: economy. Retrieved December 7, 2009.

22. Bueno de Mesquita, Bruce (2003) *Principles of International Politics: People's Power, Preferences, and Perceptions.* 2nd ed. Washington, D.C.: CQ Press.

23. Margheritis (2010), p. 26.

24. Russell and Tokatlian (2006), p. 259.

25. Ibid, p. 257.

26. Vigevani, T., Favaron, G., Ramanzini Júnior, H., and Alves Correia, R. (2008) "O papel da integração regional para o Brasil: universalismo, soberania e percepção das elites," *Revista Brasileira de Política Internacional* 51 (1): 5–27.

CHAPTER 6

FROM OBSCURITY TO CENTER STAGE: THE ARCHITECTONICS OF BOLIVIA'S FOREIGN POLICY

LARRY BIRNS AND ALEX SANCHEZ

INTRODUCTION

The 2005 election and 2009 reelection of Evo Morales to the presidency of Bolivia have significantly altered the country's domestic and foreign-policy landscape. Bolivia is a resource-rich, landlocked, and largely indigenous Andean nation, which under Morales has emerged as part of the Pink Wave and as a supporter of "21st century socialism." The aim of this chapter is to conceptualize foreign policy under Morales, arguing that Bolivia should be regarded as uniquely divorced from its traditional, Washington-friendly orientation. From this perspective, the central objective of the Morales presidency has been to break from the past and move toward an uncharted, left-leaning future, with primary attention being directed toward domestic affairs, rather than foreign policy. In his efforts he has been aided by vast natural resources, a majority in both houses and a high level of electoral support, although domestic politics remain unstable.

This is not to say that President Morales has no ideological vision as to how he will lead his country in its dealings abroad. Rather, we argue here that although an ideological vision informs his foreign policy, he is prepared to accept hard facts about what goals can be achieved and, more importantly, *how* they can be achieved. Even though Bolivia is poor and has been relatively unstable in social and political terms, unlike many other developing countries, it has good prospects, mostly due to its relatively small population and vast natural resources.

Morales's discourse in both domestic and foreign policy includes references to anti-imperialism, anticolonialism, and anticapitalism, elements that are not unique among some of the leftist leaders who have been elected to power in Latin America in the past decade. It also includes, however, a strong pro-indigenous discourse, reflecting Morales' own Aymara identity. In view of this, it is striking that his foreign policy has not been as radical or ideological as sometimes portrayed, and has actually followed a restrained, logical, and largely pragmatic pattern.

DIVORCING FROM HISTORY

The presidency of Evo Morales has afforded Bolivia a degree of political continuity that it had not enjoyed for a number of years. Hugo Banzer, who originally governed as a dictator from 1971 to 1978, was elected president in 1997, holding office only until 2001, when he resigned after being diagnosed with cancer. His vice president, Jorge Quiroga, completed his term until 2002. In the subsequent 2002 election, millionaire businessman Gonzalo Sánchez de Lozada, who had previously served as president from 1993 to 1997, was reelected, defeating Morales in a close race. However, just one year later, Sánchez de Lozada was forced to resign due to the wave of popular mobilization in defiance of his government. Key among the various issues that provoked popular unrest was the president's decision to export Bolivian gas to U.S. and Mexican markets via Chilean ports. Upon Lozada's hasty resignation, he was replaced by Carlos Mesa (2003–2005) and then Eduardo Rodríguez (2005–2006), until the late 2005 elections that resulted in Morales's triumph.

All of these administrations, to a greater or lesser degree, had followed free-market policies and had maintained the traditional close relationship with the United States, which in turn played a significant role in the domestic politics of Bolivia. For example, in the 2002 election, in which Morales and Sánchez de Lozada ran against each other, Otto Reich, the then highly controversial assistant secretary of state for Western Hemisphere Affairs, commented that, "we do not believe we could have normal relations with someone who espouses these kinds of policies," in reference to Morales' opposition to Washington's coca eradication programs.[1] Manuel Rocha, the U.S. ambassador to Bolivia, went further, threatening to cut off U.S. aid to La Paz if Morales was elected to the presidency. While Morales was deemed unacceptable, Sánchez de Lozada was clearly seen as the "golden boy" by conservative Washington policy makers, a stance that influenced Morales' view of the Bush administration.

Sánchez de Lozada sought to further deepen relations with the United States. Indeed, one of his key policy initiatives was to follow its zero-tolerance strategy regarding coca cultivation for which Lozada received economic and diplomatic recognition from the United States. Yet by the time the Bolivian president traveled to Washington in March 2003 to seek further support, large-scale protests against him in Bolivia were rapidly convincing Washington that he was an unstable ally, in danger of being overthrown. The violent protests that ultimately forced Sánchez de Lozada to resign from the presidency erupted in October 2003, and reflected nationwide Bolivian opposition to his government's decision to export gas to the United States and Mexico. While using a Chilean port as a terminus for the gas pipeline might have made eminent economic sense, it provoked strong political opposition within Bolivia due to the historical memories over the country's loss of its coastline to Chile in the late nineteenth century. Many poorer Bolivians simply did not believe that the average citizen would ever benefit from the profits accrued from the export of the country's natural gas, since very few had ever profited from such business deals in the past.

Despite distancing himself from his predecessor, Carlos Mesa did not deviate significantly in terms of his foreign-policy orientation. His main international backer, at least at first, was the United States. He also encouraged natural gas exports, signing an agreement with Argentina in 2004, and, like his predecessor, advocated gas exports to the United States and Mexico via Chile. The agreement was framed as part of a deal to enable Bolivia access to the sea.[2] The policy of exporting natural gas continued to be a controversial issue that provoked bitter resentment. Indeed, it was the reignition of protests over such exports that ultimately led to the resignation of Mesa in 2005, and provided fertile ground for the election of Morales to the presidency in late 2005.

The toppling of the Sánchez de Lozada and then the Mesa administrations exemplifies how the historical structure and subsequent direction of Bolivian foreign policy has affected the situation in which the nation now finds itself. While it is still unclear how much, if any, of the profit from the export of natural gas would have trickled down to benefit poorer Bolivians, the popular perception, based on historical experience, was that it would be foreign corporations or domestic elites who would be the primary beneficiaries. This perception made the policy untenable.

THE IMPACT OF THE DOMESTIC CONTEXT

Recent Bolivian domestic politics have been defined by almost permanent turmoil, exacerbated by poverty, inequality, regional ethnic hostility, political instability, and a historical absence of democratic tradition, including an almost constant threat of military intervention. The threat of regional separatism, ethnic conflict, and the plotting of conspiracies against the president of the day (often allegedly with the backing of the United States[3]) have been the backdrop against which Morales has sought to introduce his ambitious reforms.

At the same time, Morales has had to struggle to maintain the country's fragile cohesion throughout most of his presidency, especially in terms of long-standing tensions between the poor western highlands and the resource-rich eastern departments such as Santa Cruz, Pando, and Tarija.[4] Indeed, the wealthier eastern departments have threatened to secede from the rest of the country, spurred by opposition to Morales and his policies, in order to protect their locally based wealth, in the form of oil deposits, as well as newfound energy resources.[5] In 2008, a number of protests, along with a regional referendum that the government labeled as unconstitutional, pushed the issue of regional autonomy to the forefront of domestic politics.[6] The referendum was carried out in Santa Cruz without the consent of the Bolivian National Electoral Court (NEC), as well as without international observers, and was declared invalid by the NEC.

Such domestic instability affected foreign-policy decisions. Internal protests, which included demands that could have led to secession, or at the very least, greater autonomy, could also have undermined how the president was perceived on an international level. A president who does not control the main levers of power within his own country will find it difficult to win confidence or even support (in terms of investment and aid) abroad. More importantly, with such domestic pressures at work, it is highly doubtful that any head of state would be able to focus on developing a strong foreign policy. This was especially true in the case of Morales, who was forced to focus on domestic stability while also attempting to expand opportunities abroad.

Throughout his presidency, Morales has had to face well-organized domestic opposition forces, which have sought to destabilize his administration. This has led him to curb his more radical policies, in order to achieve greater domestic stability and be able to govern more effectively. In the same way, he is keen to construct a more pragmatic and less ideological foreign policy.[7] As a result, Morales has not been a great risk taker either in domestic or foreign-policy initiatives. Even his bold nationalization of Bolivia's natural gas fields in 2006 was ultimately a relatively controlled and pragmatic exercise. From a policy point of view, Morales sought to preserve national control over local natural resources. From a financial perspective, he recognized that Bolivia could benefit substantially if the state was able to control its gas fields.[8] "I dream of having our state company [YPFB] becoming as important as Brazil's Petrobras or Venezuela's PDVSA," Morales has stated.[9]

While he faced ideological conflicts with the Bush administration, which cost Bolivia its lucrative Andean Trade Promotion and Drug Eradication Act (ATPDEA), preferential trade agreements, anti-drug assistance, and a reduction in its share of foreign aid,[10] Morales nevertheless emerged in fairly good shape in terms of his national and international standing. As we shall see, this reflected a solid and successful pragmatism in policy implementation.

RELATIONS WITH VENEZUELA

Bolivian-Venezuelan relations have been the keystone of the so-called Pink Tide that swept across Latin America and was partially institutionalized in the creation of the Bolivarian Alternative for the Americas (ALBA). Although the two countries have not historically had markedly close ties, the relationship between Hugo Chávez and Evo Morales, combined with a shared ideological vision, has brought the countries together in an important regional alliance, reflected in significantly increased trade and diplomatic relations and military cooperation. For example, Venezuela has granted generous trade and energy concessions to Bolivia, provided funding for a large variety of social, educational, and medical projects, and offered military assistance, including the provision of military hardware.[11] However, it is the diplomatic and political alliance, centered on a shared ideology of the two leaders, including a rhetorical rejection of neoliberalism and of continued U.S. influence in the Americas, that has proven decisive in their deepening of relations.

Nevertheless, ample evidence exists that Morales does not want to be seen, either in Bolivia or internationally, merely as a protégé of Chávez. In 2008, mass protests in Bolivia and continued regional tensions led to speculation over the potential separation of the eastern provinces and an imminent coup d'etat against Morales. Chávez's response, that the Venezuelan military would intervene to protect Morales,[12] led to an outcry from Bolivian politicians as well as military officials, offended by his apparent disregard for Bolivian sovereignty.[13] Morales, for his part, was quick to distance himself from the declarations and emphasized solidarity rather than any interventionist role that Venezuela might play.[14]

Commercial relations between both countries, while not extensive, have increased significantly and appear set to grow further with Bolivia's development, particularly with its new emphasis on the economic exploitation of energy-related resources. In May 2007, the two governments signed a preferential trade agreement,[15] followed by meetings between representatives of Bolivian and Venezuelan business sectors to explore boosting investment between the two countries.[16] By the end of September 2008, Venezuela had become Bolivia's largest lender, replacing Spain and Brazil, with investments totaling upwards of $132.4 million.[17] Furthermore, Venezuela's PDVSA and Bolivia's YPFB joint venture, dubbed YPFB-Petroandina, plan to drill hydrocarbon wells in the La Paz department. The investment is projected to reach $93 million.[18]

The YPFB-Petroandina venture is an example of the use of Bolivia's available means to achieve various logical objectives: building closer relations with friendly states, exploiting natural resources, and attempting to enhance the quality of life for Bolivians. The introduction of the *Sistema Único de Compensación Regional* (Sucre) currency, at this early stage, seems mainly an ideological step with a possible practical element. In this instance, Morales is using his country's financial system to achieve two goals: to integrate policy goals with ideologically sympathetic states and to lessen the country's dependency on the U.S. dollar.

The relationship with Venezuela, in contrast with much of the rest of Latin America, is based on a shared ideological vision and other personal ties. Yet there is also a highly pragmatic element in the relationship, in the form of solid economic benefits, including trade, aid, and investment. Accompanying this relationship with Venezuela is also a more elaborate diplomatic grid, which aims to diversify foreign-policy links and make Bolivia a more involved regional player. Not surprisingly, many of the new relations revolve around Bolivia's natural resources.

RELATIONS WITH BRAZIL

Despite some ideological differences, Brazil's President Ignacio Lula da Silva and Evo Morales have maintained cordial and pragmatically stable relations, ironically due in part to a number of economic disagreements. In some ways, this has reflected their differences. Brazil has the region's largest economy and population, is an industrialized nation, and has hemispheric as well as global ambitions, including a permanent seat on the UN Security Council. In contrast, Bolivia is a small, relatively poor state, albeit with extremely important natural resources from existing as well as yet unexploited deposits. Yet, occasional clashes over Bolivia's nationalization and pricing policies have not led to a long-term deterioration of relations, but to the continuation of a pragmatic and mutually beneficial relationship in the three areas of energy, security, and trade.

The key basis for relations between these neighboring countries is trade, in which Bolivia maintains a favorable balance, due to its natural gas exports. In 2008, Brazilian exports to Bolivia totaled US$1.14 billion, while Bolivian exports to Brazil reached US$2.85 billion, making Brazil the country's most important trading partner.[19] In May 2006, as part of an energy-related nationalization program, Bolivian troops dramatically occupied a number of natural gas production facilities, including some owned by PETROBRAS (Petroleos Brasileiro SA), the Brazilian government-owned energy giant. By May of the following year, the nationalization program had been fully implemented, and Morales had issued a decree that prohibited the Brazilian company from exporting certain refined oil products.[20] Despite nationalist pressures from within Brazil and from Brazilians living in Bolivia, PETROBRAS eventually sold 100 percent of its two refineries to Bolivia, thus bringing an end to the dispute.

In early January 2009 Brasilia announced that it would shut down some of its plants that rely on Bolivian natural gas and instead promote the use of hydroelectric power.[21] However, shortly thereafter, Brazil's energy minister Edison Lobao declared that, due to economic growth Brazil would actually increase gas imports from Bolivia instead of decrease them. The mixed signals reflect Brazil's long-term aim to reduce its dependence on Bolivia's natural gas reserves alongside its short-term reliance on these same resources.[22] In February 2007 an agreement was signed, requiring Brazil to purchase between 19 million and 31 million cubic meters of gas per day at a fixed price that is favorable to Bolivia.[23] In December 2009, Bolivia announced that it would start receiving additional payments for exports of its liquefied natural gas (LNG) to Brazil—with additional payments worth between US$100 million and US$180 million a year by 2019.[24] In what is a highly pragmatic and mutually beneficial relationship, Bolivia is guaranteed an important source of revenue, while Brazil maintains guaranteed access to much-needed energy supplies.[25]

A further issue regards their common border, which extends for 2,130 miles (3,425 km) but is not heavily patrolled by either government. For example, in 2007 it was estimated that only 157 Bolivian officers were patrolling the border, averaging about one officer for every 22 kilometers.[26] In recent years there has been growing concern about the level of contraband that regularly passes through the border region.[27] In 2007, the Brazilian government donated US$9.86 million to Bolivia to develop a section of the border area that was largely inhabited by Brazilian small farmers. The donation was announced by Brasilia as part of a provisional decree reflecting growing interstate cooperation, but in reality it represented an effort by the Brazilians to persuade the Bolivians not to expel Brazilian citizens from Bolivian territory under the land reform initiatives being pushed by Morales. With viable agriculture struggling to survive in Brazil's border states, including Acre, Rondonia, and Amazonas, an influx of deported farmers would only exacerbate an already tense situation.[28]

The pragmatism demanded by daily events is far more relevant to determining the foreign-policy strategies employed by the two administrations than any ideological debate. Although Morales' ideological support for nationalization strained relations with Brazil, as did the rise in prices for LNG, these decisions were pragmatic, gaining Bolivia greater control over its natural resources and generating greater revenue from them.

RELATIONS WITH THE UNITED STATES

Historically, Bolivia has been regarded by Washington as a relatively dependable ally in South America. Bolivia under military rule cooperated in Cold War regional security, including a role in *Operation Condor*, the shared intelligence operation by military governments in the 1970s. During the transition to democracy, Bolivia stayed relatively close to the United States in terms of economic policy and political values, despite political instability and high levels of corruption, drug cultivation, and violations of human rights.

The rise to power of Morales led to a rapid deterioration of relations with Washington, and in this case, ideology does appear to have played a major role. The United States saw in Morales the threat of a nationalist leader heavily influenced by "21st century socialism," and who would bring greater instability to the region, possibly threatening U.S. interests. Morales, on the other hand, criticized the past role of the U.S. in Bolivia and called for a new relationship, best expressed by the former Bolivian ambassador to the United States Gustavo Guzman, who stated that "Morales' victory represented a defeat of past U.S. policies and a challenge to see if the United States could bend itself to the new realities of Bolivia."[29] This new reality would include reduced economic and military relations and a curtailment of U.S. influence in domestic politics, but, initially at least, not the breaking of diplomatic or economic relations.

However, tensions between the countries finally led to the crisis of September 2008, when Morales declared the American ambassador

Philip Goldberg persona non grata[30] and also ordered several Drug Enforcement Agency (DEA) agents to leave the country. The expulsion came after a period of sustained U.S. support for the political opposition, allegations that the United States was fomenting violent antigovernment protests, and Goldberg's visit to Santa Cruz to address the anti-Morales opposition. The expulsion of the DEA agents may have been based on Morales' ideological opposition to the controversial and highly unpopular policies of the United States in its efforts to combat drug trafficking, considering his *cocalero* past.[31]

The price of the conflict for Bolivia was high in terms of loss of benefits from the ATPDEA and the Andean Trade Preference Act (ATPA),[32] which gave Bolivia preferential treatment on some U.S. tariffs, worth up to US$150 million a year in terms of access to U.S. markets. Morales showed his defiance by stating, "We do not have to be afraid of an economic blockade by the United States against the Bolivian people."[33] Such statements exemplify a collision of pragmatism (external financial aid for development) with Morales' ideological stance that national sovereignty and dignity must be put before any financial agreement. Furthermore, while trade with the United States is important, the rise in value of some of Bolivia's natural resources, such as lithium,[34] and increased foreign investment by international corporations, such as the Bollore Group and Japan's Sumitomo Corp. and Mitsubishi Corp, had softened the impact of the rupture.[35]

Morales promised to uphold a robust strategy to combat drug production and domestic trafficking in Bolivia, even without Washington's aid. In part, this was an ideological statement to establish the independence of Bolivia's domestic policies from U.S. national interests. In commonsense terms, it was a popular move, given the widespread domestic opposition to U.S. anti-narcotics operations. Morales was also keen to show he had broad international support. In February 2009, Bolivia signed an agreement with Russia to purchase a number of MI-17 military helicopters to be used in anti-drug operations.[36] According to the Bolivian vice-minister of foreign affairs, Hugo Fernández Araoz, "The helicopters are to fight drug trafficking, Russia can help with this operation. The former helicopter supplier was the United States, but our relations are strained."[37]

Morales's two major conflicts with the United States marked a clear rejection of Washington's historical relationship with Bolivia. It remains debatable whether Morales' stance was based on ideology or on a more pragmatic and necessary defense of Bolivia's national interest and sovereignty. The loss of the ATPDEA income could adversely affect Bolivia's economy, and while the DEA's anti-drug operations were not always effective against drug production and trafficking in Bolivia, it is unclear if La Paz can handle the issue of narcotics on its own. Yet the crisis with Washington came about only at the end of 2008, several years into the Morales presidency, indicating that it was due less to deep-rooted ideological differences than to the perception that Washington was playing an active and highly inappropriate role in Bolivian domestic politics. Overall, it would appear that Morales' actions reflected a highly pragmatic approach, which may have reflected personal ideology and were certainly couched in the ideologically charged rhetoric of national sovereignty.

While ideology does influence the scope of foreign policy, it would be a mistake to operationally confuse Bolivia for Venezuela. While Bolivia took the somewhat extreme action of expelling the U.S. ambassador, this action did not lead to the severing of commercial links or to embedded hostility. Indeed, the defeat of President Bush and the election of President Obama was accompanied by signs of improved relations between the two nations. In May 2009, outgoing-U.S. assistant secretary of state for Latin America, Tom Shannon, visited Bolivia, the highest-level visit by a U.S. official to the Andean country in almost a year. This followed a meeting between Bolivian foreign affairs minister David Choquehuanca and Hillary Clinton in April 2009 during the Fifth Summit of the Americas, at which time they "agreed to work on a new framework agreement on such issues as commerce, cooperation and the fight against drug trafficking."[38]

How do the drugs and trade issues in U.S.-Bolivian relations fit into a discussion of pragmatism versus ideology? Should Morales have supported Washington's push for zero-tolerance of coca cultivation, it would have cut deeply into the support he enjoys from the *cocalero* unions and producers. Given that they form a base of his electoral support, such a policy could have cost him dearly in his reelection bid in December 2009. As with the issue of trade, Morales sought to maintain relations with the United States, while reducing economic and political dependency. The presentation of this to the domestic audience in ideological terms may have reflected his personal beliefs, but also reflects the complex interplay between ideology and pragmatism.

BOLIVIA AND CHILE: TALKING PAST EACH OTHER

There are some historical positions and claims that will continue, regardless of the ideological stance of the Bolivian president. Such is the case with the country's strained relationship with Chile and the persistent rumblings of the territorial dispute between the two countries that has lasted more than a century. Regardless of the party of the Chilean president, La Paz's relationship with Santiago is unlikely to improve in the near future; however a change for the worse could occur if the new president—the conservative nationalist Sebastián Piñera—turns out, as seems likely, to be indifferent to Bolivian sensibilities on the issue.

The disastrous War of the Pacific (1879–1884), which pitted Peru and Bolivia against Chile, cost Bolivia its Pacific coastline and turned it into a landlocked nation. Chile has since refused to return the disputed territory and diplomatic relations were only reestablished in 1978. The issue remains a deep-rooted source of historical resentment in Bolivia, for which only the return of lost lands and access to the coastline will compensate.[39]

With no access to the sea, Bolivia is forced to use either Peruvian or Chilean ports for vital imports and exports on which its economy depends. For financial as well as symbolic reasons, Peru has explicitly built facilities to accommodate the export of Bolivian natural gas to the international market at Ilo. Meanwhile, Morales continued to seek Chilean agreement for a Bolivian-controlled corridor to the sea, through negotiations with former Chilean presidents Ricardo Lagos and Michelle Bachelet. Despite the lack of success in these talks, a degree of pragmatism prevailed in the continuation and deepening of trade relations between the two countries, furthering the possibility of rapprochement.

The Bolivian head of state attended the inauguration of the new Chilean president, Sebastián Piñera and expressed his solidarity when a major earthquake struck Chile in March of 2010. Morales clearly aims to improve his country's relations with Chile, yet with the one goal of some kind of agreement on Bolivian access to the Pacific.

OTHER ASPECTS OF BOLIVIAN FOREIGN POLICY

At the regional level, Morales has sought to raise the profile of his country within different regional blocs. Bolivia is a key member of ALBA (Alternativa Bolivariana para América Latina) and has shown support for a number of its initiatives, including the creation of a regional currency. Morales has also expressed strong support for UNASUR (Unión de Naciones Sudamericanas)[40] in its attempts to strengthen regional cooperation and solidarity and reduce U.S. influence in the region. In a speech after a UNASUR meeting held in response to the September 2008 protests in Bolivia, Morales declared that "for the first time in the history of South America, the countries of our region are deciding how to resolve our problems without the presence of the United States."[41] Additionally, Bolivia remains a member of CAN (Comunidad Andina de Naciones), despite ideological differences with the administrations in Colombia and Peru and ideological opposition to negotiations with the European Union to achieve a free-trade agreement. Morales' backing of ALBA and UNASUR, combined with his rejection of CAN's perceived neoliberal orientation, reflects an ideological stance that backs a certain form of regional integration based more on solidarity and cooperation than free trade.

Despite historically close relations and strong commercial ties with Peru, Morales has had fractious relations with the Alan García administration over the course of the last several years.[42] As a result of tensions among indigenous communities in Peru's northern region, diplomatic and personal relations between García and Morales became tense, with Morales accusing García of following Washington's line in a conflict that has clear ideological undertones. Yet despite ideological differences between the two leaders, trade between the two Andean countries has steadily increased. A July 2010 report by the Peruvian news agency *Andina* quotes an optimistic Peruvian ambassador to Bolivia, Manuel Rodriguez Santos, as saying "[b]y the end of 2009, trade exchange between both nations was US$600 million and it could easily double in the next four years thanks to the complementarity of their economies."[43]

Morales also has sought to pursue a pragmatic and proactive policy of diversifying Bolivian relations among extra-hemispheric powers. Here he is seeking to strengthen investment with a range of nontraditional partners, including Russia, China, Vietnam, Japan, Iran, and France, as well as several Arab nations, as shown by his attendance of the Second Summit of Arab and South American Heads of State held in Qatar. Nevertheless ideology remains influential as reflected in Morales' decision to break off relations with Israel in January 2009 following Israel's invasion of the Gaza Strip.[44]

Closer relations with countries such as Iran and Russia reflect a complex mix of pragmatism and ideology. On a pragmatic level, they have certainly accounted for a positive yield in terms of trade agreements and investment opportunities; for example, Moscow has offered La Paz US$100 million in military credit with no strings attached and relations with Iran promise to bring increased trade and investment. Furthermore, a widening circle of allies and partners is a highly pragmatic policy. However, they also contain an ideological dimension, not as has been alleged, in terms of support for nondemocratic regimes, but rather to highlight Bolivia's right and freedom to establish an independent foreign policy, which provides pragmatic benefits for the nation.

A final example of the evolution and diversification of Morales' foreign policy was the hosting of the World People's Conference on Climate Change and the Rights of Mother Earth in Cochabamba in April 2010. While it is highly unlikely that the conference will change the international approach to global warming, it allowed Bolivia to put itself forward as representative of indigenous and environmental demands on a global level, and also as an important representative of the "Global South," raising its international profile, playing well to domestic audiences, and reflecting a consistent ideological stance.

CONCLUSIONS

Evo Morales was reelected to the Bolivian presidency in December 2009, obtaining 63 percent of the vote, 36 percent ahead of his closest competitor. His party, MAS, has also gained control of the county's two legislative chambers. In spite of domestic instability and powerful opposition, Morales has maintained the support of the majority of the population through a combination of political skill, artful negotiations, and strategic compromises.

Although keen to avoid the label of a protégé of Chávez and to "resist unquestioned loyalty to any single ideological bloc,"[45] Morales has maintained a special relationship with Venezuela, based on personal friendship and shared ideological positions, but also on pragmatic advantages for Bolivia in terms of economic benefits. Likewise, relations with the United States have contained a strong ideological element, yet at the same time, have remained sufficiently utilitarian in terms of upholding bilateral trade relations. This mix of ideology and pragmatism is also evident in relations with Brazil, which produced an ostensibly ideological confrontation resulting in pragmatic gains for Bolivia. Overall, while Morales' foreign-policy initiatives have often followed an ideological line, this is often intended for a domestic audience, and in reality he has consistently shown himself abroad to also be a pragmatist, ready to adjust his foreign policy if necessary.

Ideological discourse then, often combines with pragmatism in practice. Morales has a clear, long-term vision of Bolivia's revolution, of where the country should be heading, and how it will get there. He recognizes the gravity of the country's many domestic problems, as well as how its vast resources could be used to alleviate poverty, exclusion, and inequality. Above all, he appears to understand how to combine ideology and pragmatism to create a flexible, pragmatic, and ideologically coherent foreign policy aimed at limited but realistic gains, in order to further his vision of the national interest.

NOTES

1. Campbell, Duncan, and Bello, Alex. "US warns Bolivia over choice of president." *The Irish Times* (Guardian service). World News. p. 9. July 15, 2002.

2. "Bolivian president to detail to OAS Natural Gas Strategy." *Latin America News Digest.* September 20, 2004.

3. Carroll, Rory. "Bolivian president links US embassy to alleged assassination plot." *The Guardian.* April 20, 2009. Available at http://www.guardian.co.uk/world/2009/apr/20/evo-morales-bolivia-us-embassy, accessed May 24, 2009.

4. This group of separatist regions is usually referred to as the "half moon states" as their shape resembles somewhat half of a circle.

5. Raul Zibachi argues that the autonomy movement is driven by a rejection of the newfound power of the indigenous people of the Altiplano. Demands for autonomy may mask racism. See Zibachi, Raul. "The New Latin American Right: Finding a Place in the World." Report: The Right. *NACLA Report on the Americas.* January/February 2008. pp. 16.

6. "Majority in autonomy-seeking region in Bolivia vote 'yes' in referendum." *Xinhua General News Service.* June 22, 2008. Also see "Two more Bolivian provinces to demand autonomy." *Agence France Presse*—English. June 2, 2008.

7. In August 2008 Morales held a referendum on his administration. Although he won convincingly, the opposition did not reduce its criticism or activity.

8. "Bolivia sees $1.41 billion investment of oil in sector in 2010." *Oil Voice.* 15 January, 2010. Available at http://www.oilvoice.com/n/Bolivia_Sees_141_Billion_of_Investment_in_Oil_Sector_in_2010/07edba3b9.aspx, accessed March 18, 2010.

9. "YPFB announces five-year investment program of US$11bn." Business News Americas. January 12, 2010.

10. It should be stressed that President Obama denied extending ATPDEA preferences to Bolivia in 2009. "Obama pone fin al ATPDEA para Bolivia." *La Razon.* July 1, 2009. Available at http://www.la-razon.com/Versiones/20090701_006775/nota_248_837482.htm, accessed March 30, 2010.

11. Barragan, Juan Manuel. "Venezuela announces replacement helicopter for Bolivia." *Jane's Defense Weekly.* December 3, 2008.

12. Jardim, Claudia. "Venezuela reitera apoyo military a Bolivia." *BBCMundo.com.* September 13, 2008.

13. "Ejercito Boliviano rechaza ayuda military Venezolana." *ElEspectador.com.* September 12, 2008. Available at http://www.elespectador.com/noticias/elmundo/video-ejercito-boliviano-rechaza-ayuda-militar-venezolana, accessed May 24, 2009.

14. Rochlin, James. "Latin America's Left Turn and the New Strategic Landscape: The case of Bolivia." *Third World Quarterly.* Vol. 28, No. 7 (2007). pp. 13–37.

15. "Bolivia reaches Trade Preference Agreement with Venezuela." *Latin America News Digest*. May 22, 2007.

16. "Empresarios de Venezuela y Bolivia fortalecen relaciones." *TelesurTV. net*. November 11, 2008. Available at http://www.telesurtv.net/noticias/ secciones/nota/36243-NN/empresarios-de-venezuela-y-bolivia-fortalecen-relaciones/, accessed May 22, 2009.

17. "Venezuela becomes Bolivia's biggest lender." *BBC Monitoring Latin America—Political*. December 30, 2008. Reproduction of "Debt with Venezuela increased by 2.21 per cent during Evo's administration." *La Prensa* (Bolivia). December 29, 2008.

18. "YPFB-Petroandina to kick off La Paz drilling next year." *Business News Americas*. December 11, 2009.

19. Brazil to help Bolivia overcome financial crisis. Xinhua General News Service. World News; Political. March 12, 2009.

20. "Brazil's Petrobras seeking to sell refineries to Bolivia, report says." *Associated Press*. May 7, 2007.

21. Sibaja, Marco. "Brazil slashes Bolivian gas imports amid dispute." *Associated Press Worldstream*. Business News. January 9, 2009.

22. Keane, Dan. "All eyes on Bolivia in South American energy crunch." *Associated Press Worldstream*. Business News. March 10, 2008. "Brazil could not spare a single molecule [of Bolivian natural gas]," according to Sergio Gabrielli, head of state of PETROBRAS.

23. Sibaja, Marco. "Brazil to boost Bolivian gas imports." *Associated Press Worldstream*. Business News, January 10, 2009.

24. "Bolivia to receive additional payments for LNG exports to Brazil—report." *Latin America News Digest*. December 18, 2009.

25. A March 2008 article by *AP* stated that "Brazil could not spare a single molecule [of Bolivian natural gas]" according to Sergio Gabrielli, head of state of PETROBRAS. See Keane, Dan. "All eyes on Bolivia in South American energy crunch." *Associated Press Worldstream*. Business News. March 10, 2008.

26. Valdez, Carlos. "Cocaine trade growing across wild Brazil-Bolivia frontier." *Associated Press Worldstream*. June 10, 2007.

27. "Eighty percent of Bolivian drugs shipped to Brazil, says official." *BBC Monitoring Latin America*. Reproduction of "Eighty per cent of drugs produced in Bolivia destined for Brazil." *La Razon* (Bolivia). June 12, 2007. Also see "Cocaine production rises along Brazilian border: police." *Xinhua General News Service*. December 12, 2007.

28. "Brazil to donate $9.86 million to Bolivia to avoid expulsion of illegal emigrants." *Latin America News Digest*. April 2007.

29. Barclay, Eliza. "Latin America: The Mugabe of the Andes?" *The Atlantic*. April 2009. pp. 33

30. The reason for this was that Ambassador Goldberg had met with opposition-leader Ruben Costas, prefect of Santa Cruz, on August 25, 2008. Morales would declare Goldberg persona non grata the following September 10, 2008. Also see: Valdez, Carlos. Bolivia President asks US ambassador to leave. September 11, 2008. "Without fear of the empire,

I declare the U.S. ambassador 'persona non grata,'" Morales said in a speech at the presidential palace.

31. Bolivia is the world's third largest cocaine produce after neighboring Peru and Colombia.

32. "U.S. trade representative Schwab announces proposed suspension of Bolivia's tariff benefits." White House's Office of the U.S. trade representative. *US Fed News.* September 26, 2008. Also see "Bush suspends tariff accord with Bolivia over drug spat." *Agence France Presse—English.* November 26, 2008.

33. Keane, Dan. "Morales: Bolivia should not fear U.S. 'blockade.'" *Associated Press Online.* October 8, 2008.

34. Schipani, Andres. "Hard life of Bolivia's 'salt plains guardians.'" BBC News Latin & Caribbean. July 18, 2010. Available at http://www.bbc.co.uk/news/world-latin-america-10282499, accessed July 23, 2010.

35. Bajak, Frank, and Valdez, Carlos. "Bolivia pins hope on lithium, electronic vehicles." *Associated Press Financial Wire.* Business News. February 28, 2009.

36. Gutterman, Steve. "Bolivia to get Russian helicopters to fight drugs." *Associated Press Online.* February 16, 2009. Also see "Bolivia set to order weaponry from Russia—deputy FM." *RiaNovosti.* May 22, 2009.

37. "Bolivia comprara a Rusia helicopteros Mi-17V-5." *La Razon* (Peru). May 23, 2009.

38. "Bolivia to work with U.S. on commerce, anti-drug trafficking agreement." *Xinhua General News Service.* April 21, 2009.

39. Ross, Jen. "Bolivia's land-locked navy dreams of leaving lake Titicaca." *The Independent.* January 10, 2004.

40. Union of South American Nations—UNASUR.

41. Barclay, "Mugabe of the Andes?" p. 35.

42. For a list of important dates in Bolivian-Peruvian tensions lately, see "Las relaciones entre Peru y Bolivia, en zozobra permanente." *EFE.* June 15, 2009. Available at http://www.adn.es/politica/20090615/NWS-2376-Bolivia-Peru-permanente-relaciones-zozobra.html accessed June 16, 2009.

43. "Peru, Bolivia trade to total US$1.2bln in four years." Andina News Agency (Peru). July 22, 2010. Available at http://www.andina.com.pe/Ingles/Noticia.aspx?id=801+YMMCEQA=, accessed July 23, 2010.

44. "Venezuela, Bolivia break diplomatic ties with Israel." *Agence France Press—English.* January 15, 2009.

45. Shifter, "A New Politics for Latin America?" p. 17.

CHAPTER 7

IDEOLOGY AND PRAGMATISM IN THE FOREIGN POLICY OF PERU

RONALD BRUCE ST. JOHN

INTRODUCTION

With the exception of two widely separate periods, pragmatism has prevailed over ideology as the dominant influence on Peruvian foreign policy since Peru declared its independence from Spain in 1821. In the initial period that constituted the first two decades of independence, competing political forces, complicated by economic, ideological, and personal conflicts, battled to determine the future of the state. In a confused and shifting milieu, successive governments struggled to define the frontiers of Peru, not in the narrow sense of planting border markers, but in the broader sense of determining whether Peru would be divided, federate with Bolivia, or stand alone. The second period in which ideology influenced pragmatism to a notable degree was a twelve-year period of military rule, known as the *docenio* (1968–1980), during which socialist policies dominated domestic and foreign policy. This was particularly true in the first half of this period when the foreign policy of the Juan Velasco Alvarado administration (1968–1975) worked to modify the nation's commercial and diplomatic relationships with other countries, especially the United States.

This chapter examines the foreign policy of Peru from the independence era to the present time with a focus on the first administration of Alejandro Celestino Toledo Manrique (2001–2006) and the second

administration of Alan García Pérez (2006–2011). To establish the place
of Peru in the ideology-pragmatism paradigm, the analysis opens with
a brief overview of external policy from 1821 to 1990, highlighting the
prevalence of pragmatism over ideology for most of the nation's history.
The administrations of Alberto Fujimori (1990–2000), during which
Peru returned to the pragmatism-over-ideology model following modest
deviations during the first García administration (1985–1990), are then
treated in more detail because they set the stage for a wider discussion
of the foreign policies subsequently followed by presidents Toledo and
García.

    In pursuit of a largely pragmatic foreign policy, the ends and purposes
of Peruvian diplomacy have been remarkably consistent. Over the first
century of independent life, Peru generally focused on the resolution of
complicated and troublesome territorial disputes. Thereafter, the emphasis
of Peruvian foreign policy shifted to wider domestic, regional, and international issues. To achieve their goals, Peruvian politicians and diplomats
generally employed traditional attributes of power, that is, economic,
military, and political means, with the professionalism of the Peruvian
diplomatic corps, the one asset that often separated Peruvian diplomacy
from that of its neighbors. At the same time, the stature and quality
of several Peruvian presidents, notably Ramón Castilla (1845–1851,
1855–1862), Augusto B. Leguía (1908–1912, 1919–1930), Alberto
Fujimori, and Alejandro Toledo, often proved decisive in shaping political outcomes. In tandem with the professionals in the Torre Tagle (the
home of the Ministry of Foreign Affairs) strong chief executives designed
and implemented well-thought-out and coherent foreign policies that
were well suited to prevailing domestic and international milieus.

ANTECEDENTS

Between the two relatively short periods mentioned in which ideology influenced pragmatism to a notable degree, pragmatism prevailed
over ideology from the 1840s to 1968. During the administrations of
Ramón Castilla, Peru acquired for the first time the degree of internal
peace, centralized and efficient state organization, adequate and reliable public funding, and an emerging sense of national unity required
for the formation and articulation of a foreign policy. By the end of his
second term, the Ministry of Foreign Relations had begun to articulate
a coherent foreign policy founded on the principles of continental
solidarity, nonintervention, and national integrity.[1] In the process,
President Castilla influenced the content and direction of Peruvian
foreign policy to a far greater extent than any other chief executive in the

nineteenth century. Between 1862 and the end of World War II, territorial issues dominated Peruvian foreign policy. In addition to the final disposition of the Peruvian provinces of Tacna and Arica, occupied by Chile during the War of the Pacific (1879–1883), Peruvian diplomacy struggled to resolve complicated, often interrelated, boundary disputes with Bolivia, Brazil, Colombia, and Ecuador. After World War II, Peru resumed the leadership role in continental affairs that it had largely abandoned in the nineteenth century, demonstrated a growing interest in Latin American economic cooperation, and participated in multilateral conferences on maritime fishing and mineral resources. It was also a founding member of a number of international bodies, including the United Nations (UN), Organization of American States (OAS), and Latin American Free Trade Association (LAFTA). These steps toward an increasingly multilateral approach to foreign affairs paralleled a decline in the power and prestige of the United States in Peru.[2]

In the second half of the twentieth century, Peru also continued efforts to improve the professionalism of the diplomatic corps through more stringent recruitment, better training, and improved standards for advancement. The 1941 Organic Foreign Relations Bill and the 1944 Review of the Peruvian International Law Society collectively advanced a plan for educating Peruvian diplomats, leading ultimately to the establishment in 1955 of the Diplomatic Academy of Peru. One of the first such bodies in Latin America, the Diplomatic Academy developed into a premier educational institute with a strong faculty and a demanding curriculum, eventually earning university status in 2005. Over time, it became the sole avenue for entry into the diplomatic service, turning out successive generations of intelligent, well-trained, and enthusiastic young diplomats.

In the wake of the *docenio*, Peru returned to a foreign policy in which pragmatism generally prevailed over ideology. The second administration of Fernando Belaúnde Terry (1980–1985) reaffirmed the nation's commitment to subregional cooperation. At the same time, Peru continued to face a number of related concerns with regard to territorial sovereignty. The ongoing border dispute with Ecuador led to renewed fighting and a controversial cease-fire. Peru refused to sign the United Nations Law of the Sea convention on the grounds it was a hasty, unconstitutional decision, and it pursued revisions to a fishing agreement with the Soviet Union concluded during the *docenio*.[3]

The approach of the Belaúnde administration to national development goals, notably its choice of a development model dependent on the goodwill of the United States, ultimately defined its regional policies. Inheriting severe economic problems, including $9 billion in foreign debt, an International Monetary Fund (IMF) stand-by agreement, and acute unemployment, President Belaúnde pursued growth under a more open economic system that suggested a softening in the Peruvian commitment to Andean Group economic and political strategies. At the same time, he searched for a more positive relationship with the United States. Unfortunately, the growing ambiguity that characterized bilateral relations, an uncertainty stemming from the conflicting demands of Peruvian nationalism and the need for U.S. cooperation to achieve foreign-policy goals, left little room for sustained improvement.[4]

Economically, the Belaúnde administration clashed with the United States over levels of economic aid and the latter's enforcement of countervailing duties on Peruvian textiles. Politically, the issue of terrorism was an ongoing source of bilateral tension with the firm stand taken by the Peruvian government subjected to a mounting wave of criticism by human rights groups in the United States. Diplomatically, the United States rejected Peruvian support for the Contadora Group, which supported a negotiated peace in Central America, and Peru strongly criticized U.S. support for Great Britain in its war with Argentina over the Malvinas as well as the U.S. invasion of Grenada. At one point, President Belaúnde even suggested ousting the United States from the OAS.

Ideology influenced pragmatism to a larger degree during the first administration of Alan García Pérez (1985–1990). In pursuit of national development, García announced that Peru would limit interest payments on the external debt to 10 percent of the nation's export earnings and halt payments on medium- and long-term debt. In response, the IMF, World Bank, and Inter-American Development Bank (IDB) rejected new loan applications and suspended existing loan disbursements. Within the region, disarmament initiatives produced limited results as did bilateral talks with both Bolivia and Ecuador. On the other hand, Peru was a founding member of the Andean Reserve Fund and an active participant in the Latin American Economic System (SELA). Elsewhere, García took an active role in the Non-Aligned Movement, opposed apartheid in South Africa, and pursued a closer association with social democratic groups in Western Europe.[5]

The García administration tried to maintain an independent posture toward the socialist states to avoid being labeled communist; nevertheless, its activist foreign policy left little room for improvement in bilateral relations with the United States. Problems related to the external debt, a civil aviation accord, bilateral aid, and protectionist sentiments toward Peruvian imports carried over from the Belaúnde administration. At the same time, García's condemnation of U.S. policy in Central America put him in direct conflict with the Reagan administration. While his government won occasional praise from the United States, especially in response to its efforts to contain narco-trafficking and ongoing guerrilla terrorist activities, the García administration's strong language and confrontational style toward the United States strained bilateral relations.[6]

FUJIMORI ADMINISTRATIONS (1990–2000)

President Alberto Fujimori returned Peruvian foreign policy to a model in which pragmatism prevailed over ideology. At the end of García's first term, government expenditures were three times as large as government revenues, the annual rate of inflation exceeded 7,000 percent, and Peru had defaulted on some $2 billion in international loans. Inheriting a difficult situation, President Fujimori recognized that the active support of the United States would be critical in implementing an economic strategy to restore the international standing of Peru. Consequently, early contacts between the two states focused on the related issues of drug production and narco-trafficking, the policy areas of greatest interest to the United States. With Peruvians far more concerned with combating guerrilla terrorist movements than with the drug war, this approach highlighted the early pragmatism of the Fujimori administration. Drug-related issues remained a touchstone of Peruvian relations with the United States throughout the 1990s, although the bilateral agenda later expanded to include democracy and human rights, development, debt, and defense.[7]

The Fujimori administration also supported enhanced regional cooperation and development. President Fujimori attended the Andean Pact summit in late 1990 and presided over the opening meeting of the Andean Parliament in early 1991. Even as he did so, a growing political crisis in Peru increasingly conflicted with Andean Group plans to accelerate the pace of economic integration. In April 1992, President Fujimori carried out an *autogolpe* (coup d'état against himself) in which he suspended the 1979 constitution, padlocked the Congress, dismantled the judiciary, and scheduled constituent elections. In August 1992, Peru announced that it was suspending active participation in the Andean Group for two years. A renewal of the conflict with Ecuador in January 1995 further delayed plans for full-scale reentry into the group.[8]

Following its withdrawal from the Andean Group, the Fujimori administration negotiated bilateral trade agreements with Colombia, Ecuador, and Venezuela. It also concluded an agreement with Bolivia that gave the latter a duty-free port and industrial park at the Peruvian port of Ilo in return for similar facilities at Puerto Suarez on the Paraguay River. After Peru returned to full-scale participation in the Andean Group, the Fujimori administration in October 1998 concluded a Global and Definitive Peace Agreement with Ecuador, ending the longest standing boundary dispute in the Americas. In December 1999, Peru and Chile signed an agreement that also resolved outstanding issues from the Tacna and Arica Treaty and Additional Protocol concluded in 1929.[9]

With the core objectives of Peruvian foreign policy largely unchanged throughout the decade, the Peruvian government in the 1990s enjoyed more success in advancing its external policies than at any other time in the second half of the twentieth century. The Fujimori administration restructured the foreign debt on highly favorable terms and restored Peru's standing in the international community, setting the stage for the pursuit of a more autonomous national development policy. Moreover, bilateral relations with the United States, throughout much of the decade, were the most positive since the *oncenio* of Augusto B. Leguía (1919–1930). The resolution of the Ecuador-Peru border dispute, on terms favorable to Peru, and the settlement of the issues outstanding from the 1929 treaty with Chile achieved goals pursued by successive governments for well over half a century. The stature and worldview of President Fujimori was central to this success as his administrations repeatedly demonstrated both perseverance and pragmatism in the pursuit of bold policy initiatives.

THE TOLEDO ADMINISTRATION (2001–2006)

President Alejandro Celestino Toledo Manrique actively pursued nine related foreign-policy goals. First, he promoted democracy and human rights inside and outside Peru. Second was the struggle against poverty, especially extreme poverty. Third, he worked to create a preferential association with neighboring states, and in so doing, to promote economic development in the borderlands. Fourth, he promoted a reduction in regional arms spending with the expressed intent to spend the money saved to reduce poverty. The fifth goal of the Toledo administration was increased unity and stronger integration within the Andean Community (CAN). Sixth, President Toledo aimed to strengthen relations with the major industrialized states and the Asia-Pacific region. The seventh goal of the administration was to make the Ministry of Foreign Affairs more effective in promoting the Peruvian economy abroad. The eighth objective was to do a better job of serving Peruvians overseas, and finally, the Toledo administration targeted a thorough reform of personnel practices within the Ministry of Foreign Affairs, stemming in part from a scandal concerning the treatment of professional diplomats during the Fujimori years.[10] In pursuit of these goals, the Toledo administration largely continued the pragmatism-over-ideology model employed by President Fujimori.

President Toledo's desire for Peru to play a wider, more visible role overseas was a notable aspect of his foreign policy. Articulating a broad goal to better connect Peru with the outside world, one of the first tasks he set for his administration was to reaffirm Peru's place in the international community in the wake of the discredited Fujimori regime. A central component of his approach was the articulation of a foreign policy that projected democratic values and respect for human rights as integral components of any viable strategy to reduce poverty.[11] While previous governments had generally supported both human rights and democracy, Toledo's emphasis on these issues reflected both personal persuasion and a reaction to the policies of the Fujimori administration.

In a related albeit more idealistic initiative, President Toledo pressed for reduced arms spending in Latin America. Less than three weeks after his inauguration, he made an impassioned speech to the Rio Group in which he rejected regional arms expenditures totaling some $26 billion annually, arguing that the money should be spent on the education, health, and social well-being of the Latin American people. Thereafter, the Toledo administration continued to emphasize arms control in a variety of bilateral and international forums, often linking democracy, poverty reduction, and reduced arms expenditures. Over the ensuing five years, President Toledo continued to emphasize these issues, although he made little real progress in reducing regional arm purchases or sales, a policy objective Peru simply lacked the means to achieve.[12]

Other pragmatic elements of the foreign policy of the Toledo administration included a multilateral emphasis that involved broader integration with subregional, regional, and extra-regional bodies, from the CAN to the OAS to the UN, as well as enhanced relations with select states, like Brazil and China, and multilateral economic groupings, like MERCOSUR.[13] Relations with the industrialized world, especially the United States and the European Union (EU), centered on pragmatic efforts to increase aid, trade, and investment through the promotion of democracy and human rights, together with cooperation in the fight against narco-trafficking and terrorism.[14] Like Fujimori, President Toledo recognized that he would need the support of the U.S. government to pursue successfully many of the foreign and domestic policies he had articulated during the 2000–2001 election campaign.

Commercial and diplomatic ties with neighboring states have been of concern to successive Peruvian governments, and the Toledo administration was no exception. In dealing with its Andean partners, the foreign policy of the Toledo administration enjoyed both success and failure with the former far outstripping the latter. In the process, pragmatism remained the dominant characteristic of Peruvian foreign policy with ideology intervening periodically to play a relatively minor role.

The achievement of a strategic alliance with Brazil was probably the major foreign-policy success of the Toledo administration. A strategic relationship with Brazil had been under consideration by the career diplomats at the Peruvian Ministry of Foreign Affairs for some time, and several important developments, in addition to the vision and determination of President Toledo, led to its conclusion at this time. For many years, the two neighbors had tended to look in opposite directions with Brazil generally focused on the Atlantic Ocean and Africa; however, with the creation of MERCOSUR, Brazil began to take a heightened interest in South American issues. At the same time, Peruvian involvement in Asia-Pacific Economic Cooperation (APEC) and its growing participation in Asian markets, made improved access to the Pacific Basin increasingly attractive to Brazil.

In August 2003, President Toledo met with the Brazilian head of state, President Luiz Inácio Lula da Silva, and concluded a strategic understanding with an ambitious set of objectives. First, they agreed to promote increased economic cooperation within the framework of the Initiative for Integration of Regional Infrastructure in South America (IIRSA), a multiyear plan to crisscross Latin America with 10 hubs of economic integration. Second, they agreed to promote bilateral trade and investment within the context of a bilateral free-trade agreement between Peru and MERCOSUR. Third, Brazil agreed to give Peru access to two surveillance systems it was developing to track illicit activities in the Amazon Basin. Fourth, the parties agreed to develop the South American Community of Nations (CNS) with the aim of creating within South America a region of peace, economic development, and political dialogue. Over the next three years the implementation of the pragmatic goals of the newly formed strategic alliance remained center stage.[15]

In tone and content, Peruvian relations with Colombia after 2001 often resembled those with Brazil in that the dialogue focused on pragmatic issues such as terrorism and narco-trafficking. Related national security concerns included the incursion into Peruvian territory by the Revolutionary Armed Forces of Colombia (FARC) guerrilla movement, together with defense and police cooperation, and frontier security. The Toledo administration also worked with Colombia to improve economic conditions in the borderland.[16]

With Ecuador, the Toledo administration immediately acknowledged the validity of the 1998 Brazilia Accords, even though Toledo had suggested during the presidential campaign that he might renegotiate them, and made repeated efforts to energize borderland development. In an excellent example of issue-based pragmatism, neither Peru nor Ecuador after 2001 showed any inclination to return to the state of belligerency that had largely characterized bilateral relations from independence to 1998. On the contrary, President Toledo joined his Ecuadorian counterparts in reiterating their commitment to peace, emphasizing the need to reduce poverty, and decrying the failure of the international community to provide the financial assistance allegedly promised when the Brasilia Accords were concluded in 1998.[17]

Peruvian relations with Bolivia were generally positive during the first 54 months of the Toledo administration, but they deteriorated sharply following the inauguration of Bolivian President Evo Morales in January 2006. In the early years, talks were held on a variety of pragmatic issues, including Ilo as an exit port for Bolivian energy, labor migration, economic integration, free trade, and the perennial question of a sovereign Pacific port for Bolivia. With the elevation of Morales, who questioned the benefits of globalization and advocated socialism, Bolivian foreign and domestic policy moved in new directions that were often antithetical to policies long advocated by President Toledo.[18] In so doing, rhetoric increasingly characterized the discourse between the two states with ideology intruding on bilateral relations long characterized by pragmatism. The leftward tilt in Bolivian politics, when combined with a contentious 2006 presidential campaign in Peru in which a nationalist candidate, Ollanta Humala Tasso, looked set to take Peru into the Bolivia-Venezuela camp, made meaningful cooperation impossible.[19]

Since independence, Peru had enjoyed prolonged and mostly cordial relations with Venezuela. However, with the election in early 1998 of President Hugo Chávez Frías, bilateral tensions increased, peaking in the latter years of the Toledo presidency. The progressive deterioration in relations that took place was not surprising as the personalities, philosophies, and policies of the two presidents could not have been more different. Specific bilateral issues involved a mix of pragmatic and ideological concerns, including Venezuelan support for Vladimiro Montesinos, President Fujimori's disgraced spy chief, when he was evading an arrest warrant, Peruvian support for democratic processes in Venezuela, and Venezuelan interference in the domestic politics of Peru. That said, the real issue from the outset was the opposing visions that Toledo and Chávez had for the region as a whole. Where Toledo promoted orthodox economic policies and free-market reforms, Chavez questioned the benefits of globalization, advocating nationalization and socialism. Where Toledo concluded a free-trade agreement with the United States, Chavez signed people's trade pacts with Bolivia and Cuba. Where Toledo cultivated stronger ties with a wide variety of states, including the United States, Chavez allied with a smaller number of mostly left-leaning states, including Bolivia, Cuba, Ecuador, and Nicaragua. Where Toledo expanded ties with established international trade and finance organizations, Chavez promoted alternative trade and finance structures.[20]

Often an irritant, the regional policies of President Chávez were particularly troublesome in the final days of the Toledo presidency when Chávez joined Evo Morales in supporting the presidential candidature of left-leaning Ollanta Humala Tasso. When Chávez threw himself into the Peruvian presidential campaign, openly criticizing other candidates, President Toledo responded by withdrawing the Peruvian ambassador to Venezuela, declaring that the Venezuelan president was not the president of Latin America, and promising to teach him the Peruvian national anthem. Undeterred, Chávez continued to speak out, prompting the Toledo administration to withdraw its ambassador to Venezuela a second time and later to denounce Venezuelan involvement in the internal affairs of Peru before the OAS.[21]

In contrast to Venezuela, where pragmatic and ideological concerns frequently intermingled, long-standing pragmatic issues dominated bilateral relations with Chile during the Toledo presidency. In addition to the full implementation of the 1929 Tacna and Arica Treaty and Additional Protocol, the chief policy concerns were the Peru-Chile maritime boundary and Chilean arms purchases that threatened to provoke a regional arms race. Other issues included an open-skies agreement, the return of the Peruvian warship *Huáscar*, the Lucchetti case, a social agenda, and the extradition of former Peruvian President Fujimori, all of which fell into the pragmatic category.[22] While the negotiation of a social contract could be counted a success, the Toledo administration failed to gain from Chile any commitment to a wider policy of regional disarmament. Peruvian diplomacy also failed to achieve a solution to its maritime dispute with Chile. Failure in both cases was the product of Chilean intransigence as much as any policy deficiency on the part of the Toledo administration.

In terms of an elevated engagement with the outside world, the foreign policy of the Toledo administration was a success in large part due to the president himself. From very humble beginnings, Toledo had become fluent in English, earned undergraduate and graduate degrees from U.S. universities, including a PhD from Stanford University, and worked for several international bodies, including the World Bank, before being elected president. As a result, Peru in 2001–2006 was a highly visible, often effective player in a variety of international conferences, forums, and organizations.

At the same time, critics of the foreign policy of the Toledo administration argued with good reason that its initiatives sometimes lacked substance and purpose. There was a tendency to advance broad themes, like democracy and human rights, but then failure to bring them to practical application and implementation. There was also a tendency to pursue themes of questionable viability, like multilateral disarmament and reduced arms expenditures, which were admirable in their own right but almost certainly incapable of execution. Concerning subregional and regional integration, the Toledo administration took important steps to strengthen traditional ties and to develop new ones, but was also criticized for sometimes failing to take the concrete economic steps necessary to advance the political side of the equation.

These criticisms aside, the Toledo administration was notably successful in the pursuit of its subregional, regional, and extra-regional objectives. In pursuing largely pragmatic policies that reflected both the internal and external interests of Peru in a wide variety of international gatherings, it demonstrated a profound understanding of the growing interconnection of domestic and foreign policies in the new millennium. Not afraid to fail, the Toledo administration launched fresh initiatives that increased awareness of important issues even when they did not lead to diplomatic breakthroughs or the conclusion of firm agreements.[23]

THE GARCÍA ADMINISTRATION (2006–2011)

The former president Alan García Pérez successfully reinvented himself in the course of the 2006 presidential campaign. Depicting himself as an elder statesman who had learned from his mistakes, he gained favor with voters when he targeted his message at younger Peruvians with no memory of his disastrous first administration. Admitting his free-spending policies and refusal to repay Peru's foreign debt were major mistakes, he painted himself as a moderate leftist no longer hostile to the United States. Having come second in the first round of elections, narrowly ahead of Lourdes Flores Nano, García overcame Ollanta Humala Tasso in the second round with 52 percent of the vote.[24]

In the course of the campaign, García promised to continue macroeconomic stability, promote worker rights, and levy a windfall profits tax on mining companies. Pushing an austerity program that included a reduction in public sector salaries, he offered conditional support for a free-trade agreement with the United States and pledged to maintain open relations with the IMF. In a backhanded complement to the Toledo administration, García in June 2006 told a columnist that "Peru's foreign policy has not been the most misguided part of Toledo's government. So we must continue with [current policies] in issues such as opening up to the world market and drawing investments in a framework of democracy."[25]

At the same time, his approach to the Andean Community as a means to strengthen subregional integration was less clear, especially after Venezuela announced its withdrawal in April 2006. In the course of an election campaign in which President Chávez had openly supported Ollanta Humala Tasso, President García exchanged barbs with Chávez after the latter termed García "a swine, a gambler, and a thief" and characterized García and Toledo as "two alligators from the same swamp."[26]

As is sometimes the case with newly elected officials, García, the president, was not always the same as García, the candidate. Once in office, he pursued a foreign policy that was a blend of the old and the new, but in its totality, mirrored the policies of the Toledo administration. In an interview in early August 2006, José Antonio García Belaúnde, the newly appointed foreign minister of Peru, was mildly critical of the foreign policy of the Toledo administration, yet outlined a set of goals little changed from those of President Toledo.[27] In so doing, the foreign policy of the second García administration stood in marked contrast to that of the first, in that it largely continued the pragmatism-over-ideology model pursued by both Fujimori and Toledo.

The inaugural address of President García focused almost exclusively on domestic issues. In one of the few references to foreign policy, he pledged to maintain economic growth and development at a rate equal to or greater than his South American neighbors. Where President Toledo was generally viewed as an internationalist who was not so good on domestic policy, President García was determined to be considered stronger on domestic concerns.[28] In line with the emphasis on thrift in government, the Ministry of Foreign Affairs soon announced that it would close six embassies, a small but symbolic rejection of Toledo's policy of promoting a wider, more visible international role for Peru. Ironically, President García was later criticized for not traveling abroad enough.

President García's support for market-friendly economic policies was welcomed in the White House where President George W. Bush greeted him in October 2006. In the joint news conference following their meeting, García invoked the Alliance for Progress, arguing free trade today could accomplish what the Alliance had failed to do in the 1960s. García also embraced the free-trade agreement with the United States negotiated by the Toledo administration and approved by the Peruvian Congress before García took office. Following their White House meeting, President Bush pledged to work with the U.S. Congress to pass the free-trade pact. The U.S. president eventually made good on his promise but not until mid-January 2009 when he signed a proclamation enacting the agreement.[29] However, García never achieved the close personal relationship with Bush that Toledo had enjoyed, a rapport Toledo once described as "a chemistry at the level of skin."[30] That said, President García was invited to the Bush White House a second time in April 2007 and a third time in December 2007, notable achievements given his difficult relationship with the United States in the 1980s.

García pledged early on in his second administration to give priority to diplomatic and commercial relations with neighboring states. With Ecuador, for example, efforts continued to implement fully the multiple agreements constituting the 1998 Brasilia Accords, including a pact to regularize labor migration across the border and an ongoing struggle against contraband. Progress continued even after the November 2006 election of Rafael Correa to the presidency of Ecuador, despite Correa's tendency to support Bolivia and Venezuela in subregional and regional issues. In spite of clear policy differences, both Ecuador and Peru refused to return to the state of belligerency that had long hampered mutual relations, focusing instead on borderland development. At one point, Ecuador did appear to side with Chile in Peru's maritime boundary dispute with the latter; however, the Correa administration later assumed a seemingly neutral position in the Chile-Peru dispute.[31]

In the case of Chile, President García finalized a new commercial accord, largely negotiated by the Toledo administration, which widened bilateral ties. Other agreements included one covering domestic employees from Chile and Peru working in the country of the other. The disposition of the ex-president Fujimori was a contentious issue for more than a year until the Chilean Supreme Court finally authorized his extradition to Peru in September 2007 to face charges of corruption and abuse of human rights. Finally, García also supported Toledo's decision to take the maritime issue with Chile to the International Court of Justice, a judicial process well under way in 2010 but expected to take several more years to complete. Other areas of discord included the Chilean purchase of high-tech weaponry when Peru was advocating reduced arms purchases in the region, and a case of espionage in which a Peruvian air force officer admittedly sold national security information to the Chileans.[32]

With Brazil, the diplomacy of the García administration focused on strengthening the process of bilateral integration initiated by President Toledo in 2003. In February 2008, President García was the first head of state to visit Brazil following President Lula's election for a second term in office. In the course of the visit, the two countries reached 12 new accords, including agreements on technical cooperation, health, education, biotechnology, energy-mining, and Amazon security. A product of a Toledo administration initiative, the latter agreement gave Peru access to the Amazon Surveillance and Protection System (SIVAM/SIPAN), a combination of fixed and mobile radars, meteorological stations, and airborne surveillance developed to provide real-time information on illicit activities, such as drug trafficking and illegal deforestation. In July 2008, presidents García, Lula, and Uribe concluded a tripartite memorandum of understanding aimed at combating narco-trafficking in the Amazon region. Presidents García and Lula reaffirmed their strong bilateral ties in December 2009, concluding 17 new commercial and other agreements in the course of a state visit by Lula to Peru.[33]

As for Colombia, the foreign policy of the García administration continued to focus on pragmatic border issues, most of which related to questions of security and national defense. They included economic development in the frontier zone, increased commercial exchange, and additional collaboration against narco-trafficking. On the latter issue, mounting evidence surfaced to suggest that FARC units engaged in the illicit drug trade were operating on both sides of the Peru-Colombia border.[34]

In the course of the presidential campaign, García had responded in kind to the harsh criticism of presidents Chávez and Morales, but after his inauguration, he reached out to both heads of state in an effort to calm the rhetoric. At the same time, he cast his administration as the regional antithesis of Chávez and Morales, arguing in Washington that a bilateral free-trade pact was necessary to thwart the threat of "Andean Fundamentalism" in South America.[35] With observers inside and outside the region viewing Chávez and Morales as threats to democracy, García's approach played well in many circles in Peru—and also in Washington—but not in Caracas or La Paz. Management of the ongoing tension between discourse and action proved a difficult balancing act for García and made a permanent reconciliation with either Bolivia or Venezuela very difficult.

An early source of concern with Bolivia was its agreement with Venezuela for the latter to fund Bolivian military bases along the Peruvian border, an issue the Morales government later sought to defuse by terming them "frontier posts." Peruvian officials were also frustrated by Bolivia's reluctance to accept the modifications to the CAN agreement necessary to implement Peru's free-trade agreement with the United States, as well as its refusal to negotiate a common CAN trade agreement with the EU. While some cooperation in areas such as combating narco-trafficking and terrorism was evident, unproductive rhetoric continued to characterize bilateral relations well into the fourth year of García's five-year term. On the other hand, the appointment of Manuel Rodríguez Cuadros, an ex-foreign minister of Peru (2003–2005), as the Peruvian ambassador to Bolivia in early 2010 offered the promise of improved diplomatic and commercial relations between the two states.[36]

Regarding Venezuela, there was an ongoing concern in Peru with the activities of the Bolivian Alternative for the Americas (ALBA). Funded by Venezuela, its activities in and around Peru sparked concerns of regional hegemony. In mid-January 2007, while attending the formal inauguration ceremony for President Correa, presidents García and Chávez did agree to renew diplomatic ties, formally ending the rift that began during the 2006 presidential campaign. However, by March 2008, after Peruvian police arrested nine people alleged to be militants bankrolled by Venezuela, the García administration was again accusing Chávez of meddling in the domestic affairs of Peru. Venezuela returned its ambassador to Lima in August 2009, restoring full diplomatic relations; nevertheless, the relationship between the García and Chávez administrations remained problematic.[37]

President Toledo had worked hard to increase trade with China, together with Chinese investment in Peru, and the García administration supported these initiatives, building on the bilateral agreements in place, ranging from education to health to transportation. In March 2010, foreign minister José Antonio García Belaúnde traveled to China to discuss a variety of commercial subjects of mutual interest, including implementation of the free-trade agreement in operation from March 1, 2010. At the same time, the García administration continued the efforts of its predecessor to broaden commercial relations with both Japan and South Korea.[38]

Elsewhere, the García administration continued the participatory policies of the Fujimori and Toledo administrations in regional and international bodies, such as the OAS and the UN. However, it did not pursue as aggressively as the Toledo administration initiatives in areas such as the promotion of democracy and the reduction of regional arms expenditures. On the contrary, President García in the early months of his second administration committed to a major rearmament of the Peruvian armed forces, reversing the arms control policy pursued by his first administration. Thereafter, the García administration continued to articulate a policy of arms control and reduced arms spending, but at the same time, it looked to acquire new weapons for the Peruvian armed forces, including jet fighter planes and armored tanks.[39]

CONCLUSIONS

Over the last two centuries, pragmatism has tended to prevail over ideology in the content and expression of Peruvian foreign policy, and this trend has continued over the past two decades. Issues of sovereignty, continental solidarity, regionalism, territorial integrity, and economic independence were central to the foreign policy of Peru throughout this period, and they have remained prominent in the contemporary era. The Fujimori, Toledo, and García administrations were active participants in international and regional organizations, such as the UN and the OAS, as they worked through subregional bodies, like CAN, to promote cooperation and development. Territorial issues also stretched into the present century as successive administrations sought to tie up loose ends related to the 1929 Tacna and Arica Treaty and Additional Protocol with Chile, the 1998 Brasilia Accords with Ecuador, and the still unresolved maritime dispute with Chile. This is not to say that ideology did not play a role from time to time, but rather that it only occasionally influenced pragmatism, and seldom overshadowed it.

As to the factors that have influenced this mix of pragmatism and ideology, the professionalism of the Peruvian diplomatic corps has been one of the most important influences in the Peruvian case. Attempts to improve the structure of the Ministry of Foreign Affairs and the professionalism of the diplomatic service began as early as the mid-nineteenth century and have continued to the present time. Occasionally, the executive branch has sought to politicize the Ministry of Foreign Affairs, with the Fujimori regime being the most recent example, but more often than not, the executive has relied on the professionals resident in the Torre Tagle to guide the external affairs of the state. A second important influence has been the central place of territorial issues in the foreign policy of Peru since independence. Essentially pragmatic in form and content, these issues were subject to rhetoric on occasion but not to ideology in resolution.

In recent times, the mounting rejection of neoliberalism and the consequent ideological divide in Andean America that presently separates Bolivia, Ecuador, and Venezuela from Chile, Colombia, and Peru has heightened the tension between pragmatism and ideology. Nevertheless, the mounting complexity and increasing fragmentation of the global environment would appear in the Peruvian case to support the continuation of pragmatism in most instances with no sharp breaks anticipated between past, present, and future. Pragmatism therefore may be expected to continue to prevail over ideology in the foreign policy of Peru for the foreseeable future.

NOTES

1. Rosa Garibaldi de Mendoza, *La Política Exterior del Perú en la era de Ramón Castilla: Defensa hemisférica y defensa de la jurisdicción nacional* (Lima: Fundación Academia Diplomática del Perú, 2003).
2. Ronald Bruce St. John, *The Foreign Policy of Peru* (Boulder, CO: Lynne Rienner, 1992), 67–184, 188–89, 193–98.

3. Fernando Belaúnde Terry, President of Peru (1963–1968, 1980–1985), interview with author, Lima, Peru, July 11, 1983.
4. St. John, *Foreign Policy of Peru*, 206–9.
5. John Crabtree, *Peru under García: An Opportunity Lost* (Pittsburgh, PA: University of Pittsburg Press, 1992), especially 25–68, 121–51.
6. Ibid.
7. David Scott Palmer, "Relaciones entre Estados Unidos y el Perú durante el decenio de 1990: dinámicas, antecedentes y proyecciones," *Política Internacional* 53 (July–September 1998), 23–45; St John, *Foreign Policy of Peru*, 213–16.
8. Catherine M. Conaghan, *Fujimori's Peru: Deception in the Public Sphere* (Pittsburgh, PA: University of Pittsburgh Press, 2005), 27–76; Julio Cotler and Romeo Grompone, *El fujimorismo: ascenso y caída de un régimen autoritario* (Lima: Instituto de Estudios Peruanos, 2000).
9. Ronald Bruce St. John, *La Política Exterior del Perú* (Lima: Asociación de Funcionarios del Servicio Diplomático del Perú, 1999), 218–27.
10. Diego García-Sayán, foreign minister of Peru (July 2001–July 2002), interview with author, Lima, Peru, March 11, 2008; Ambassador Manuel Rodríguez Cuadros, deputy foreign minister of Peru (July 2001–December 2003), foreign minister of Peru (December 2003–August 2005), interview with author, Lima, Peru, March 14, 2008.
11. Perú, Presidencia de la República, *Mensaje a la Nación*, 28 July 2001; Perú, Ministerio de Relaciones Exteriores, *Un Líder sin Fronteras: Diplomacia Presidencial, 2001–2006* (Lima: Oficina General de Comunicaciones, 2006), 29–49, 451–52, 489–91.
12. "Toledo relanzará propuesta para limitar compras militares," *El Comercio*, August 17, 2001; "Paises latinos invierten más en Defensa," *El Comercio*, June 2, 2006.
13. Allan Wagner Tizón, Foreign Minister of Peru (July 2002–December 2003), interview with author, Lima, Peru, May 9, 2003; Oscar Maúrtua de Romaña, Foreign Minister of Peru (August 2005–July 2006), interview with author, Lima, Peru, April 18, 2006.
14. Alejandro Celestino Toledo Manrique, President of Peru (2001–2006), interviews with author, Lima, Peru, May 9, 2003, April 19, 2006; Perú, Ministerio de Relaciones Exteriores, *Un Líder sin Fronteras*, 453–65, 505–9.
15. Diego García-Sayán, *Una Nueva Política Exterior Peruana: Democrática, moderna, independiente y al servicio de la gente* (Lima: Comisión Andina de Juristas and Academia Diplomática del Perú, 2002), 131–37; Perú, Ministerio de Relaciones Exteriores, *Memoria Institucional, Agosto 2005–Julio 2006* (Lima: Ministerio de Relaciones Exteriores, 2006), 77–78.
16. Allan Wagner Tizón, foreign minister of Peru (July 2002–December 2003), interview with author, Lima, Peru, May 9, 2003; Perú, Ministerio de Relaciones Exteriores, *Memoria Institucional*, 77–78.

17. Ambassador José Antonio Arróspide del Busto, director for the Binacional Plan for Development, Peru-Ecuador, interview with author, Lima, Peru, March 13, 2008.

18. Alejandro Celestino Toledo Manrique, president of Peru (2001–2006), interviews with author, Lima, Peru, April 19, 2006, Palo Alto, CA, September 12, 2008.

19. Ambassador Oscar Maúrtua Romaña, foreign minister of Peru (August 2005–July 2006), interview with author, Lima, Peru, April 18, 2006; "Toledo es un hipócrita, dice el Gobierno," *La Razón*, May 23, 2006.

20. "Chávez: El Simón Gorila," *Caretas* 1675, June 21, 2001; Alejandro Celestino Toledo Manrique, president of Peru (2001–2006), interview with author, Lima, Peru, May 9, 2003.

21. "Toledo: 'Chávez no es presidente de América Latina,'" *El Comercio*, January 11, 2006; Ambassador Oscar Maúrtua Romaña, foreign minister of Peru (August 2005–July 2006), interview with author, Lima, Peru, April 18, 2006; "Toledo advierte que se gestaría 'alboroto pagado' para el 4 de junio," *La República*, May 28, 2006.

22. Ambassador Oscar Maúrtua Romaña, foreign minister of Peru (August 2005–July 2006), interview with author, Lima, Peru, April 18, 2006; Ambassador Manuel Rodríguez Cuadros, deputy foreign minister of Peru (July 2001–December 2003), foreign minister of Peru (December 2003–August 2005), interview with author, Lima, Peru, March 14, 2008.

23. Alejandro Celestino Toledo Manrique, president of Peru (2001–2006), interview with author, Palo Alto, CA, September 12, 2008.

24. Ronald Bruce St John, "Politics of Peru in Flux," *Foreign Policy in Focus*, June 29, 2006. http://www.fpif.org.

25. Quoted in Andres Oppenheimer, "Peru's next leader vows to support free trade," *Miami Herald*, June 11, 2006.

26. Quoted in Cynthia McClintock, "An Unlikely Comeback in Peru," *Journal of Democracy* 17, 4 (October 2006): 104.

27. Sheilla Díaz, "Estrecharemos relación con Chile," *Caretas* 1936, August 3, 2006.

28. Augusto Alvarez-Rodrich, Journalist and Editor (*Perú21*), Lima, Peru, March 12, 2008.

29. Adriana Garcia, "Bush eyes Peru's Garcia as Latin American ally," *Washington Post*, October 10, 2006; "Estados Unidos declara la entrada en vigor del TLC con Perú," *La República*, January 16, 2009.

30. Alejandro Celestino Toledo Manrique, president of Peru (2001–2006), interview with author, Lima, Peru, May 9, 2003.

31. "García y Correa buscarán impulsar el desarrollo en las zonas de frontera," *El Comercio*, June 1, 2007; "El Perú espera fortalecer relaciones económicas y políticas con Ecuador," *El Comercio*, February 18, 2008; "Ecuador dice podría acudir a La Haya por diferendo entre Perú y Chile" *El Comerico*, October 22, 2009; C. Toro, "Ministro de Defensa de Ecuador destaca 'paz y amistad profunda' con el Perú," *La República*, March 19, 2010.

32. "ExPresident Is Returned to Peru," *New York Times*, September 22, 2007; "Wagner señala que el Perú debe confiar en que demanda marítima será bien sustentada," *La República*, January 29, 2009; Andrew Whalen, "Peru, Chile presidents trade barbs in spy spat," *Washington Post*, November 17, 2009; "Equipo peruano inició el análisis de la contramemoria chilena, *El Comercio*, March 12, 2010.

33. Antonio José López Rengifo, "Peru-Brazil Cooperation Goes Forward," February 9, 2008. http://english.ohmynews.com; "Uribe, García y Lula firmaron un acuerdo para combatir el narcotráfico," *Perú21*, July 20, 2008; "Presidentes Lula y Alan García suscribieron 17 acuerdos de cooperación," *El Comercio*, December 11, 2009.

34. "Uribe y García ampliarán los acuerdos entre Colombia y Perú," *La República*, December 11, 2007; "Miembros de las FARC habrían ingresado infiltrados al Perú," *Perú21*, March 19, 2008; "Correos de 'Raúl Reyes' revelan presencia de las FARC en el Perú," *El Comercio*, August 30, 2009.

35. "García pide poner freno al "fundamentalismo andino," *La Razón*, October 11, 2006.

36. "García lamenta intención de Bolivia de construir bases en frontera," *El Comercio*, October 11, 2006; "Opinan que Evo Morales debilita a CAN con doble discurso," *La República*, January 18, 2009; "'Evo Morales no tiene autoridad para criticar al Perú'," *El Comercio*, October 1, 2009; "Perú quiere que relaciones con Bolivia recuperen niveles históricos," *La República*, March 18, 2010.

37. Andrew Whalen, "Peru says Chavez backs domestic revolt," *Miami Herald*, March 22, 2008; "Correa viajará mañana a Venezuela para asistir a cumbre de la ALBA," *El Comercio*, February 1, 2008; "El Perú y Venezuela tendrán relaciones plenas con llegada de embajador," *El Comercio*, August 12, 2009.

38. "APEC El Ojo de Tormenta," *Caretas* 2055, November 27, 2008; "Alan García llegó a Japón con la premisa de acelerar TLC y mejorar relaciones," *El Comercio*, November 10, 2009; M. Carrion, "Canciller viajará a China para fortalecer asociación estratégica," *La República*, March 20, 2010.

39. "Invertirán US$650 millones en las FFAA hasta el 2011," *El Comercio*, March 3, 2007; "Alan García demanda frenar compra de armas," *Perú21*, May 17, 2008; "Rey: Perú está a punto de comprar tanques chinos," *El Comercio*, December 8, 2009; "En enero se reanudarán misiones contra el armamentismo," *La República*, December 10, 2009; "Perú adquirirá dos aviones super tucano de Brasil, confirmó ministro Rey," *El Comercio*, December 20, 2009.

CHAPTER 8

The Continuing Pull of the Polar Star: Colombian Foreign Policy in the Post–Cold War Era*

Stephen J. Randall

Introduction

The tension between ideology and pragmatism in the making of foreign policy exists to some degree in all nations, including Colombia. Some analysts would point to the fact that Colombia has largely adhered to a close relationship with the United States since World War I as evidence of a predominantly conservative ideological orientation in the nation's foreign policy. That perspective would be further reinforced by the fact that during the Cold War years Colombian governments, without exception, adhered to the Western, anti-Communist position dominated by the United States. There were administrations during which that orientation was more pronounced than others, as for instance during the conservative-dominated 1950s, when Colombia was the only Latin American country to commit troops to the Korean War, and other administrations that adhered to a more multilateral position, such as the governments of Carlos Lleras Restrepo (1966–1970) or Alfonso López Michelsen (1970–1974), which opened up trade relationships with Soviet bloc countries and took a moderate position on Cuba's place in hemispheric affairs. However, overall there is little debate over the fact that Colombian governments in the Cold War years were intensely anti-Communist.

Yet, as this chapter suggests, the orientation of Colombian foreign policy in the post-1945 years was driven largely by pragmatic consider-ations, in particular the realistic perspective that the United States was the hegemonic power in the hemisphere, with the result that it was in Colombian interests to maintain a reasonably balanced and positive rela-tionship with the "polar star." Colombian foreign policy has thus been predominantly pragmatic, but this does not mean that it was devoid of values and ideas. Colombian leaders, regardless of party affiliation, have placed a high degree of importance on the nation's adherence to the principles of international law.

Foreign policy has also been multilateral in its orientation, consis-tent with the policies that most smaller nations tend to pursue, and Colombia has been a strong supporter of the United Nations and the Organization of American States (OAS). The country's foreign policy has also tended to be dominated by a small foreign-policy elite, of which the president has without exception been the most significant player. Many Colombian presidents have viewed themselves as essentially their own foreign ministers, at least in terms of setting the agenda, leaving Congress and public opinion with little real influence and the Foreign and Defense ministries with the responsibility to implement rather than design policy. This chapter focuses on Colombian foreign policy from the 1990s to 2010, a year in which the two terms of President Alvaro Uribe Vélez will come to an end; but the chapter also places those years in a larger historical context in order to stress the continuities in Colombian foreign policy.

THE HISTORICAL CONTEXT

Colombian foreign policy since the end of the Cold War must be under-stood within the larger context of its evolution since World War I.[1] Over the past century two fundamental forces have shaped Colombian foreign policy. The first and foremost has been relations with the United States, a relationship that has been above all economic, strategic, and pragmatic rather than ideological, even though there have often been shared values and shared assumptions about the nature of the world in which they operated. To the extent that Colombian policymakers have adhered to principles in foreign policy it has been the unwavering com-mitment to international law; yet that commitment has not imposed any degree of rigidity in the Colombian approach to its international relations. The loss of Panama in the first decade of the twentieth century, for which Colombians continue to hold U.S. actions responsible even if they grudgingly acknowledge Colombian mismanagement, represented a significant turning point in Colombia's external relations. Colombian leaders recognized they had a choice between pragmatism, which would align Colombian interests with the interests of the United States as the hemispheric and ultimately global superpower, or they could pursue policies that would be more balanced and multilateral in nature. They might even have pursued a kind of Bolivarian vision of leadership within Latin America, a notion long dormant but which Hugo Chávez has rekindled in Venezuela. Colombian leaders chose the pragmatic course, with the result that since the World War I era, relations with the United States have dominated Colombia's orientation even during those administrations that have sought to play more significant roles on the regional and world stage.

Other forces that have driven Colombian foreign policy have been the internal insurgency since the late 1940s and the international implications of illegal narcotics cultivation and trafficking since the 1970s. Both factors, the guerrilla insurgency and the narcotics industry, have been politically and economically destabilizing forces domestically, but they have also contributed to regional security challenges and to tensions with Colombia's immediate neighbors.[2] Responding to those challenges has served primarily to reinforce Colombia's ties to the United States at the same time that, perhaps paradoxically, they have been sources of friction between the two nations. In this sense Colombia is hardly unique. Middle powers tend to be consistently torn between responding to the demands of their hegemon at the same time that they seek to engage the larger world. As with other middle powers that have a high degree of dependency on a single nation, Colombia has consistently sought to balance the dominance of the United States with a quest for multilateral ties and commitment to major international organizations, such as the UN, the OAS, the Andean group, and to support such international agencies as the International Court of Justice.

Such an orientation has been driven primarily by realpolitik and a belief in the fundamental importance of international law. Whatever the factors that led Colombian elites to choose the course they did over the past century, these were Colombian choices as much as decisions driven by Washington, but the latitude within which those choices were made was very limited. The result has been a high degree of economic, military, and political dependency on the United States, a dependency that, in the decade on which this chapter focuses, has significantly increased.[3]

Colombia's economic linkages have reinforced its foreign-policy orientation. The United States has traditionally been the dominant trade partner, but regional trade also represents an important component of the Colombian economy, in particular the relationship with Venezuela, which is the second largest market for Colombian products. In 2007, for instance, the United States exported more than $8.5 billion in goods to Colombia and imported more than $9.4 billion.[4] By contrast, total Colombian trade with Venezuela in that year was approximately $4.1 billion, while with Brazil it was $2.5 billion, with Mexico $3.3 billion, and with Germany $1.5 billion.[5] It is evident where Colombia's primary trade interests reside, and the protection as well as expansion of that market has been a logical foreign-policy goal, including the negotiation of a still to be ratified Free Trade Agreement with the United States.

In addition to the consistent, even if sometimes reluctant, adherence to the "Polar Star" fixation that has characterized Colombian foreign policy, scholars have identified other features of Colombian policy formation that have determined its orientation. One factor has been the extreme elitism of policy formation, normally limited to the president and an inner circle of advisors. Although Congress has committees that debate foreign policy they have had relatively little impact on policy. That has also been true of the Advisory Commission of the Ministry of Foreign Relations, composed of all former presidents and a few appointees.[6] Nor has the Foreign Ministry exercised a degree of influence equal to that of the British Foreign Office or the U.S. Department of State.

As in other nations, the importance of military issues in the Colombian context has further eroded the influence of the Foreign Ministry and increased the relative importance of other ministries, particularly Defense. Nor has domestic public opinion tended to be a significant factor in policy formation. It is arguable that in the decades since drugs trafficking and the domestic insurgency became a major international issue, foreign opinion has been a far more significant force in shaping Colombian policy responses on such critical issues as human rights than has domestic public opinion, including even such organized entities as the trade unions, the coffee federation, and ANDI, the industrial association.[7]

Preoccupation with the relationship with the United States has not precluded some administrations from pursuing more multilateral policies, an approach that in the Cold War years tended to be more characteristic of Liberal than of Conservative governments. That multilateralism was evident in the orientation of President Carlos Lleras Restrepo (1966–1970), who sought to open diplomatic and commercial ties with the Soviet Union and other countries of Eastern Europe from 1968. Lleras's position was strongly supported by his foreign minister and later president Alfonso López Michelsen (1974–1978), who also supported normalization of relations with Cuba, with the result that once the OAS reversed its earlier policy of isolating Cuba, López's administration established full diplomatic relations with Castro's government. López Michelsen and most of his presidential successors recognized that Colombia had paid a high price for its opposition to Fidel Castro under Alberto Lleras Camargo, especially given the Cuban links to the ELN guerrillas (National Liberation Army) and Castro's capacity to play a broker role in the region (which continued into the twenty-first century during the Uribe crisis with Ecuador and Venezuela). Certainly the Lleras and López Michelsen approaches were driven more by the pragmatic desire to diversify Colombian trade and international relations than by any ideological empathy for Cuba or the countries directly within the Soviet sphere.

Virgilio Barco as president (1986–1990) took an even more pronounced direction in his government's foreign policy, at times appearing to take positions that would be deliberately opposite to those of the United States. His administration, along with other members of the nonaligned movement, opposed the U.S. bombing of Libya, opposed U.S. intervention in Panama in 1989 to overthrow Manuel Noriega, and criticized Israel's occupation of Arab territory. Colombian governments in the 1980s also pursued through the Contadora Group a negotiated settlement of the Central American crisis and specifically the U.S.-backed Contra war against the Sandinista government in Nicaragua.[8] Such approaches derived less from ideological opposition to the United States than from Colombia's consistent opposition to interventionism.

The end of the Cold War alleviated tensions over foreign-policy orientation between the more traditionally anti-Communist Conservative and Liberal parties, a tension that at times in the past had imposed some degree of constraint on strictly pragmatic Colombian policy. César Gaviria Trujillo (1990–1994) came to power as the Cold War ended. In his inaugural address he called on Colombia to recognize the new international reality as an opportunity to put divisive international politics aside and focus on economic issues.[9] In practice his administration, led in the international arena by foreign ministers Luis Fernando Jaramillo and subsequently Noemí Sanín (1991–1994), pursued policies similar to those of the Barco administration, further opening the economy to the international community, supporting international law, and strengthening regional and global linkages. In 1991 his government reestablished diplomatic relations with Cuba, a decision that reflected the presidentialist nature of Colombian policymaking, since there was a negative reaction from Colombian Conservatives as well as some Liberals, from the military, and some sectors of the press. To some degree the decision to restore relations with Cuba did reflect the specific orientation of the Barco administration, but taking into consideration a longer view of Colombian policy toward the place of Cuba in the inter-American system, the decision was consistent with perceived Colombian principles and the national interest.[10] On the whole, the administration pressed forward with a strong internationalist orientation. As the foreign minister, Noemí Sanín was vigorous in pursuing a prominent place for Colombia in the international arena, seeking a seat on the UN Security Council, obtaining for Colombia the presidency of the G-77 as well as the nonaligned movement, and effectively lobbying for President Gaviria to be elected secretary-general of the OAS at the end of his presidential term. In 1994 Colombia also joined the newly established Association of Caribbean States, consistent with a role that López Michelsen had earlier viewed as a logical one for the country. The association included Cuba but none of the U.S. dependencies.[11]

YEARS OF CRISIS: THE SAMPER ADMINISTRATION

The election of the Liberal Ernesto Samper-Pizano as president in 1994 ushered in a four-year period of uncertainty and tensions with the United States. He came to power with the stated intention of pursuing the multilateralist and pragmatic foreign policies of his Liberal predecessor, and his appointees as foreign minister, Rodrigo Pardo (1994–1995) and María Emma Mejía Vélez (1995–1998), were equally committed to those goals. Unfortunately, the early allegations that Samper's campaign had accepted funds from the Cali narcotics cartel severely compromised his government's credibility both domestically and abroad. This development was particularly unfortunate since Samper's first foreign minister, Rodrigo Pardo, who resigned in 1995 during the crisis, brought lengthy foreign-policy experience, expertise, and insight to the position.[12] At the outset of his tenure as foreign minister, Pardo indicated in an interview that the government's priority was the traditional emphasis on the basic principles of Colombian foreign relations: peaceful resolution of conflict; respect for international law; nonintervention; and the self-determination of people. The secondary goals were to continue with the previous government's pursuit of further integration with Latin America and the Caribbean and the increased "universalization" of Colombia's international relations.[13] Pardo added that there would also be attention to some of the nontraditional issues that had gained increased significance in Colombian foreign relations, including narcotics trafficking, international trade, the environment, and human rights. On the issue of relations with the United States, he suggested that he believed that two friendly nations could disagree on issues but still work constructively together. He also contended that it was critical that narcotics trafficking not become the all-consuming issue in the country's international relations given the greater importance of trade liberalization, investment, and social progress. Pardo also added a significant observation on the relative significance of foreign policy in Colombian politics and society, noting that it was not an electoral issue, nor was it an issue in the relationship between the presidency and Congress, and that the Colombian political elite had not become engaged in the issues.[14]

Pardo's successor, María Emma Mejía, had little choice except to focus on improving relations with the United States as well as with Venezuela, although the concerns over Venezuelan relations did not intensify until the election of Hugo Chávez as Venezuelan president in 1998, at the end of the Samper presidency. Mejía stressed in a 1998 interview that she was concerned that the United States might engage in sales of more advanced fighter aircraft to Venezuela, something that she felt would destabilize the bilateral relationship, might require Colombia to improve its weapons systems, and in the process divert resources from badly needed social and economic programs. She also expressed the Colombian government's consistent perspective that in spite of the Clinton administration's decision to lift sanctions against Colombia on the sale of military equipment for reasons of national security, the decertification process had been immensely damaging to the bilateral relationship.[15]

The Samper administration from the outset indicated a commitment to maintaining the neoliberal trade and investment policies of previous governments, continuing to expand the country's international engagement, and collaborating with the United States and Colombia's immediate neighbors to minimize the international impact of combined guerrilla insurgency and drug-trafficking. In spite of the presidentialist nature of Colombian policymaking and the increasingly beleaguered nature of the Samper administration, these foreign-policy goals reflected a general consensus among Colombian elites over the national interest. Revelations about Samper's relationship with the Cali Cartel, however, rapidly weakened his government's capacity to achieve its goals. Relations with the United States thus began on a sour note and remained that way throughout his four years in office. U.S. policy became increasingly aggressive, pressing his administration to address human rights violations, the war on drugs, and allegations of corruption in the civilian and military sectors. The Clinton administration went so far as to deny the president a visa in 1996 and decertify the country for failing to meet U.S. expectations in terms of human rights and the war on drugs.[16] Such policies effectively denied the legitimacy of Samper's government and destabilized the government at a time that strong leadership and credibility was needed. The bilateral relationship was made even more acute by the fact that the U.S. ambassador for a portion of the Samper administration, Myles Frechette (1994–1997), was particularly outspoken publicly and interventionist on issues that while domestic in nature also impacted U.S. interests.[17]

What U.S. officials appear to have neglected, failed to understand, or ignored in the Samper years was that given the presidentialist system of government in Colombia, by undermining Samper, who though weakened domestically and internationally, remained in power, they were in fact acting in a way that reduced the likelihood of achieving their own policy goals, goals that were not going to be achieved without a strong Colombian executive with both domestic and international support. By the time President Samper left office in August 1998, to be succeeded by the Conservative Party candidate Andrés Pastrana Arango, U.S. officials appeared to have grasped that dilemma. At the same time, the Samper experience once again underlined the extent to which Colombian domestic and foreign policy remained highly dependent on the United States. Unlike the presidencies of Carlos Lleras Restrepo and Alfonso López Michelsen, or even that of Gaviria that preceded his, the Samper administration had neither the will nor the latitude to pursue a more aggressive multilateral foreign policy, hamstrung as it was by its lack of domestic and international credibility.

THE PASTRANA TRANSITION

Domestic and international observers viewed the election of Andrés Pastrana to the Presidency in 1998 as an opportunity to restore some degree of normalcy to Colombian politics, and in particular to its relations with the United States. On one level there was little change in the fundamentals of Colombian foreign policy from Samper to Pastrana. Certainly there was no ideological shift, in part because although Pastrana was the official candidate of the Conservative party, he was in fact the candidate of a Conservative-Liberal coalition, *Gran Alianza por el cambio*. What changed was the attitude of the Clinton administration toward Colombia's new government. Thus, relations with the United States continued to dominate the agenda, but the relationship shifted from one of confrontation and distrust under Samper to close collaboration under Pastrana. Pastrana tended to pursue a dual policy.

On the one hand, in an effort to defuse the domestic conflict and reduce its impact on international relations, he pursued dialogue with FARC as part of a larger strategy of "diplomacy for peace." Rather than turn initially to the United States for support of his peace initiative, he sought support from Colombia's immediate neighbors and from European countries. In the critical year 2001 Colombia held the chair of the UN Security Council, and the foreign minister Fernandez de Soto was secretary-general of the Andean Community in 2002.[18] Pastrana also took the initiative to pay an official visit to Cuba, the only Colombian president to do so, thus seeking to offset years of bitterness on Fidel Castro's part.

Ultimately, however, it was the ties with the United States that dominated. The most critical initiative undertaken by the Pastrana administration was the development in 1999 and implementation the following year of what became Plan Colombia. The initiative came from the Pastrana administration and its original concept, as presented in 1998, was a broad-based one, designed to address social and economic challenges in the country as well as to undermine the production and distribution of illegal drugs. Even after his inauguration, President Pastrana did not appear to have viewed the initiative as one that would involve the further militarization of the conflict against the guerrillas or aerial fumigation of illicit crops. Indeed, the administration had serious doubts about the efficacy of aerial spraying.[19] The orientation changed significantly once serious negotiations began with the Clinton administration. When completed, the Clinton administration's aid package to Colombia targeted the war on drugs, and the majority of the funds were directed to the Colombian military and police to enhance their capacity to meet U.S. and, presumably, Colombian goals. Between 2000, when Plan Colombia aid began to flow into Colombia, and 2008, the country received approximately $600 million per annum in U.S. support. By mid-2003 the United States had provided $2.5 billion in military, economic, and humanitarian aid to Colombia, while Colombian taxpayers had contributed more than $4 billion to the plan.[20]

In contrast with its approach to the issue of international narcotics traffic, the Pastrana administration viewed the insurgency as a domestic issue and pursued negotiations with FARC.[21] In April 2000, speaking before the Association of Newspaper Editors in Washington, Pastrana stressed the international implications of the war on drugs, not the guerrilla insurgency:

> There is a growing awareness in Colombia, the United States and around the world, that the threat of drug trafficking is no longer a national or a regional issue . . . I have taken the message of greater burden-sharing in the fight against drugs to the international community . . . I have called our efforts "Diplomacy for Peace," because if we have learned anything from the recent progress in Northern Ireland, Central America and the Middle

East, it is that the international community must be actively engaged in order for peace to prevail.[22]

This focus evolved again after 9/11 with the Bush administration's shift to a focus on counterterrorism, eliminating the distinction between rolling back the guerrillas on the one hand and eradicating drug crops and controlling narcotics trafficking on the other. Before the end of the Pastrana administration, with the failure of negotiations with FARC, it was evident that there was a clear contention that one could not control narcotics without destroying the guerrillas, who both benefited from and supported the industry.[23]

ÁLVARO URIBE VÉLEZ AND THE POLITICS OF DEMOCRATIC SECURITY

The election of the independent Liberal Álvaro Uribe Vélez in 2002 inaugurated a decidedly new chapter in Colombian foreign policy, a policy focus that was even more closely oriented toward the goals of U.S. policy than at any previous time in Colombian history. As with previous administrations, Uribe's foreign policy was to a large extent a projection of the domestic situation. It was also consistent with the long-established primacy of the bilateral relationship with the United States, even if Uribe took that relationship to new heights. He, like his predecessors, identified the linkage with the United States as in the Colombian national interest. Even more than those presidents who preceded him in recent years, Uribe's foreign policies have been definitively presidentialist in nature, and his government has been widely viewed as highly centralized and conservative, verging on the autocratic.

Yet, distinctions of left and right, do not readily apply to Uribe. His officials stress that any attempts to define Uribe in ideological terms are misleading. His is a pragmatist, and his efforts in early 2009 to build closer links with Brazil and President Lula have been precisely that, to create a counterweight against the regional influence of Chávez, who like Uribe embodies many of the characteristics of the traditional Latin American *caudillo*.

The earlier crisis of legitimacy of the Samper government and the implementation of Plan Colombia had provided the United States with an opportunity to wield greater influence in Colombian domestic policies, but the Uribe government pressed ahead far more vigorously with what has come to be considered the internationalization of the domestic conflict. Uribe's policies led, to use a now popular term, "intervention by invitation,"[24] which Arelene Tickner has argued undermined national autonomy and compromised Colombia's relations with its neighbors, in particular Ecuador and Venezuela.[25] The Uribe administration came to be viewed as the closest partner of the United States in Latin America during the Republican administration of George W. Bush, endorsing the Bush administration's war on terror in the aftermath of 9/11 and supporting the U.S.-led invasion of Iraq. His administration vigorously pursued the conflict against FARC, supported the war on drugs and continued to benefit from U.S. assistance under Plan Colombia. U.S. forces also assumed a more direct role in the counter-insurgency efforts,[26] while President Uribe also provided full cooperation to U.S. authorities on extradition requests.

The Uribe administration continued to press, against considerable opposition in the U.S. Congress, for ratification of a Free Trade Agreement. Uribe stressed in an address to the Council on Foreign Relations in September 2008 that the agreement was not as important to trade as it was to encourage foreign investment in Colombia. "With a Free Trade Agreement approved," he argued, "many investors from several countries in the world will come to make investments."[27] However, the agreement remained an elusive goal. Although the Bush administration was understandably supportive of the agreement, the administration was unable to convince the majority Democratic Party, and the newly elected administration of Barack Obama has continued to emphasize its concerns with Colombian human rights.[28]

Analysts have tended to present the orientation and policies of the Uribe administration as indicative of an ideological as well as tactical shift, in part because of the perceived similarities between the worldviews of presidents Bush and Uribe.[29] The events of 9/11 made it possible to view the internal Colombian guerrilla insurgency as part of the international terrorist threat, and that perception was adopted not only by the Bush administration but also by European countries and Canada. There was also a shift in style under the Uribe presidency, which fits more clearly into the presidentialist, centralized, model of policymaking than that of his two immediate predecessors. That orientation was embodied not only in Uribe's approach to foreign policy, but in his capacity to have the Constitutional Court permit him to run for reelection in 2006, a departure from Colombia's longstanding constitutional practice and one that led such former presidents as Lopez Michelsen to criticize the decision publicly.

Uribe's first appointment as foreign minister was Carolina Barco Isakson, who was born and primarily educated in the United States. Her selection in itself spoke of the importance the newly elected president placed on the bilateral relationship. Barco served with considerable distinction until 2006 when she was appointed ambassador to the United States, a further signal of the importance of the relationship. Her three successors between 2006 and 2008 were less successful, in part because of the growing domestic and international concerns over the ties of individuals close to the President with the paramilitary groups.[30]

Uribe's appointments of ambassadors to the United States reflected his recognition of the need to have representation in Washington that had the respect and the ear of both the executive and Congress. Former President Andrés Pastrana, closely identified with the Clinton administration and with a generally pro-United States position, served as ambassador briefly in 2005–2006 in an effort to strengthen Colombia's image in Washington.[31] Shortly after the election of Barack Obama as president-elect of the United States, Pastrana indicated that Colombia had lost a significant opportunity to conclude the Free Trade Agreement while the Republicans were in control of the White House and were stronger in Congress. Colombia's only hope, he argued, was to seek to restore some degree of bipartisan support for such an agreement in Congress, in return for Colombian support for Plan Colombia and the U.S. counternarcotics program.[32]

President Uribe came to be widely viewed as the closest ally in Latin America of the Bush administration. As a member of the UN Security Council, Colombia supported the Bush administration's Iraq policies and the UN resolutions on the issue of Weapons of Mass Destruction. As a show of support for the often beleaguered Colombian president, President Bush twice visited Colombia during his presidency, once to Cartagena in 2004 and on the second occasion in 2007 for a short, high security, seven-hour visit to Bogota, the first to the Colombian capital by a serving U.S. president since 1982.[33] Although Uribe's support for the War on Terror and for the invasion of Iraq in 2003 paralleled the policies of Tony Blair's Labour government in Great Britain, it was a source of some tension with other Latin American countries. Yet he worked throughout his two terms in office to maintain strong ties with more leftist Latin American governments, including Lula de Silva in Brazil. He was a regular participant in multilateral and bilateral meetings with his Latin American colleagues, he maintained relations with Cuba as well as with the People's Republic of China, he concluded a trade agreement with Mercosur in 2005, and the Free Trade Agreement that was negotiated with the United States also included Peru and Ecuador.

Nonetheless, his vigorous and increasingly successful pursuit of the war against FARC and his rather ambiguous policy toward the various paramilitary organizations resulted in some serious regional challenges for his government, particularly with Hugo Chávez's Venezuela. In 2004 there were rumors that Colombian paramilitaries were involved in a plot to overthrow Chávez's government. In December of the same year, a senior member of FARC, Rodrigo Granda, considered FARC's foreign minister, was captured in Caracas while attending the Second Bolivarian People's Congress, transported to Colombia, and arrested by Colombian officials. Although the Venezuelan foreign ministry indicated that it would have cooperated officially with Colombia in the arrest of Granda, it viewed the private action as a violation of Venezuelan sovereignty, recalled its ambassador and suspended bilateral commercial relations. The Uribe government contended that Venezuela was knowingly harboring Colombian guerrillas, and the Bush administration strongly endorsed the Colombian position. Cuba, Brazil and Peru worked to mediate the dispute and in February the following year, Uribe and Chávez resolved the conflict at a bilateral summit, thus restoring commercial relations.

More serious were the reactions to the early 2008 Colombian military incursion into Ecuadoran territory to attack a major FARC base, and the killing of Raul Reyes, FARC's second in command, along with a number of other guerrillas. The action created a regional crisis. Ecuador withdrew its ambassador, while Chávez ordered the deployment of several battalions of Venezuelan troops and tanks to the Colombian border and warned Colombian authorities that any comparable incursion into Venezuelan territory would be a cause of war. The Venezuelan minister of defense presented the mobilization not as an action against the Colombian people but against U.S. expansionism. The only hemispheric government to publicly support Uribe was the Bush administration. The OAS on March 5 passed a resolution declaring the Colombian military raid a violation of Ecuador's sovereignty, although in an effort to allow both countries to save face, the resolution did not explicitly condemn the Colombian action. The resolution did not satisfy President Chávez, however, and bilateral tensions persisted, although Colombia's defense minister Juan Manuel Santos did not respond to the Venezuelan military mobilization.[34]

Within days of the crisis, Latin American leaders met in a summit in the Dominican Republic in an effort to resolve the dispute before it could escalate further. It was not until July that tensions eased when Uribe and Chávez met in Paraguaná, Venezuela. Both parties were driven by practical economic considerations as well as the need for a resolution of the conflict. Colombian-Venezuelan bilateral trade was valued at some $6 billion per annum, with Venezuela relying on significant imports of foodstuffs, natural gas, and manufactured goods from Colombia, where those enterprises were a significant source of employment.[35]

The crisis with Venezuela and Ecuador did not divert Uribe from his efforts to defeat FARC and to press ahead with the demobilization of the paramilitaries. In response to persistent criticism by Colombian as well as international groups for an overly lenient approach to the demobilization, in May 2008 his government extradited to the United States fourteen already imprisoned paramilitary leaders, including the major figure of Salvatore Mancuso. The move was in part an effort to defuse allegations of paramilitary ties to senior members of his government, Congress, and his own family. Although the extradition was also an effort to ensure that the paramilitaries would receive punitive judicial treatment in the United States on drug-trafficking charges, the action left the administration open to the criticism that the paramilitary leaders would neither be punished for their human rights violations, nor their victims and victims' families compensated.[36]

The Venezuelan crisis also raised the issue of Colombia's capacity to pursue a multilateral foreign policy in the Andean region. When he met with the Council on Foreign Relations in New York in September 2008, President Uribe was asked: "What is the room for multilateral action in the context of the challenges in the region—the recent violence in Bolivia, the tensions that arose between Colombia, Ecuador and Venezuela in the context of the Reyes situation?" In response, Uribe indicated that he preferred not to speak about the nation's neighbors, but rather the challenges Colombia faced from the guerrillas, drugs traffickers, and paramilitaries. At the same time he stressed that it was important in the region to support other democratic governments, as for instance that of Evo Morales, who had recently been confronted by violent opposition. He studiously avoided any reference to Hugo Chávez and Venezuela. Reflecting his objective of balancing Colombian foreign relations in the region, Uribe also pursued a major initiative to strengthen relations with Brazil in an effort not only to enhance economic relations, but also in recognition of Brazil's armament industry's importance to Colombian security.

The two terms of the Uribe presidency are drawing to a close as the final draft of this chapter is written, and it is likely that there is too little distance from those years to draw any final conclusions about the successes and failures of his foreign policies. At the same time, it can be said that his government pursued in an almost single-minded manner its intention to contain and destroy guerrilla insurgencies within the country and to demobilize and reinsert armed combatants into the mainstream of society. Those policies contributed to serious diplomatic and economic tensions with Ecuador and Venezuela but solid relations with Brazil, Panama, and the United States during the presidency of George W. Bush. With the election of Barack Obama and the dominance of the

Democratic Party in the U.S. Congress, however, the aggressive policies pursued by Uribe, which have brought so much domestic success, have led to negative reactions in the United States and Canada to what is perceived to be a weak human rights record, to the extent that neither of the North American nations have ratified already negotiated free-trade agreements with Colombia. Historians should refrain from attempting to predict what the future will bring, but in the case of Colombia it is reasonably safe to suggest that continuity in the direction, values, conduct, and control of foreign policy is far more likely than discontinuity.

CONCLUSION

In the post–Cold War years it is evident that Colombian foreign policy has been fundamentally pragmatic in its orientation, even during the administration of Álvaro Uribe Vélez, who has been viewed as the most ideologically oriented of the past three presidents. It could be argued that the continued effort to defeat the guerrilla insurgency is a remnant of the Cold War, which would also help explain the fact that only the Uribe government in Latin America supported the Bush administration's war in Iraq. Yet, even support for the Iraq war should be viewed as based on pragmatic rather than ideological factors, and there are contradictions to this, such as the Colombian vote in the UN General Assembly in 2007 to recognize the right of the Palestinian people to self-determination, a vote that was opposed by the United States and Israel.[37]

Colombian foreign policy has sought to adhere consistently to international law and multilateralism, in spite of the dominant influence of the United States. To a significant degree, practical domestic political considerations have driven foreign policy, in particular, because the two dominant domestic issues, drugs trafficking and the guerrilla insurgency, have had international implications. Although a link between the narcotics cartels and the guerrillas, particularly FARC, had long been identified by both Colombian and U.S. officials, it was not until the Bush administration and the post-9/11 environment that Colombia was caught up in the War on Terror, and this response was based on pragmatic rather than ideological considerations.

Colombian policymakers have also sought to respond positively to the international community's more general concerns with human rights. In addressing these issues, Colombian officials consistently sought, with varying degrees of success, to adhere to their basic foreign-policy principles of respect for international law and the international system, as well as balance the response to U.S. goals and demands with the need to address domestic challenges.

As the orientation of Colombian foreign policy has since World War I been premised on the assumption that it is in the national interest to maintain a positive relationship with the United States, it is difficult to escape the conclusion that the pragmatism that has characterized Colombian policy is a permanent feature. Such pragmatism has at times, of course, been tempered by ideology, as for instance in Colombia's definitive adherence to the West during the Cold War and its anti-Communist domestic policies. It would be mistaken, however, to confuse pragmatism in the Colombian case with any tendency to be inconsistent in foreign policy. On the contrary, Colombian policy has been remarkably consistent.

NOTES

*The author would like to express his appreciation to a number of individuals who kindly gave their time to discuss Colombian foreign policy: former president Cesar Gaviria; foreign minister Jaime Bermudez, vice-minister of foreign relations Clemencia Forero, former vice-minister Camilo Reyes, former foreign minister Guillermo Fernandez de Soto, Senator Rodrigo Rivera, and Rodrigo Botero, former finance minister. Above all, the author is grateful to his long-time friend and colleague Alfonso López Caballero for his generous assistance and insights. Juliana Ramírez, a former graduate student in Political Science at the University of Calgary and a graduate of Universidad Externado de Colombia, provided excellent assistance with the initial literature review for this chapter.

1. For two insightful synthetic assessments of Colombian foreign policy and scholarship in the field see: Arlene Tickner, "Colombia: U.S. subordinate, Autonomous Actor, or Something in Between," in Frank Mora and Jeanne Hey, eds., *Latin American and Caribbean Foreign Policy* (Boulder: Rowman and Littlefield, 2003), 165–84; Roberto Gonzalez Arana, "La Política Exterior de Colombia a finales del Siglo XX," *Investigacion y Desarrollo* 12, no. 2 (2004), 258–85.

2. For discussion on the regional implications of the Colombian security challenges, see the following: María Clara Izaza, "Colombia y sus vecinos," pp. 63–68, and Fernando Ribadeneira, "Relaciones Colombo-Ecuatorianas," pp. 69–76, in Martha Ardila, compilador, *Colombia y la seguridad hemisférica* (Bogotá: Universidad Externado de Colombia, 2001). Luz del Socorro Ramírez, "Colombia y sus vecinos," *Nueva Sociedad,* no. 192 (July–August, 2004), 144–56; Socorro Ramírez, "Colombia-Brasil: Distante Vecindad se Fortalece en la Seguridad y el Comercio," *Análisis Político.* No. 58 (September–December, 2006), 3–34; Socorro Ramírez, "El gobierno de Uribe y los paises vecinos," *Análisis Político,* no. 57 (May–August, 2006), 65–84; Richard Millet, "Colombia's conflicts: the Spill-Over Effects of a Wider War," in *The North-South Agenda,* no. 57 (2002).

3. For discussion of Colombian dependency, see: Gerhard Drekonja, *Retos de la política exterior colombiana* (Bogotá: CEREC-CERI, 1983); Drekonja, "Autonomía periférica redefinida: América Latina en la década de los noventa," in María Mercedes Gómez, Gerhard Drekonja, Juan Gabriel Toklatian, Leonardo Carvajal H. "Redefiniendo la autonomía en política internacional," *Documentos Ocasionales* (CEI), 31 (July–September, 1993); Fernando Enrique Cardoso y Enzo Faletto, *Dependencia y desarrollo en América Latina. Ensayo de interpretación sociológica* (Mexico D.F.: Siglo XXI, 1969); Helio Jaguaribe, "Autonomía periférica y hegemonía centrica," *Estudios Internacionales*, 46 (April–June, 1979), 91–130; Tickner, "Colombia: U.S. subordinate." Not all are agreed that dependency is a negative. See, for instance, the analysis by Carlos Escudé, *El realismo de los Estados débiles* (Buenos Aires: GEL, 1995) as referenced by Tickner, "Intervención por invitación: Claves de la política exterior colombiana y sus debilidades principales," *Colombia Internacional*, no. 65 (January–June, 2007), 90–111.

4. http://www.census.gov/foreign-trade/balance/c3010.html#2007. Accessed December 18, 2008. Note that Colombia has been a member of the World Trade Organization since 1995.

5. http://www.mincomercio.gov.co/eContent/NewsDetail.asp?ID=764& IDCompany=1. Colombian export data in this data set includes only the period January to August, 2007.

6. Socorro Ramírez, and Luís Alberto Restrepo (compiladores), *Colombia: entre la reinserción y el aislamiento* (Bogotá: Siglo del Hombres Editores, 1997), p. 68.

7. See Tickner, "Colombia: U.S. subordinate." On Silva, see http://juanvaldez.com/menu/news/Releases/Colombian_Coffee_Growers_Election.pdf.

8. Arana, "La Política Exterior de Colombia," p. 275. On López Michelsen as both foreign minister and president, see Stephen J. Randall, *Alfonso López Michelsen, su vida su época* (Bogotá: Villegas Editores, 2007). Colombian relations with Cuba quickly became strained, however, when Cuba supported a failed M-19 initiative to establish a rural insurgency. The Liberal government of Julio César Turbay Ayala broke relations in 1981.

9. Author interview with former President Gaviria, Bogotá, February 16, 2009.

10. Arana, "La Política Exterior de Colombia," p. 277.

11. Colombia, Ministerio de Relaciones Exteriores (Ministra Noemí Sanín), *Actuar en el mundo: la política exterior de Colombia frente al siglo XXI* (Bogotá: MRE, 1993). Alberto Lleras Camargo was the first secretary-general of the OAS. Gaviria served two terms as secretary-general, 1994–1999 and 1999–2004. See also Randall, *Alfonso López Michelsen, su vida su época*.

12. See *Washington Post*, March 21, 1996.

13. See Arana, "Política Exterior," p. 266n.2, 274–75. On the nonaligned movement, see República de Colombia, Ministerio de Relaciones

Exteriores, *La política exterior de Colombia y el movimiento de Países No Alineados* (Bogotá: Tercer Mundo, 1995); Ramirez y Restrepo (compiladores), *Colombia: entre la reinserción y el aislamiento* (1997). For early analyses of the Colombian relationship with nonhemispheric regions, see José Luis Ramírez, *Las Relaciones Internacionales de Colombia con el Medio Oriente: Evolución, Desarrollo y Perspectivas* (Universidad de Los Andes: CEI, Nov-dic. De 1988); Dora Rothlisberger, *Las Relaciones Internacionales de Colombia con los Principales Países Asiáticos de la Cuenca del Pacífico* (Universidad de Los Andes: CEI, Enero-Febrero de 1989). On Colombian security issues and the European relationship, see Diego Cardona C., Bernard Labatut, Stephanie Lavaux, and Rubén Sánchez, eds., *Encrucijadas de la seguridad en Europe y las Américas* (Bogotá: Universidad del Rosario, 2004).

14. Rodrigo Pardo, "Algunos aspectos de la política exterior colombiana en la administración Samper," *Colombia Internacional,* no. 27 (September, 1994), 3–8.

15. Interview with Maria Emma Mejia, *Army Times, Defense News,* April 27–May 3, 1998, http://www.colombiasupport.net/199804/0427AT. html. Accessed November 17, 2008. The author also met with Mejia as foreign minister in 1997 when she expressed similar views on relations with the United States.

16. Robert Gelbard, "Certification for Drug Producing Countries," March 7, 1997, testimony before the House of Representatives, International Relations Committee, Sub-Committee on the Western Hemisphere.

17. On Zuñiga's resignation, see *New York Times* March 12, 1996. On the policy implications of U.S. certification, see Juan Gabriel Tokatlian, "Condicionalidad y Certificación: El caso de Colombia," Nueva Sociedad, no. 148 (March–April, 1997), 98–107.

18. See Guillermo Fernández de Soto, *La Nueva Integración Andina* (Comunidad Andina, 2003).

19. Author interview with Fernández de Soto, February 17, 2009.

20. Russell Crandall notes the irony of the fact that although Plan Colombia was a Clinton initiative, the actual military aid in the form of two counternarcotics brigades and helicopters was delivered by the Bush administration. See *Driven By Drugs: U.S. Policy Toward Colombia* (Boulder: Lynne Rienner, 2002), p. 165. The data on Plan Colombia is from the foreign minister Carolina Barco's address to the Council on Foreign Relations, September 29, 2003, http://www.cfr.org/publication/6326/address_by_ the_honorable_carolina_ barco. Accessed December 16, 2008.

21. After his presidency Pastrana wrote about the collapse of the negotiations with FARC. See Andres Pastrana Arango, *La Palabra bajo fuego* (Bogotá: Planeta, 2005).

22. Pastrana address, April 12, 2000, http://www.asne.org/kiosk/archive/ convention/2000/pastrana.htm. Accessed November 28, 2008. On Pastrana, see Diana Marcela Rojas, "La política exterior del gobierno Pastrana en tres actos," *Análisis Político,* no. 46 (May–August, 2002), and

Rojas, "Balance de la política internacional del gobierno Uribe," *Análisis Político*, no. 57 (May–August, 2006), 85–105.

23. Diana Marcela Rojas, "Balance de la política internacional del gobierno Uribe," *Análisis Político*, no. 57 (May–August, 2006), 89.

24. Leonardo Carvajal y Rodrigo Pardo, "La internationalización del conflicto doméstico y los procesos de paz," in Martha Ardila y Diego Cardona, eds. *Prioridades y desafíos de la política exterior colombiana* (Bogotá: Editorial Planeta, 2001).

25. Arlene Tickner has argued effectively that even during those administrations that had sought to expand Colombian foreign relations internationally, relations with the United States remained paramount. See, for instance, Tickner, "Intervención por invitación: Claves de la política exterior colombiana y sus debilidades principales," *Colombia Internacional*, revista no. 65 (January–June, 2007), 90–111.

26. This increase was approved by the U.S. Congress. U.S. forces participated primarily in Plan Patriota, which was a major offensive in the Putumayo region against FARC strongholds.

27. http://www.cfr.org/publication/17336/meeting_with_president_alvaro_ uribe_velez_of_colombia.html. Accessed December 17, 2008.

28. Canada on the other hand concluded a Free Trade Agreement with Colombia in 2008, an agreement that was actively pursued by the Uribe administration to offset the opposition from the U.S. Democratic Party. Author discussions with Rodrigo Botero, former Colombian Finance Minister, 2007–2008.

29. See, for instance, Rojas, *Análisis Político*, no. 57 (May–August, 2006), 92.

30. Maria Consuelo Araujo served only briefly in 2006–2007, and was succeeded by Fernando Araujo, who in turn was succeeded in 2008 by Jaime Bermúdez, a former Colombian ambassador to Argentina.

31. Pastrana resigned in 2006 in protest against President Uribe's offer of the Spanish ambassadorship to Ernesto Samper.

32. Interview with Pastrana, *El Tiempo*, November 10, 2008

33. *New York Times*, March 12, 2007. On the Bush visit to Bogotá, see *El Tiempo*, 3 de febrero de 2007; *El Tiempo* editorialized on the Bush visit: "Seis años después de que Bush prometió que América Latina sería clave en su política exterior, el mandatario estadounidense emprende una gira continental que muchos han calificado no solo de tardía sino de irrelevante." March 11, 2007.

34. *New York Times*, March 6, 2008

35. *New York Times*, July 12, 2008.

36. Between 2002 and 2008 Uribe's government extradited approximately seven hundred Colombians to the United States. *New York Times*, May 14, 2008.

37. http://domino.un.org. Accessed February 17, 2009.

CHAPTER 9

VENEZUELAN FOREIGN POLICY UNDER CHÁVEZ, 1999–2010: THE PRAGMATIC SUCCESS OF REVOLUTIONARY IDEOLOGY?

DIANA RABY

INTRODUCTION

No country in Latin America (and arguably in the world) has adopted a more proactive, innovative, and controversial foreign policy than Venezuela in the last 12 years. The process proclaimed by Hugo Chávez as the "Bolivarian Revolution" has brought far-reaching change to Venezuela itself, and has placed that country at the center of international controversies and tensions that resonate far beyond the Latin American and Caribbean region.

The prevailing view in Western diplomatic circles and in the media is that Chávez has polarized both Venezuela's domestic politics and her international relations, using inflammatory rhetoric and ill-conceived "populist" projects to inflate his personal popularity at the expense of the country's long-term economic interests and democratic stability.[1] But with the passage of time it has become apparent that the Bolivarian Republic is at least as stable and prosperous as its neighbors, and that

Venezuelan foreign policy has achieved results that would have seemed inconceivable ten years ago.

Venezuela's proclaimed goals have become more radical with time, with the domestic agenda changing from "participatory and protagonistic democracy" to "21st Century Socialism," and the international vision expanding from multipolarity and regional integration to the promotion of a new anticapitalist regional project (ALBA—Alianza Bolivariana para los Pueblos de Nuestra América) and a new international economic order. What is quite remarkable is that these goals have begun to assume concrete form and have transformed the political map of the entire region.

In terms of the ideology-versus-pragmatism template, Bolivarian Venezuela appears to represent a clear case of the primacy of ideology. However, it would be misleading to assume that this implies a complete absence of pragmatic adaptability. The considerable degree of success in translating revolutionary ideology into practice has only been made possible by highly inventive, pragmatic, and strategic flexibility combined with the determined pursuit of long-term goals. The radical and far-reaching character of Chávez's foreign-policy agenda would test Venezuela's capacities to the limit. At best a medium-sized country, its one great asset on the international stage is, of course, oil; its position as a leading petroleum exporter gives it the means in pragmatic terms to play a role out of proportion to its size.

Regarding the process of formation and implementation of foreign policy, fundamental decision-making was clearly concentrated from the beginning in the hands of President Chávez himself and a small leadership group in the government and the Bolivarian Movement. Their ideological position implied a radical break with previous policies and probable tensions with international partners such as the United States. In this sense, determined agency, in the form of the president and his immediate circle, was crucial. This policy reorientation also encountered resistance from the existing Venezuelan diplomatic corps, a factor that would cause significant problems of implementation for several years.

Finally, the international context was problematic. The collapse of the Soviet bloc had resulted in the apparently complete triumph, by the mid-1990s, of neoliberal economic policies and electoral democracy, combined in George Bush senior's "New World Order." This clearly made any serious challenge to U.S. hegemony that much more difficult.

INITIAL STEPS ON THE ROAD TO CHANGE

At the time of Chávez's inauguration on February 2, 1999, the price of oil was at a record low of US$9 a barrel and socialist Cuba was widely regarded as a kind of dinosaur that was doomed to collapse before the inexorable advance of the free market and Western-style polyarchy. Francis Fukuyama had proclaimed "The End of History" and Jorge Castañeda had consigned the entire Latin American left to Clio's dustbin unless it meekly accepted Blairite social democracy as its maximum program.[2]

Not surprisingly, under the circumstances, Chávez was cautious in his early declarations, even suggesting an admiration for Tony Blair's "Third Way." But at the same time, he took decisive actions that laid the groundwork for future advances, appointing Alí Rodríguez Araque as minister of energy and mines and dispatching him to tour all the major oil-producing countries in order to begin the revival of OPEC (the Organization of Petroleum Exporting Countries). Within a few months, the OPEC countries plus Mexico and Russia had agreed to limit production, and by March 2000 the oil price had more than tripled.[3] It was this, well before the further explosion of oil prices sparked by the Afghanistan and Iraq wars, that laid the financial foundations for Venezuela's subsequent social, economic, and diplomatic programs.

Second, Chávez took discrete but crucial measures to reassert Venezuelan political and military sovereignty. Beginning in late 1999, he refused permission for over-flights by U.S. aircraft engaged in anti narcotics surveillance.[4] Following the catastrophic landslides of December 1999 in Vargas state, Venezuela rejected U.S. offers of assistance, which entailed naval ships and helicopters.[5] Widely seen as an oversensitive nationalist gesture, this nevertheless helped to establish the principle that foreign military intervention of any kind would not be accepted. Then in September 2001, Venezuela announced its intention to cancel the IMET military cooperation agreement (although the actual cancellation did not occur until early 2004).[6]

Also, in the late 1990s a U.S. company with CIA and military connections, SAIC (Science Applications International Corporation), had acquired control of the software governing operations by PDVSA, the national oil company (this would cause major problems during the opposition strike/lockout of 2002–2003). Potentially even more seriously, in 1998 SAIC was negotiating a similar contract to run all the electronic systems for the Venezuelan Ministry of Defense. If this had been implemented, the outcome of the April 2002 coup attempt would almost certainly have been different, but Chávez canceled the deal soon after taking office.[7] Such measures, combined with the ideological transformation of the armed forces through their incorporation in social programs, such as Plan Bolívar 2000 and the Bolivarian Schools, ensured that Chávez had the necessary margin of maneuver when it came to later confrontations with the United States (although the coup showed that it was a very close-run thing).

A third area in which Chávez took important steps early in his presidency was in diversifying Venezuela's international relations as part of the quest for multipolarity. Already before his inauguration he had visited several Latin American countries including Cuba, as well as the United States and Western Europe. In October 1999 he visited China, Japan, South Korea, and other Asian nations, signing several bilateral trade agreements; in China he declared that just as the People's Republic had "stood up," so Venezuela was beginning to "stand up" for its rights, arguing that "this world cannot be run by a universal police force that seeks to control everything."[8]

Similarly, Alí Rodríguez's tour of oil-producing countries was followed up by further overtures to the Arab world and Iran, culminating in the Second OPEC Summit held in Caracas in late September 2000.[9] Iran, in particular, would become a strategic partner, with important economic agreements including Venezuelan acquisition of industrial technology from the Islamic Republic. Another key partner would be Russia, not so much as oil producer but for arms and military technology.[10]

The fourth area in which Chávez took swift action to lay the foundations for much more ambitious later moves was in relations with Latin America. The crucial relationship with Cuba, as representing "the dignity of Latin America," began to take concrete form in November 1999 when Chávez stayed in Havana for several days after the Ibero-American Summit that took place there. The two countries signed the first of several bilateral agreements based on the exchange of Venezuelan oil on favorable terms for Cuban educational, health, and sports services.[11] But Venezuela was also active in forging links with other Latin neighbors such as Brazil and Argentina with a view to promoting regional integration and independence from Washington. Thus the initiative of the Brazilian president Fernando Henrique Cardoso in convening the First Summit Meeting of South American Presidents in Brasilia in 2000 was vigorously supported by Venezuela,[12] and this prepared the ground for the crucial stand taken by the two countries at the III Summit of the Americas in Quebec City in May 2001. This was where the U.S. agenda of the FTAA (Free Trade Area of the Americas) was formally launched, and the only countries to voice public reservations at this early stage were Venezuela and Brazil.[13]

These early initiatives were all part of a broad vision consisting of five components: (1) national sovereignty; (2) Latin American integration; (3) multipolarity (and rejection of U.S. hegemony); (4) construction of an alternative social and economic order (ALBA, XXI Century Socialism); and (5) a new concept of hemispheric security.[14] For our purposes, however, Venezuelan policy can be discussed under four headings: (1) national sovereignty and relations with the United States;

(2) relations with Colombia, a key U.S. ally; (3) Latin American integration and the promotion of an alternative social and economic order; and (4) the promotion of multipolarity.

NATIONAL SOVEREIGNTY AND RELATIONS
WITH THE UNITED STATES

Relations with the United States were difficult from the start. Washington refused Chávez a visa in 1998 when he was still a candidate, ostensibly because of his armed revolt in 1992, and the then U.S. ambassador John Maisto is alleged to have said "I don't know anyone in Venezuela who thinks that Chávez is a democrat."[15] But following his electoral victory the visa was granted, and in January 1999 as president-elect he did visit Washington. Nevertheless his reception by President Clinton was distinctly cool, among other things because Chávez had just visited Cuba, in itself a clear assertion of independence.[16]

With the Clinton administration, relations remained cool but correct, and open friction was kept to a minimum. But with the inauguration of George W. Bush in January 2001, relations rapidly deteriorated. Following the open but civil expression of differences at the Quebec Summit of the Americas in May, there followed Venezuela's announcement in September of its intention to cancel the IMET agreement, and then in October Chávez's public criticism of U.S. actions in Afghanistan, arguing that "terror cannot be fought with more terror."[17] The U.S. responded by recalling Ambassador Donna Hrinak for consultations.

The following months were dominated by internal tensions leading up to the anti-Chávez coup of April 11–14, 2002, with increasingly overt U.S. support for the opposition. The appointment on February 25, 2002, of Charles Shapiro as ambassador was symptomatic of Washington's growing hostility, given his long interventionist record.[18] U.S. approval of the coup (if not actual responsibility for it) is a matter of public record,[19] and in a sense this phase must be seen as the nadir of *chavista* foreign as well as domestic policy, when it came within a hair's breadth of total failure. It is possible to argue that, given the intrinsic hostility of the Bush administration, Chávez had little alternative if he were not to abandon his entire project; but the drama of those critical April days clearly transcends any normal policy analysis.

However, the defeat of the coup and of the opposition strike/lockout eight to ten months later transformed the situation both internally and externally. In the two years beginning in January 2003, the Bolivarian Revolution was consolidated, meaning that it became a reality that could no longer be ignored. With the effective renationalization of PDVSA, the imposition of exchange controls and the launching of the social "missions," national sovereignty was consolidated and the foundations were laid for open adoption of a much more ambitious agenda, "XXI Century Socialism," first proclaimed in December 2004 at a solidarity meeting in Caracas.[20] It is no accident that the ALBA, hitherto easily dismissed as mere *chavista* rhetoric, also took concrete form with an agreement signed in that same month by Cuba and Venezuela.

During 2003–2004 there were signs that Venezuela was trying to improve relations with Washington, hoping no doubt that the United States had also learned from the failure of the coup. But overt U.S. support for opposition parties and NGOs such as *Súmate* and for renewed violent destabilization tactics in the months preceding the August 2004 recall referendum appear to have convinced Chávez that there was little hope of improved relations.[21] It was this that led to some of the Venezuelan leader's most colorful and untempered rhetoric, describing Bush as *burro* (a donkey, i.e., stupid), *pendejo* (a fool) and "the most dangerous man on the planet," as well as the notorious reference to the sulfurous fumes left by this devilish character at the United Nations podium.[22]

Continued tense relations, and the suspicion in Venezuela that Washington was planning more serious destabilization moves or even invasion, led to statements by Chávez (for example early in 2005) to the effect that any aggression would lead to an immediate suspension of oil shipments.[23] But such threats were usually followed by a reduction of tension and indications of the desire to maintain good commercial relations, including oil supplies. Pragmatism, then, continues to prevail; some 60 percent of Venezuelan oil exports continue to be destined to the U.S. market (about 1.5 million barrels a day),[24] and U.S. corporations continue (or continued until the onset of the global recession) to invest in Venezuela.

A particularly significant development in terms of commercial relations was the Exxon/PDVSA case. Chávez's decision in 2007 to impose full national control on the remaining concessions in the Orinoco oil belt was accepted by most multinationals but not by Exxon, which took PDVSA to court in London and sued for US$12 billion. The case had major implications for Venezuela and potentially for other Third World countries, and the British High Court decision in Venezuela's favor in February 2008 was rightly celebrated as a landmark victory.[25]

The growth of ALBA and related counterhegemonic initiatives has led to further serious diplomatic issues between Caracas and Washington. In September 2008 the separatist destabilization attempts by right-wing leaders of the *Media Luna* departments in Bolivia led the government of Evo Morales to expel the U.S. ambassador, adducing evidence of

Washington's involvement. Venezuela then followed suit, both in solidarity and claiming evidence of similar U.S. support for Zulia separatism and a possible assassination plot.[26]

Relations had scarcely been restored with a renewed exchange of ambassadors in June 2009 when another ALBA-related incident, the coup against President Manuel Zelaya in Honduras, led to further tensions. In this case open rupture was avoided, in part because of the more conciliatory approach of the new Obama administration in Washington, but the incident only confirmed the underlying divergence of interests between Venezuela and the United States.[27]

The Honduran episode initially seemed to confirm some possibility of improved U.S.-Venezuelan relations insofar as Washington went along with all the other hemispheric nations in condemning the coup. The significance of this in terms of Obama's new approach should not be underestimated, and it should also be seen as a further diplomatic success of Venezuela and the ALBA countries. But subsequent differences over what practical action to take in relation to Honduras revealed tensions once again, and when Washington changed its position to de facto acceptance of the coup regime and its new president Porfirio Lobo, the Honduran issue became the focal point of a diplomatic polarization affecting the entire Latin American and Caribbean region.

It soon became clear that the Honduran coup was only the most dramatic manifestation of a general reassertion of U.S. regional hegemony, displayed also in the reestablishment of the Fourth Fleet to patrol the southern seas, the establishment of new U.S. military bases in Colombia and Panama, and the creation of an atmosphere favorable to right-wing electoral successes in both those countries and in Chile.

These developments undoubtedly constitute a setback for Venezuelan diplomacy, although the ALBA alliance has survived (minus Honduras), and other major regional actors, such as Brazil and Argentina, have continued to take an independent stance that accords in most respects with that of Venezuela. In the longer run a shared pragmatic interest in conflict avoidance and mutually beneficial trade may make it possible for the United States and the Bolivarian Republic to find a modus vivendi, but fundamental ideological differences have also created divergent de facto interests (in terms of trade, investment, and geopolitical alliances) that cannot be ignored.

RELATIONS WITH COLOMBIA

As immediate neighbors with close cultural and historical ties and a thriving cross-border trade, Colombia and Venezuela have little option but to coexist. Both are acutely aware that conflict would be disastrous, and despite the dramatic divergence of their political trajectories (a divergence that became more acute under Presidents Uribe and Chávez, but that dates back at least 50 years), they have thus far succeeded in avoiding the worst. The roller-coaster pattern of Colombo-Venezuelan relations reveals the tension between ideology and pragmatism at its most acute.

In some ways, tensions between the two countries can be traced back to philosophical and material differences between the liberator Simón Bolívar and the more conservative Francisco de Paula Santander, *el hombre de las leyes* (the Man of the Laws), seen by the establishment as the real founding figure of independent Colombia. But in recent times, the tensions have resulted above all from the chronic Colombian internal conflict and the country's role as a key U.S. ally in Latin America.

The low-intensity war between the Colombian state and left-wing insurgents (the FARC, ELN, and others) has often threatened to spill over into Venezuela and other neighboring countries, and Colombian accusations of Venezuelan complicity with the rebels did not begin with the rise of Chávez. With over 2,000 km of shared border, often traversing difficult mountain, swamp, and jungle terrain, it is scarcely surprising that different participants in the conflict should at times enter Venezuelan territory. Indeed, Venezuela often has reason to complain of violations of its sovereignty.

The Colombian government and the Colombian establishment media have repeatedly alleged that Venezuela provides sanctuary for the FARC and ELN, and that Chávez provides financial and military support for the insurgents as part of a strategy for internationalizing the Bolivarian Revolution. In reply Venezuela has always insisted that it wants good relations with Colombia and has no interest in that country's internal conflict other than to facilitate a peaceful solution, should that be possible.

One of the most serious incidents in this respect arose in December 2004 and caused open tension for several months. "Rodrigo Granda," described as the foreign secretary of the FARC, was kidnapped on the streets of Caracas by Colombian agents and smuggled across the border into Colombia where he was officially arrested. The Colombian government accused Venezuela of supporting terrorism, to which Venezuela replied that it had no official responsibility for Granda's presence in the country, which in any case was perfectly legal since he (along with some four million Colombians resident in Venezuela) had dual citizenship. Chávez also demanded that Colombia issue an official apology for having violated Venezuelan sovereignty. Tension continued to escalate, and Venezuela closed the border, a measure that caused serious problems for Colombia since it exports large quantities of industrial and agricultural products to Venezuela (and Venezuelan exports to Colombia consist largely of petroleum that can easily be diverted elsewhere). Faced with growing protests from his own commercial supporters, Uribe had little choice but to back down and concede to Venezuelan demands.[28]

Another serious incident arose early in 2008 when the Colombian military launched an armed raid on a FARC camp across the Ecuadorian border. Ecuador protested vigorously at the violation of its sovereignty, Caracas immediately backed Quito, and both countries announced troop mobilizations to their respective borders with Colombia. Contrary to Colombian expectations, both the Rio Group of South American countries and the Organization of American States rejected Bogotá's arguments in what was another diplomatic victory for both Ecuador and Venezuela.[29]

Other illegal armed actors in the Colombian conflict also have a problematic presence in neighboring countries, in particular, the right-wing paramilitary. In May 2004 Venezuela announced the detention on a farm near Caracas of some 80 heavily-armed Colombian paramilitaries, allegedly linked with extremist sectors of the Venezuelan opposition in a conspiracy to assassinate President Chávez.[30] More recently there have been numerous reports of intimidation, violence, and mafia-type activities by Colombian *Águilas Negras* (Black Eagles) in the Venezuelan border states of Táchira, Mérida, and Zulia.[31]

Despite such ongoing sources of friction, the two countries until recently went out of their way to maintain vigorous commercial relationships and to seek to reduce tensions. Venezuela has been promoting a project for a pipeline through Colombia and Panama for oil exports to the Pacific Rim.[32] As recently as June 2009, the new Venezuelan ambassador in Bogotá proposed a formal security agreement between Colombia, Venezuela, and Ecuador.[33] But relations took a serious turn for the worse with the Colombian decision in July 2009 to concede several new military facilities to the United States, a decision that led Chávez to instruct his foreign minister to "undertake a thorough revision" of Venezuelan-Colombian relations, reducing diplomatic relations to the lowest level possible without complete rupture and once again restricting cross-border trade.[34] At the time of this writing, relations remain very tense, with little apparent prospect of improvement.

LATIN AMERICAN INTEGRATION AND THE PROMOTION OF AN ALTERNATIVE ECONOMIC AND SOCIAL ORDER

The Bolivarian ideal of Latin American unity, to which most countries in the region subscribe in theory, has been a keystone of Venezuelan policy since Chávez's inauguration. From early in his presidency, and in practice since late 2004, Chávez has also been active in promoting an alternative regional development model, expressed most clearly in the ALBA.

This ambitious ideological agenda is very clearly presented in a recent document published by an official think tank:

> The proposal formulated by our country consists of the following aspects: a Strategic Plan for the Union of Peoples and Republics; the clarification of why we consider that existing schemes of regional integration are defunct, and the preparation of a plan for food supplies, health and economic development; encouragement of direct negotiation between states, the creation of an autonomous power bloc in South America or Latin America and the Caribbean; the construction of a Pact between Republics, the coordination of the Armed Forces of the different countries, and finally, the preparation of a Founding Charter for the Union of the South.[35]

Such an agenda seems anything but pragmatic, and it is instructive to note how it has been applied in practice. Once again, we can observe here a considerable degree of pragmatic flexibility combined with single-minded adherence to long-term ideological or programmatic goals.

From the outset, the Chávez government participated in existing regional forums such as the Andean Community (CAN, Comunidad Andina de Naciones), but this soon proved problematic because key members, such as Colombia and Peru, were committed to a neoliberal agenda, including free-trade agreements with the United States; when it proved impossible to change this, Venezuela withdrew from CAN.[36] Venezuela also expressed interest in joining Mercosur, and by 2006 Venezuelan membership was approved in principle, but ratification of the agreement has been held up by opposition in the Paraguayan Senate. However, Mercosur is also based on conventional capitalist principles of free trade among its members, with little attention to social issues; hence Venezuela has placed much greater emphasis on its own alternative project, the ALBA.[37]

If economic integration with the major South American countries has proved difficult, political and diplomatic unity has been much more successful. This is largely because Venezuela's Bolivarian agenda converged to a considerable extent with Brazilian priorities. In 2000 the Brazilian president Fernando Henrique Cardoso convened the First Summit of South American Presidents in Brasilia, and further such summits followed in Guayaquil (2002), Cuzco (2004), and so on. In Cuzco, leaders declared the aim of creating a South American Community of Nations, which would officially become UNASUR, the South American Union, in April 2007.[38]

A closely related project, also launched by Venezuela and Brazil, is the South American Defense Council, which creates a common forum for the armed forces of all member countries. While its operational capacity is so far nonexistent and its diplomatic role quite limited (given, for example, the different perspectives of Colombia and other members), it is hugely symbolic, above all because it explicitly excludes the United States.[39]

If UNASUR and the Defense Council, at least as they exist at present, might be described from a Venezuelan point of view as corresponding to a minimal concept of integration, ALBA represents the maximum concept. Based on principles of equitable exchange (as against free trade), mutual benefit (as against competition), cooperation, social justice, national sovereignty, and sustainable development, ALBA is a direct rejection of neoliberalism and is tendentiously anticapitalist.

On December 14, 2004, in Havana Venezuela and Cuba signed a formal pact as founding members of ALBA. This confirmed and extended existing arrangements for the exchange of Venezuelan oil (on favorable terms) for Cuban medical, educational, and sporting services, but also initiated much broader collaboration between the two countries in agriculture, manufacturing, and technology.[40] Then in the first few months of 2005, Venezuela signed bilateral agreements with Brazil, Argentina, and Uruguay for mutually beneficial exchanges based on noncommercial or barter principles, including shipbuilding and cattle (Argentina), cement and oil (Uruguay), and an agreement between PDVSA and Petrobras, the Venezuelan and Brazilian national oil companies, respectively.[41]

Following Evo Morales's electoral victory in December 2005, Bolivia officially joined ALBA in April 2006 and added a new institutional agreement, the TCP or *Tratado de Comercio de los Pueblos* (Peoples' Trade Agreement), which reinforces the ALBA principles of social inclusion, food security, technology transfer, and ecological sustainability.[42] With the return of the Sandinista leader Daniel Ortega to the presidency of Nicaragua in late 2006, that country also joined ALBA in January 2007. In 2008–2009 the consolidation of ALBA as a pole of attraction, at least for the smaller countries in the region, seemed to be confirmed with the adhesion of the Anglophone Caribbean island of Dominica, followed by Honduras, St Vincent and the Grenadines, Ecuador, and St Kitts & Nevis, giving a total of nine member states.

ALBA is not limited to formal membership, but includes other agreements sponsored by Venezuela. This applies to the aforementioned bilateral agreements with Argentina, Uruguay, and Brazil (and further similar agreements with these and other countries), but also to the very important parallel initiative of Petrocaribe. Created on June 29, 2005 by

Venezuela and 13 other countries (mainly from the CARICOM group of Anglophone Caribbean states), by 2009 it had grown to 18 members including Haiti, the Dominican Republic, Honduras, Costa Rica, and Guatemala, with Venezuela providing over 200,000 barrels a day of petroleum and derivatives on favorable terms.[43] Petrocaribe clearly provides substantial economic benefits to its smaller members, valued at approximately US$4 billion by the Venezuelan minister of energy and petroleum, Rafael Ramírez.[44]

Critics argue that these are simply Venezuelan handouts and are unsustainable, especially with lower oil prices.[45] They also claim that other than subsidized oil, ALBA trade is insignificant and that Venezuelan trade continues to be overwhelmingly with non-ALBA nations such as the United States, Colombia, and China. But this fails to take into account the fact that much inter-ALBA trade may not be registered in normal commercial statistics because it occurs through partnership and cooperation agreements under which goods and services are not necessarily assigned a monetary value.[46] Thus, Alí Rodríguez, then Venezuelan ambassador to Havana, declared that in 2006 ALBA exchanges between Cuba and Venezuela were worth over US$3 billion; this would include not only the cheap oil provided by Venezuela but also the services of tens of thousands of Cuban medical, educational, and sports personnel.

Moreover, as ALBA develops it has been promoting structural integration between members in unprecedented forms. The aforementioned Petrocaribe joint energy company is one example of what are described under ALBA as *Compañías Grannacionales* (Grand National Companies), regional joint ventures created by the public sectors of member states, which in the case of Cuban-Venezuelan relations, since 2007 has included joint ventures in cement, petrochemicals, liquefied gas, a refinery for heavy crude oil in Cuba, improvement of the Venezuelan fishing fleet, nickel mining, undersea hydrocarbon exploitation, and telecommunications.[47]

Several other integration initiatives, more or less closely linked to ALBA, have also been sponsored or supported by Venezuela: for example, Telesur, the University of the South, the Bank of the South, and the Sucre common currency (thus far existing only as a unit of account among ALBA countries). Telesur, the TV news channel sponsored by Venezuela, Cuba, Argentina, and Uruguay, has already become a reference point for serious radical journalism in the region, and the Bank of the South has begun to function as an alternative source of development aid for the poorer countries. Despite the setback of the loss of Honduras, ALBA continues to grow and is increasingly seen as a genuine alternative project.

PROMOTION OF MULTIPOLARITY

For Chávez and his team it was clear from the beginning that their vision of integration and regional development could not advance without the broadest possible global alliances as a counterweight to the United States. Hence their very active diplomatic campaign to forge relations with other powers as diverse as China, Russia, India, Iran, the European Union, and the OPEC countries. While this was certainly an integral part of the Bolivarian program, it could be considered less markedly ideological and allowed ample scope for pragmatic adjustment in practice.

Relations with China—primarily commercial—partly reflect growing Chinese interest in Latin America as a whole; Venezuela is China's fifth most important partner in the region in this respect, with binational trade reaching US$10 billion in 2008.[48] In April 2009 Chávez made his sixth visit to the country, pointing out that Venezuelan oil exports to China had risen from zero to 380,000 barrels per day in five years (already over a quarter of what Venezuela exports to the United States), and are projected to reach 1 million barrels per day by 2013, while PDVSA and the Chinese state oil company are working on a joint refinery and tanker fleet. In return, Chinese investments in Venezuela (which include a significant element of technology transfer) include mobile phones, domestic appliances, irrigation equipment, and railways, while in November 2008 Venezuela's first telecommunications satellite was launched by China.[49] However, while Venezuela sees the relationship as also having geopolitical (counterhegemonic) implications, it is doubtful whether the Chinese attach great importance to this aspect.

The Russian Federation has become an important partner in commercial, but also in military and political terms. Its relevance for Chávez quickly became apparent, as a major non-OPEC oil producer whose collaboration was important in maintaining petroleum prices and also as an alternative source of advanced technology, particularly in the military sphere. Although Russia is now clearly capitalist, the West continues to view it with distrust and thus, when in 2005 Venezuela signed an agreement to purchase significant quantities of military equipment from Moscow, both the United States and Colombia expressed concern. For Venezuela it was clearly desirable to reduce its military dependence on Washington, especially when the Bush administration attempted to veto arms sales to Caracas by other Western countries (in particular by Spain).[50]

While Venezuelan-Russian exchanges were not purely military, it soon became clear that the 2005 deal was only the beginning of a military relationship with Moscow. In July 2008 it was announced that Venezuela would buy more than US$1 billion worth of anti-aircraft weapons, torpedo-equipped submarines, and tanks from Russia, and by August 2009 total arms purchases from the Russians were estimated at US$4 billion.[51] This has to be kept in perspective (the total size of the Venezuelan armed forces is still modest in regional terms), but the message is clear: although the United States still has overwhelming military dominance, Caracas does have powerful allies. This was brought home in November–December 2008 when, coinciding with a visit by the Russian president Dmitri Medvedev, Russian and Venezuelan naval vessels conducted joint maneuvers in Venezuelan waters (this was the first time that Russian warships had visited the Caribbean since the early 1990s).[52]

The Islamic Republic of Iran has become another significant—and controversial—Venezuelan ally. Not only is it a leading member of OPEC but it has attained a certain level of industrial and technological development, and its independent and indeed antagonistic stance in relation to the United States makes it a logical partner for a counterhegemonic project. Iranian oil technology was useful for PDVSA as it struggled to restore production after the damaging opposition strike/lockout.[53] Venezuela has signed several cooperation agreements with Iran that include the establishment of plants for the manufacture of cars and tractors with Iranian technology. Since September 2006 the Iranian state oil company Petropar has been participating in exploration of the Orinoco oil belt along with state companies from China, India, Vietnam, and other Latin American countries.[54]

The Iranian connection has aroused criticism from many leftist sympathizers of Venezuela who point to repression in Iran and question the country's democratic and/or revolutionary credentials. This issue came to the fore again when Chávez went out of his way to defend the Iranian president Ahmadinejad's reelection in May–June 2009 in the face of intense Western criticism. Chávez (and Venezuela) may well feel that this is simply a matter of opposing Western double standards, but it does highlight the complexity of the question of how far Venezuela regards Iran in terms of pragmatism or ideology (as a genuine popular revolutionary regime).

The quest for multipolarity has also given a new impulse to relations with India, another major developing power that previously had minimal contact with Venezuela. In March 2005 Chávez led a delegation to India and signed six cooperation agreements in areas including petroleum, biotechnology, railways, and space technology. In 2008 these agreements were extended and it was reported that bilateral trade had boomed, from US$60 million in 2004 to almost US$1 billion in 2006. As in other cases the new ties went beyond purely commercial concerns, with both governments calling for a revitalization of the Non-Aligned Movement and

Venezuela pledging support for India's campaign to become a permanent member of the UN Security Council.[55]

Indeed, Venezuelan diplomacy has scarcely left any stone unturned in the quest to diversify the country's international relations and promote both a multipolar world and counterhegemonic alliances. Africa is now being prioritized and other non-Western countries, such as Malaysia, Vietnam, and both Koreas, have also received attention. Western European countries have not been neglected either, with France and Spain having the closest relations with Caracas, but other countries, including the UK, also maintaining important commercial exchanges.

CONCLUSIONS

For more than ten years now Venezuela under President Hugo Chávez has pursued a vigorous and independent foreign policy, with active—one could even say hyperactive—diplomatic activity in pursuit of a series of ambitious and interrelated goals. The international agenda of the Bolivarian Revolution is clearly ideological, but this has not prevented the country's leadership from making appropriate pragmatic adjustments in its implementation.

By conventional criteria, *chavista* foreign policy has been anything but pragmatic. To proclaim visionary goals, such as the reaffirmation of national sovereignty, the promotion of regional integration, social justice and an alternative development model, and the quest for multipolarity and counterhegemonic alliances, might in 1998 have been seen as purely populist rhetoric that could lead to a few symbolic achievements, but little substantive change. Many administrations might have claimed to fulfill these goals by modest increases in petroleum royalties, minor changes in military agreements with the United States, joining Mercosur, and negotiating commercial agreements with China, India, and one or two other countries. But the Bolivarian Republic has in effect renationalized oil and nationalized other key industries, reinvigorated OPEC, replaced the United States with Russia as its main defense partner, led the way in opposing the U.S. free-trade agenda and forged a radical new regional socioeconomic alliance with socializing tendencies, sponsored new independent regional financial, political, defense, and communications institutions, reoriented its trade on a massive scale on a South-South perspective, and negotiated far-reaching commercial, political, and military agreements with a diverse range of countries. In the process it has of course had to make pragmatic concessions on specific issues and shown flexibility at moments of crisis. In general, however, ideology—or perhaps one should call it strategic vision—has prevailed, to an extent that no one could have anticipated ten years ago. In its regional and global impact, Venezuelan foreign policy is indeed revolutionary.

NOTES

1. A good example of this type of critique is Michael Reid, *Forgotten Continent: The Battle for Latin America's Soul* (New Haven: Yale University Press, 2007).

2. Francis Fukuyama, *The End of History and the Last Man*, London: Hamish Hamilton, 1992; Jorge Castañeda, *La Utopía desarmada: la izquierda latinoamericana después de la Guerra Fría* (New York: Vintage, 1994).

3. Bart Jones, *¡Hugo! The Hugo Chávez Story: From Mud Hut to Perpetual Revolution*, (London: The Bodley Head, 2008), pp. 278–79.

4. Christopher I. Clement, "Confronting Hugo Chávez: US 'Democracy Promotion' in Latin America," in Steve Ellner and Miguel Tinker Salas (eds.), *Venezuela: Hugo Chávez and the Decline of an "Exceptional Democracy"* (Lanham, MD: Rowman & Littlefield, 2006), p. 190; Nicholas Kozloff, *Hugo Chávez: Oil, Politics, and the Challenge to the U.S.* (New York: Palgrave Macmillan, 2006), p. 149.

5. Gregory Wilpert, *Changing Venezuela by Taking Power* (London: Verso, 2007), p. 168.

6. Ibid., pp. 169, 176–77.

7. Eva Golinger, *The Chávez Code: Cracking U.S. Intervention in Venezuela* (Havana: Editorial José Martí, 2005), pp. 136–38.

8. Jones, *¡Hugo!*, p. 249.

9. Wilpert, *Changing Venezuela*, p. 97.

10. Ibid., p. 160.

11. Jones, *¡Hugo!*, pp. 251–24; D. L. Raby, *Democracy and Revolution: Latin America and Socialism Today* (London: Pluto Press, 2006), p. 162.

12. *Fundamentos Filosóficos de la Nueva Integración del Sur* (Caracas: Instituto de Altos Estudios Diplomáticos Pedro Gual, 2007), p. 60.

13. Ibid., p. 60; Wilpert, *Changing Venezuela*, p. 169.

14. Ibid., p. 152 and Ch. 5n1.

15. Richard Gott, *Hugo Chávez and the Bolivarian Revolution* (London: Verso, 2005), p. 187.

16. Golinger, *The Chávez Code*, p. 52.

17. Wilpert, *Changing Venezuela*, p. 169.

18. Golinger, *The Chávez Code*, p. 84.

19. Clement, "Confronting Hugo Chávez," pp. 193–97.

20. Raby, *Democracy and Revolution*, pp. 176–77.

21. Golinger, *The Chávez Code*, pp. 147–68.

22. Wilpert, *Changing Venezuela*, pp. 169, 176–77.

23. Juan Forero, "Venezuela Cautions U.S. It May Curtail Oil Exports," *New York Times,* February 27, 2006 (commondreams.org/headlines06/0227-01.htm) (consulted July 26, 2009).

24. Ibid.
25. James Suggett, "London Court Rules in Favor of Venezuela in Dispute with Exxon," March 18, 2008, www.venezuelanalysis.com/news/3283 (consulted July 24, 2009); and "Entrevista con el Embajador Samuel Moncada," *Boletín Especial* del Instituto de Altos Estudios Diplomáticos Pedro Gual, marzo 2008, www.institutopedrogual.edu.ve/index.php?option=com_remository&Itemid=136&func=fileinfo&id=81 (consulted June 23, 2009).
26. "Chávez expulsa a embajador de EE.UU.," por Carlos Chirinos, September 12, 2008, news.bbc.co.uk/hi/spanish/latin_america/newsid_7611000/7611655.stm (consulted June26, 2009).
27. See, for example, José Vicente Rangel, "Anatomía de un golpe," *Últimas Noticias* (Caracas), July 6, 2009, p. 16; Gilberto Lopes, "Zelaya vs. Micheletti, ¿Chávez vs. EE.UU.?" July 9, 2009, www.bbc.co.uk/mundo/america_latina/2009/07/090709_1130_honduras_crica_glopes_wbm.shtml (consulted August 26, 2009).
28. "Cronología: Colombia vs. Venezuela," February 4, 2005, http://news.bbc.co.uk/hi/spanish/latin_america/newsid_4182000/4182195.stm (consulted July 24, 2009); Sarah Wagner, "Venezuela and Colombia Patch-up Relations, Vowing Closer Cooperation," February 16, 2005, www.venezuelanalysis.com/news/941 (consulted August 25, 2009).
29. "Colombia-Ecuador: OAS Rejects Military Incursion," by Constanza Vieira, March 18, 2008, www.ipsnews.net/news.asp?idnews=41639 (consulted August 26, 2009).
30. Carlos Chirinos, "Capturan 'paramilitares' en Venezuela," May 9, 2004, news.bbc.co.uk/hi/spanish/latin_america/newsid_3698000/3698989.stm (consulted September 26, 2009).
31. James Suggett, "Venezuelan Government: Separatist Opposition Uses Paramilitaries for Social Cleansing, Destabilization," June 15, 2009, www.venezuelanalysis.com/news/4521 (consulted August 30, 2009).
32. "Cancilleres de Venezuela y Panamá conversan sobre oleoducto," January 13, 2005, minci.gob.ve/noticias/1/2481/cancilleres_de_venezuela.html (consulted July 26, 2009).
33. "Acuerdo de seguridad entre Colombia, Ecuador y Venezuela, propone nuevo embajador venezolano," *El Tiempo* (Bogotá), Junio 6 de 2009, www.eltiempo.com/archivo/documento/CMS-5375928 (consulted July 26, 2009).
34. Constanza Vieira, "Colombia: Uribe Agrees US 'Access' to Military Bases," Bogotá, July 17, 2009, ipsnews.net/news.asp?idnews=47714; "Gobierno de Colombia defiende acuerdo militar con EE UU," *El Universal* (Caracas), July 17, 2009, pp. 1–16; "Chávez pidió revisar relaciones con Colombia," *Últimas Noticias* (Caracas), July 21, 2009, p. 17.
35. *Fundamentos Filosóficos*, pp. 10–11.
36. Kiraz Janicke, "Venezuela Considers Re-Joining Andean Community of Nations," September 4, 2007, www.venezuelanalysis.com/news/2584 (consulted August 30, 2009).

37. Jason Tockman, "Chávez, Morales Seek Transformation of MERCOSUR Trade Bloc," January 22, 2007, www.venezuelanalysis.com/analysis/2187 (consulted August 30, 2009).

38. The South American Community of Nations was established at the III Summit of South American Presidents in Cuzco, Peru on December 8, 2004; it adopted the name of UNASUR (Union of South American Nations) at the First South American Energy Summit in Porlamar, Venezuela, on April 16–17, 2007, and established a Secretariat in Quito, Ecuador, www.sela.org/sela/csnaciones.asp (consulted July 25, 2009).

39. "Unasur aprueba creación del Consejo Sudamericano de Defensa," December 16, 2008, www.noticias24.com/actualidad/noticia/21542 (consulted July 26, 2009).

40. Antulio Rosales, "Democracia y participación de la sociedad civil en los procesos de integración ALBA-TCP," unpublished paper presented at the meeting of the Alianza Social Continental, October 2007, p. 4. Consulted by courtesy of the author.

41. Raby, *Democracia y Revolución*, pp. 244–45.

42. Antulio Rosales, "Democracia y participación," p. 5.

43. "Petrocaribe en tiempos de crisis," BBC Mundo, June 12, 2009, http://www.bbc.co.uk/mundo/america_latina/2009/06/090611_2252_petrocaribe_cumbre_gm.shtml (consulted November 6, 2010); Hedelberto López Blanch, "PETROCARIBE y el combustible integrador," *Rebelión*, July 21, 2008, http://www.rebelion.org/noticia.php?id=70570 (consulted November 6, 2010).

44. Iban Campo, "Guía subsidio eléctrico," September 14, 2008, *El Caribe* (Santo Domingo), www.elcaribe.com.do/site/index.php?option=com_content&view=article&id=183715&catid=141:sociales&Itemid=162 (consulted August 30, 2009).

45. José Toro Hardy, quoted in "Petrocaribe en 3 preguntas," BBC Mundo.

46. "Claves sobre el ALBA," BBC Mundo, April 28, 2007, news.bbc.co.uk/go/pr/fr/-/spanish/business/newsid_6602000/6602409.stm (consulted October 8, 2008).

47. Nadeska Silva Querales y Stiven Tremaria Adan, *La Revolución Bolivariana en América Latina: 2007, un año de avances* (Caracas: Ministerio del Poder Popular para la Comunicación y la Información, 2008), pp. 16–20.

48. *El Universal* (Caracas), July 21, 2009, "Comercio con China alcanzó $10 millardos durante 2008."

49. James Suggett, "Venezuela and China Strengthen Energy-Based Economic and Political Alliance," April 10, 2009, www.venezuelanalysis.com/news/4362; and "Venezuela and China Expand Joint Oil and Investment Accords," September 24, 2008, www.venezuelanalysis.com/news/3828 (both consulted August 30, 2009).

50. Alex Holland, "Venezuela May Buy Elsewhere if Spain Cannot Overcome US Pressure," February 2, 2006, www.venezuelanalysis.com/news/1596 (consulted August 31, 2009).

51. James Suggett, "Venezuela Strengthens Alliance with Russia to Promote 'Polycentrism'," July 23, 2008, www.venezuelanalysis.com/news/3666 (consulted August 30, 2009).

52. Russ Dallen, "Chávez Says Venezuela and Russia Will Build a Nuclear Reactor in Oil-Rich Zulia," *Latin American Herald Tribune*, in www.venezuelanalysis.com/newsbrief/3961 (consulted August 30, 2009); "Militares de Venezuela y Rusia formalizaron programa de ejercicios navales," November 29, 2008, www.aporrea.org/tiburon/n124838.html (consulted August 30, 2009).

53. Alex Holland, "Venezuela Iran's Best Friend?" March 11, 2006, www.venezuelanalysis.com/analysis/1654 (consulted July 26, 2009).

54. Steve Ellner, "Using Oil Diplomacy to Sever Venezuela's Dependence," *NACLA Report on the Americas* 40:5 (Sept–Oct 2007).

55. Sarah Wagner, "Venezuela opens a 'New Dimension' in its Relationship with India," March 7, 2005, www.venezuelanalysis.com/news/984 (consulted August 31, 2009); "Venezuela and India Sign Joint Project in Orinoco Oil Belt," AFP, April 10, 2008, www.venezuelanalysis.com/newsbrief/3338 (consulted August 31, 2009).

CHAPTER 10

DEFYING EXPECTATIONS: THE EXTERNAL PROFILE AND ACTIVISM OF THE CUBAN REVOLUTION

ANTONI KAPCIA

INTRODUCTION

While one might expect ideology in foreign policy to be the preserve of the stronger developed countries and pragmatism to be the lot of smaller developing countries, Cuba's external profile, since 1961, appears to have often been more obviously ideologically driven than most. Cuban foreign policy between 1962 (the Second Declaration of Havana) and 1968 (when the erstwhile "heretical" Fidel Castro endorsed the Soviet invasion of Czechoslovakia) was seemingly based on an active commitment to continental revolution, regardless of U.S. hostility, Soviet exasperation, and regional isolation. Later, between 1975 and 1989, a policy of active "internationalism," including active support for Angola, while initially seen as following Soviet dictates, actually seemed to demonstrate a continuing commitment to revolutionary principles. In the 1990s, as Latin America moved to the left, this stance seemed to be maintained despite economic weakness.

On closer analysis, however, what becomes clear is that the ideological ends and purposes of Cuba's foreign policy (and its pragmatic dimension) differed somewhat in each period: early on, the impulse to "spread revolution" also offered the pragmatic prospect of breaking Cuba's U.S.-imposed isolation; in the middle period, the aim of "defending revolution" elsewhere also brought new allies in the process; while, after 1990, the stalwart defense of revolutionary principles had two clear pragmatic purposes—to strengthen domestic ideological resolve and to tune in to the emerging regional ideological consensus.

Therefore, to portray Cuban foreign policy as purely ideological is to misunderstand the complexity of both pragmatism and ideology in a revolutionary process that has always had to make the best of the means available, of the spaces, both predictable and unexpected, allowed by a world dominated first by the Cold War and later by unipolarity (under a hostile United States) and globalization. This has tended to mean not only that, throughout the 50 years of revolution, seemingly ideological policies often had a pragmatic dimension, and vice versa, but also that Cuba's active foreign policy has ultimately been determined by what is possible, by what the best means happen to be at any one time and in any one context, while being tempered by the need to ensure that any external stance (i.e., the possible) does not undermine the basic principles of the Revolution (i.e., the desirable). Within the ideology that has driven the Revolution since 1959, which includes the defense of national sovereignty, the pursuit of active nationalism and the notion of active solidarity specifically with developing countries, pragmatism has also been inherent in long-term adherence to Soviet global objectives, as well as the desperate search for new markets and allies in the face of economic collapse and a tightening of the U.S. embargo in the 1990s.

This uneasy balance has been the outcome of several complex internal processes of policy formulation, the particular and changing characteristics of the Cuban leadership (visible at home and abroad), and, of course, the fundamental shifts in the global context over all five decades, which significantly shaped the extent and nature of the parameters for Cuba's independent foreign policy.

THE ROOTS OF IDEOLOGY

The trajectory described indicates three characteristics of the Revolution's complexity. First, the seeming contradiction between different periods of either pragmatic or ideological motivation implies either an inherent inconsistency or, more likely, an unusual vulnerability to external pressures. Second, any given policy (such as internationalism) can be interpreted in two entirely opposite ways, according to one's reading and preconceptions. Third, therefore, it suggests that simple answers following preordained paradigms are misleading, obliging us to address the underlying complexity and contradictions, as well as the unpredictability of Cuban foreign policy. Hence the starting point is to go beyond the obvious on the basic question of the Revolution's ideology over the past decades. For, if Cuba's drift to Communism arose from a pragmatic alliance with the Soviet Union, how can we explain the continuing commitment to socialism after 1991? Moreover, even before 1991, how firm was Cuba's ideological adherence to Soviet models and dictates?

One answer to these questions lies in the essentially indigenous nature of Cuba's socialism, often overlooked by foreign observers in 1959, given the obsessive U.S. search for "reds under the bed" and assumptions about Soviet links. The reality was that many of the rebels came from a radical tradition of a redistributive nationalism, which included the Cuban People's (Orthodox) Party—to which Castro belonged—other more heterodox groups echoing a Rooseveltian "New Dealism" and espousing a vague notion of revolution,[1] and the Communists as well.[2] All of this created what has been called *cubanía* (the ideology of an active belief in *cubanidad*), which, reacting to the recent history of U.S. domination, became increasingly radical,[3] adopting fundamentally anti-imperialist (and thus equally anticapitalist) explanations. After 1959 this *cubanía* drove a new process of nation-building, which was revolutionary in its commitment to egalitarian redistribution, collectivist participation, and an interventionist state. Therefore, what really drove the Revolution was often less the overt Marxism-Leninism than *cubanía*, radicalized with each year of successful transformation, survival, and resistance to U.S. hostility.

This *cubanía* also affected Cuba's external redefinition. Since prerevolutionary foreign policy had revolved exclusively around the world sugar economy and the United States, the break with the United States in 1961 created a new set of urgent problems and a new set of challenges for Cuban foreign policy; these especially included the need for new markets and the growing prospect of intervention, both of which encouraged gravitation toward the Soviet Union. This new alliance was a stark example of the pressures determining that policy: uniquely placed within a Cold War geography, wherein Cuba's leaders faced the choice of abandoning their goals (by continuing to accept U.S. hegemony) or gravitating toward the alternative superpower (and needy sugar market), their characteristic determination not to compromise left them with only one means available, albeit one with which they increasingly came to share some ideological affinity.

However, post-1961 foreign policy was by no means dictated by Soviet interests, ideas, or policies;[4] indeed, until 1969, Cuba's policy of fostering insurrection and confronting the United States in its own back-yard ran directly counter to Moscow's preferences. Even after 1972, when Cuba joined the Socialist Bloc's trading network, Comecon,[5] and when Cuba's structures, policies and definitions seemed more "Sovietized," the involvement in Angola after 1975 was, despite appearances, largely driven by Havana rather than Moscow.[6]

However, beyond both the new relationship with the USSR and the U.S. embargo, Cuba's new foreign policy was driven by cubanía in another sense: the desire to redefine Cuba's place in the world, reclaiming a national identity hitherto denied by colonialism and neo-colonialism and complicated by Cubans' own uncertainty about which wider context Cuba rightfully belonged—a community of former Spanish colonies (given Cuba's unusually late independence) or some sort of formal affinity with the United States. Hence, after 1959, those many actors and institutions shaping foreign policy had three purposes: the search for allies, the pursuit of trading partners, and the need to redefine Cuba's "world."

The twin aims of the search for allies and new trading partners were, in the short term, settled easily through the Soviet connection. After February 1960 (and increasingly thereafter), sugar sales were guaranteed through a pragmatic alliance with a sugar-hungry Soviet Union, which ensured economic security. As the threat of an impending U.S. invasion grew, Soviet promises of military aid and protection also increasingly answered the need for new protective allies. The redefinition of Cuba's "world," however, took much longer.

Initially, Cuba's leaders seemed to rediscover Latin America, rapidly seeking to understand something previously ignored.[7] Equally, the concept of solidarity with developing countries, soon becoming a kind of "Third Worldism," was also part of this redefinition, reflected through a political, military, and cultural internationalism that seemed to fuse the pragmatic and the ideological by offering the prospect of leverage against both superpowers within a rapidly decolonizing world, with which Cuba's leaders clearly empathized. After 1972, once the material benefits of Comecon membership became clear, stability at home and abroad then meant a new self-definition—as part of a socialist context, almost confirming Western images of Cuba as a Caribbean version of the "second world." This generated a new internal debate on foreign policy, between the desirability of an environment bringing concrete rewards and institutional consolidation, on the one hand, and continuing internationalism (especially in Africa) on the other. Meanwhile, as Latin America fell increasingly under the shadow of military authoritarianism, involvement in Africa brought a reassessment of Cuba's African roots and a new awareness of Cuban cultural affinity with other Caribbean islands sharing many of the same economic and psychological preoccupations; as a result, the revolution's ideology—cubanía—began to be reshaped to take a deeper account of an element in *cubanidad* previously neglected or downplayed.

Furthermore, the idea of a homogenous and coherent Cuban foreign policy should not overshadow the divisions, tensions, and pressures that were present in a policy-making apparatus that included several different, and occasionally contradictory, agents: the Foreign Ministry, the Revolutionary Armed Forces (FAR), Guevara's clandestine unit to train Latin American guerrillas, the country's different economic managers, and those always leaning more towards Moscow, to name only a few. Hence, Cuba shifted between a "Third Worldist" strategy (led by the foreign minister Raúl Roa), the concept of continental insurrection spearheaded by Che,[8] and greater integration within Comecon and a closer adherence to Socialist Bloc models, advocated by those in the leadership who had always argued for closer Soviet links (principally the pre-1959 Communists but also an increasing lobby in the military, security, and educational apparatus). The existence of multiple perspectives in foreign policy was perhaps best demonstrated in 1975, when Cuba asserted its independence of action in Angola in what was a unilateral response to the MPLA's request for assistance, which was not initially supported by the USSR. Indeed, this dimension also demonstrated another critical feature of Cuban foreign policy: the special characteristics that Fidel Castro brought to that policy. For the evidence seems to indicate that not only was he instrumental in deciding on active support for the MPLA, but also that this came in the midst of a period when his personal relationship with other Third World leaders seemed to transcend ideological affinities, most notably in the cases of Indira Gandhi and several Caribbean leaders, adding a further dimension to unusual alliances.

THE INTERNAL DIMENSIONS OF FOREIGN POLICY

The Revolution's external profile has also consistently reflected internal debates and also occasionally served distinctly internal purposes, especially because Cuba's freedom of action abroad has often been circumscribed by very specific global and regional contexts, that is, by varying alliances, changing trade imperatives, or the equally variable limits of deterrence. For example, the insurrectionary policy in Latin America, by challenging both the United States and Soviet policy, helped strengthen the evolving collective self-image of "the embattled enclave," of David confronting two Goliaths, reinforcing the siege mentality that helped sustain loyalty and patriotism. Conversely, collective material benefits flowed from the Soviet and Comecon links, which helped to underwrite the social revolution. Pragmatism also underwrote the policy of internationalism that, while enlisting young Cubans in a new collective struggle to fortify their ideological commitment (given their decreasing awareness of the pre-1959 hardships or the "heroic" 1960s), also allowed thousands to travel and either acquire materials goods or hard currency or, by working in poorer countries, appreciate Cuba's relative merits.

The events of 1961 and 1962 marked a significant turning point. First, they removed the issue of U.S.-Cuban relations from Cuba's foreign policy. While 1961 witnessed the end of a 60-year long dependent relationship (a major psychological boost), the October 1962 U.S. guarantees not to invade Cuba (the so-called secret protocol to the Missile Crisis agreement) removed the real threat of direct intervention. Second, they ended the need for Soviet military protection, aroused briefly by the threat of U.S. invasion. Indeed, after the 1961 victory and the 1962 guarantees, it became clear that the Soviet link could actually be exploitable rather than simply a dependent one. Third, as a result of both these effects, Cuba's leaders found an unusual freedom to pursue an actively insurrectionary policy that was openly ideological (a praxis of active revolution against "U.S. imperialism") and also to exercise considerable leverage with the Soviet Union. In fact, it was ideological in the most pragmatic way; Cuba had nothing to lose from pursuing an otherwise ideologically driven and dangerous path, because there was no penalty, while it had everything to gain at home and abroad.

Moreover, the Cuban leaders remained aware of the fundamental differences between Cuban and Soviet socialism, with cubanía informing their increasingly revolutionary definition. Indeed, however much Cuba seemed to return to orthodoxy between 1970 and 1986, the emergence of Gorbachev's reforms resurrected that latent awareness, engendering the new drive for "Rectification" (of "errors and negative tendencies" imported from the Socialist Bloc) and a return to cubanía.

The post-1990 crisis then plunged the Revolution into its deepest (and potentially terminal) recession. Deprived of Soviet protection and with Washington's policy of democracy promotion seemingly rampant, Cuba's leaders now had three urgent tasks abroad: the search for new commercial links, the search for new allies, and the need to confront the United States alone. The first two of these needs were unquestionably pragmatically motivated, albeit with the clear purpose of protecting the ideologically driven process and achievements of the Revolution; those achievements, of course, if successfully defended, could be a critical component of the third task—confronting Washington—if a sufficient consensus could be built for ideological reinforcement at home.

The search for trading partners was, of course, something entirely new. Between 1962 and 1972, external trade had been relatively limited, with the Soviet oil-for-sugar agreements forming the major part, and with the symbolically important trade with Western Europe being somewhat marginal. After 1972, trade expanded to include all of the Socialist Bloc (via the familiar Comecon bilateral barter arrangements) but also increasingly with Latin America. This meant that, between 1972 and 1989, Cuba's policy-makers had little need to think outside the new, and apparently propitious, means available to them.

The year 1990 therefore brought a totally new situation, forcing a complete reassessment of policy, the disappearance of those propitious means implying a new search for the possible. First, without Soviet and Socialist Bloc purchases, Cuba's access to preferential markets disappeared, throwing the sugar industry—characterized by plummeting production due to desperate shortages of fuel and fertilizer—to the mercy of an already crowded market. Tourism (with nickel and biotechnology in subordinate roles) was soon determined to be the mainstay to replace sugar at least in the short term, and this indeed opened up possibilities of trade with new partners.

These huge changes clearly altered the balance and relationship between the pragmatic and the ideological. Since 1963, there had been a close and integrated relationship between the two, since Cuba's economic development was ensured within a framework in which Cubans felt ideologically comfortable. In the post–Cold War environment, the essential aim of all policy was to survive, and to save the Revolution, by whatever steps were deemed necessary and acceptable (including, for example, developing the tourist industry, which had previously been seen as dangerous to the essential values and coherence of the Cuban political culture).

Likewise the search for new allies was different. Since there was no chance of a new protector being found to replace the economic, political, and military alliance with the Soviet Union, the search focused on building up a diplomatic defense that might restrict the United States' freedom of action against Cuba. This meant courting developing countries, as before; capitalizing on the kudos gained from the preceding decades of internationalism, and doing so by stressing "Third World solidarity" (not least within the fading Non-Aligned Movement); and by still offering the opportunities of education in Cuba to foreign students. This took advantage of a changing international context that saw developing countries becoming increasingly willing to vote together in international forums and enter into new alliances.

It also meant seeking support from other countries, in an attempt to drive more of a wedge between the EU and the United States, sometimes through offering commercial advantages in joint ventures and tourism and sometimes simply by skillful diplomacy. This soon bore fruit in the steady building of a growing majority in the UN for the annual Cuban motion against the U.S. embargo; by the 2000s, the EU had moved into the anti-embargo camp and the United States was regularly supported by only Israel and one or two Pacific microstates.

Relations with the EU also underline the subtlety of the interplay between pragmatism and ideology. The resistance by Cuba in 2003–2005 to the EU's new pressure to conform to EU and U.S. demands on human rights made little pragmatic sense if Cuba wished to receive increased aid and investment. However, Cuba's leaders reasoned that it was not worth jeopardizing the fundamentals of the revolutionary system simply to meet the demands of what they judged to be a short-term and changeable shift on the part of the EU toward a pro-United States position (and later events rapidly bore out that judgment). Hence what seemed ideological in motivation was actually a pragmatic assessment.

Similar campaigns were waged in other forums, such as UNCTAD, Caricom, and even the UN Human Rights Commission, where U.S. moves to condemn Cuba were regularly countered by Cuban accusations against Washington, usually appealing to anti-U.S. sentiment among developing countries. The purpose of all this was simple: to partially counter the United States' military and economic encirclement of Cuba by a diplomatic encirclement of the United States that might give Washington some food for thought in any plans for active hostility. It was therefore both nakedly pragmatic (to provide some protection against U.S. actions) but also curiously ideological, in that Cuba was able to fly the flag of anticolonialism and, increasingly, of antiglobalization, especially as the "Pink Tide" developed, with many of the emerging leaders of that wave looking toward Cuba—and especially to the person of Fidel Castro—as something of a "spiritual" mentor as well as practical model of resistance.

RELATIONS WITH THE UNITED STATES

From 1962 (except for a brief hiatus in 1977–1980 when Carter's détente diplomacy partially opened relations) until the end of the Cold War, Cuban-U.S. relations had largely been a nonissue. The collapse of the USSR, however, not only deprived Cuba of its protector but also removed from the United States any obligation to adhere to the guarantees given to Moscow in October 1962, opening up the possibility of military intervention. However unlikely that possibility might have been (given both other, more pressing, concerns and the Pentagon's assessment of the unacceptable human [and thus political] costs of any invasion), many Cubans genuinely feared invasion, mindful of the ease with which U.S. troops had been sent to Panama in 1989. After 2003, of course, seeing the extent to which Washington was willing to invade a sovereign country against fierce international opposition and with questionable legality, those fears increased.

In reality, the U.S. option of invasion had been replaced by two other strategies: the tightening of the embargo and active support for the internal and external groups opposing the Revolution. The former took shape almost immediately, with the Cuba Democracy Act (the so-called Torricelli Act) of 1992, which extended the terms and scope of the existing embargo to affect third parties. This was followed by the Helms-Burton Act (1996), which took the embargo to a new level, with its draconian legislation designed to deter foreign countries from trading with, and investing in, Cuba. Finally, 2004 saw measures to limit the flow of Cuban-American remittances and family visits, in the hope of starving the Cuban economy of much-needed dollars.

Support for the opposition had begun in the 1980s, with the funding of Radio Martí and TV Martí, and the Republicans' close links with the Cuban American National Foundation (CANF), but it took on a new aspect after 2000, when the U.S. Interests Section began to fund dissident groups directly, host dissident gatherings, and generally promote active opposition. One purpose of this was to provoke a Cuban reaction against dissidents, which might force the EU away from its position of dialogue with Cuba, a strategy that proved successful in spring 2003, when the arrests of 75 dissidents provoked the EU into imposing diplomatic sanctions for two years.

In response to the post-1991 challenge, Cuba deployed three strategies. The first was simply to prepare for the worst. Given that the Revolutionary Armed Forces (FAR) had already been almost halved in response to the crisis, the tasks of defense were now devolved to the civilian population, through the militias and Committees for the Defense of the Revolution (CDR). Since the effectiveness of this civil defense relied on popular commitment, this also meant the need to strengthen the population's ideological resolve, by continually mobilizing and promoting the nationalist elements of defense by implying that U.S. hostility was directed against Cuban sovereignty as much as against the Revolution, and that it threatened to deprive Cubans of their right to the "gains of the

Revolution" in terms of social provision, as had occurred in post-1989 eastern Europe and as was explicitly posited (via privatization) in the various U.S. plans for a transition. Indeed, the latter was the essence of the post-2000 "Battle of Ideas," which, although usually seen abroad as a domestically focused drive to strengthen ideological resolve, had clear international dimensions. In every sense, therefore, this aspect of U.S.-Cuban relations was strongly linked to internal factors and fiercely and deliberately ideological, not least because a purely pragmatic response to the crisis and the increase in U.S. hostility could easily have been to surrender and develop an acceptable transition to capitalism and multiparty democracy.

The second strategy was to seek low-level practical cooperation with U.S. agencies, engaging in "confidence building measures" by regularly negotiating and meeting with the U.S. armed forces, the Drug Enforcement Agency, and the Immigration and Naturalization Service. Until 2001, this cooperation reaped considerable benefits for both sides, and, even after 9/11, Cuba's offer to support the Guantanamo Bay Camp X-Ray, through the provision of further facilities, indicated a willingness to continue this pragmatic modus vivendi. However, with Cuba included as an adjunct of the new "axis of evil," this cooperation was halted by Washington, thus closing the door on pragmatic relations.

The third strategy involved the prosecution of low-level cooperation with U.S .academic institutions and news agencies, as Cuba allowed the entry of an increasing number of U.S. students and researchers, as well as inviting CNN among others to set up a base in Havana. While the latter policy survived, the former came to an end, partly due to Cuba's fears (of the U.S. "Track Two" policy of engaging with civil society in order to subvert it), and then definitively by the Bush administration in 2004, when travel was cut to a minimum. With the failure of the more pragmatic strands, all that remained of Cuba's approach to U.S.-Cuban relations by 2008 was the strictly ideological—resistance and defense of the Revolution.

What relations with the United States reveal is that for much of the time the pragmatic has been constrained by the limits posed by the ideological, and that pragmatic policies may be pursued, but only if they do not fundamentally contradict deeply held ideological beliefs. Hence, in the 1990s, although tourism and self-employment were reluctantly accepted as short-term pragmatic domestic solutions to the crisis, there was actually little attempt abroad to court the United States' favor, as a means of evading the tightening encirclement. The reason was clear in that the costs of any rapprochement (inevitably on U.S. terms) would have undermined the bases of Revolution, while the peculiarities of the

U.S. "Fidel-centric" policy toward Cuba meant that Washington was unlikely to accept any Cuban approach other than abject surrender; indeed, curiously, it was actually Washington's Cuba policy that proved more ideological (in its fixation on the personality of Castro) than Havana's reciprocal policy. Hence, as with the Latin American policy of the 1960s, Havana had nothing to gain and everything to lose by pursuing what at the time may have seemed to be the pragmatic course of action.

The possibility of some sort of *detente* with an Obama-led United States (however far off that possibility might be, given constitutional, political, and electoral constraints in the United States on any intention to weaken, let alone end, the embargo) raises the specter of an unfettered influx of U.S. tourists, which Cuban policy-makers are certain to resist or at least limit. While opening up to a vast U.S. tourist market makes clear pragmatic sense, as a lucrative solution to Cuba's economic ills and pent-up domestic frustrations, such an influx would threaten to destabilize so many aspects of the Revolution's value-system that ideology is certain to remain paramount in at least that aspect of foreign policy.

"IDEOLOGICAL PRAGMATISM" IN FOREIGN POLICY

U.S.-Cuban relations highlight that Cuba's foreign policy seeks noncon-flictive and potentially advantageous relationships with neighbors, allies, and powers, despite ideological disagreements, but that, when pragma-tism is impossible, Cuba stresses the ideological roots and purpose of that policy. However, where Cuba differs from other countries is in the constraints (as well as the possibilities and means available) under which foreign policy is designed and implemented.

First, Cuba's position as a small, dependent, sugar-exporting, and underdeveloped economy has given it much less leeway than developed nations. Cuba trades to survive and cannot afford to damage trading relationships. While there have been periods when this imperative has not dominated, they have been short-lived. Second, Cuba's unusual geo-political location in the Cold War allowed it both less space and more space for maneuver. While U.S. policy-makers perceived Cuba as a threat to its Latin American interests, Cuba was obliged to use the Soviet link as a deterrent to U.S. intervention. However, not only did the 1962 agree-ment allow Cuba more space within the region, but, as long as Cuba has not seriously threatened to undermine U.S. interests, it has enjoyed a relative freedom to operate.

Hence, although Cuba's Angolan involvement might not have won initial Soviet approval, Cuba's successes (and popularity across the developing world as a result) brought advantages to Moscow. What began as a foreign-policy action that unquestionably followed the leaders' ideological preferences (active solidarity with the anticolonial struggle, however costly) soon brought practical advantages to Havana, in forcing the Soviet Union's hand and also in creating a deep reservoir of international support and sympathy. Although some speculated that the whole involvement was driven by the search for Angolan oil, it now seems it was after all wholly ideological in its motivation.

However, when, after 1979, Castro attempted to persuade Moscow to support both the Nicaraguan and Grenadian revolutions, Moscow remained unconvinced about the costs of new commitments in the agreed U.S. "sphere of influence." Cuba, therefore, continued to pursue its own ideological agenda alone, supporting both governments (curiously advising caution and moderation), albeit giving Washington a pretext to justify intervention, confirming Soviet fears and the limits of Cuban action.

Those Cuban involvements were, however, part of the wider policy of internationalism, which became the mainstay of Cuba's foreign policy for the next fifteen years, allowing Cuba to parallel the oil-producing nations' capacity to act externally beyond their objective limits, in Cuba's case based not on oil but rather human capital. Indeed, the high levels of skill and commitment of the "internationalists" became an invaluable resource in which to trade diplomatically, winning hearts and minds abroad and eventually paying dividends in terms of UN support and diplomatic recognition, as well as domestic loyalty and ideological commitment.

However, the one essential factor that has defined Cuban foreign policy has been the highly pragmatic priority given to the protection and continuation of the Revolution. While this has occasionally meant a willingness to seek extreme means to achieve that end (such as the Soviet link or accepting post-1992 reforms), this objective has not necessarily been pursued at all costs, but rather within the parameters set by what is acceptable ideologically. In other words, the pragmatic has always been constrained by the ideological, generally ensuring that the means adopted do not conflict with what are deemed the fundamentals of its ideology.

Therefore, the key to determining foreign policy has often been the balance between what is possible and what is desirable, as well as the balance between those internal forces arguing about and shaping that policy. During the Cold War, the possible was both necessarily constrained and curiously permissive, allowing protection and a remarkable leeway to negotiate a space free from Soviet dictates and allowing leverage between the two superpowers that was possible only while the Soviet Union needed Cuba's sugar and the Revolution's survival. Therefore, since

Cuba's need for the Soviet Union was greatest between 1960 and 1962 (given the U.S. withdrawal and threat), Cuban foreign policy between 1962 and at least 1986 was actually able to balance the possible and the desirable comfortably. After 1990, however, that space closed dramatically, returning Cuba to the pre-1962 position of vulnerability and forcing it to develop policies that pursued what was deemed best for Cuba (and thus for the Revolution) on both a matter of principle and on the grounds of feasibility.

The result has been that the obvious has not necessarily or always been what is seems. For example, Castro's apparently pragmatic support in 1968 for the Warsaw Pact invasion of Czechoslovakia arose from ideological and not nakedly pragmatic motives, since Castro saw Dubcek's talk of leaving the Warsaw Pact as an even more serious and reprehensible betrayal of a front (against imperialism) than Moscow's much-criticized abandonment of its world responsibilities to socialism. Hence, ideology clearly overrode pragmatism. Similarly, Castro's 1973 description of the USSR as the Third World's "natural ally" (at the Non-Aligned Movement's Algiers summit), pushed many to assume an abandonment of revolutionary idealism and the acceptance of a role in support of Soviet policy. Yet, a more accurate reading would be that Cuba's leaders were not so much abandoning their commitment to revolution as making a practical judgment about the poor prospects for revolution in Latin America in the 1970s, and the decision was less to do with Soviet links than with Latin America, as became clearer following Cuba's support for leftist and even revolutionary governments in both Africa and the Anglophone Caribbean, and by1979, Nicaragua.

These examples highlight that ideology in Cuba has often had less to do with conventional readings of Marxism than with the basic principle of the defense of the Revolution and, through that, of national sovereignty—the essence of cubanía. The Revolution's roots in a radicalized nationalism made that defense of Cuba a foregone conclusion for any subsequent ideology, with the early years adding a revolutionary dimension in the redefinition of the nation (to include a population empowered through participation, equality, and social justice) and in an ethical commitment to revolution outside Cuba. What really mattered, however, was Cuba, and, increasingly, the Revolution—gradually taken to mean one and the same thing. In other words, Cuban foreign policy was less about making "the world safe for revolution"[9] than making it safe for "the Revolution." While the Soviet relationship was alive and functioning, the safety of the Revolution was guaranteed. However, after 1990, nation-building became even more urgent as a collective task of rebuilding following the collapse of the Soviet Union.

CUBA AND THE PINK TIDE

However, the emergence of the "Pink Tide" of center-left governments throughout Latin America in the new millennium created a totally new external context, reopening possibilities abroad that few Cubans thought likely in the "special period" of 1989–1994. With the election of Hugo Chávez in late 1998, the prospect of an economically benevolent and ideologically supportive regional context began to arise, something that no Cuban policy-makers had envisaged in 1990. When this was followed by the seemingly relentless rise of other center-left and socialist governments (Brazil, Argentina, Uruguay, Chile, Panama, Paraguay, for the former, and Bolivia, Ecuador, Nicaragua, and, most recently, El Salvador, for the latter) the possibility of regional solidarity and support for Cuba became a reality. As a result, the dominance of simple pragmatism over ideology that had characterized the post-1990 years was replaced by a greater fusion of the two, returning Cuba to pre-1989 patterns of behavior, and, in the process, relating Cuban nationalism to this "continentalism," in the form of José Martí's concept of "Nuestra America" and *nuestramericanismo*.

Indeed, in 2004, with the Cuban-Venezuelan agreement to create ALBA (the Alternativa Bolivariana para los Pueblos de Nuestra América), ideology seemed to marry pragmatism in the most explicit way. However, this marriage is perhaps not quite as clear as it seems, as few Cuban politicians seem ready yet to place their faith in the practical possibilities of a broadened ALBA. While they seem ready to commit to ALBA in political terms, and to develop schemes that use Cuba's human resources (especially teachers and doctors) in both a pragmatic and ideological sense, and that bring Cuba some trade advantages, few Cuban leaders view ALBA as offering long-term solutions. Indeed, it is the Venezuelan exchange (of oil for internationalist aid) that offers the most concrete fusion between the practical and the ideological, and, while ALBA seeks to generalize this pattern of exchange wherever possible, few current or potential ALBA members can offer Cuba what Venezuela can. Hence, Cuba's commitment to ALBA once again reflects ideology being played out in the most practical way. In the post-1990 search for a new protective carapace, a new balance might just have been found, sufficient to last for a few years until other changes in Cuba can find a firmer economic footing.

CONCLUSIONS

Where then does this leave the Cuban case? As exceptional, unexceptional, or simply unusual at times? What is clear is that the balance between the evidently ideological and the evidently pragmatic has changed substantially over the Revolution's 50 years, reflecting shifting internal debates, pressures, and imperatives, changing external contexts that changed the means available to Cuba, and evolving aims and purposes. As we have seen, in the 1962–1989 period, political proximity to the Soviet Union, combined with Cuba's unusual position in the geopolitics of the Cold War, allowed Cuba's leaders a remarkable freedom to be both ideological and pragmatic; pragmatism and ideology determined economic and political alliances, but those alliances in turn allowed an overtly ideological foreign policy in the region, although generally with a clear pragmatic purpose and dimension.

From 1990, however, that freedom disappeared, and the priority of political and economic survival dictated a more explicitly pragmatic orientation. Pragmatism thus dominated the post–Cold War period even though from the late 1990s political shifts toward the Left in the region did create new options and a greater space for the return of ideological positions. Indeed, the rise of the "Pink Tide" and ALBA have allowed again a degree of freedom for Cuba's foreign policy to be ideological while acting pragmatically—witnessed above all in the mutually beneficial exchange with Venezuela.

However, what this exposition has revealed is that, beyond the obvious (of labels, alliances and public rhetoric), the whole history of the Revolution's foreign policy has been one of a more subtle interplay between two different motivations and two different directions, encapsulated in the alternative answers to the two questions: "Why?" and "Towards what?" While, at times, the pragmatic (what is possible) has determined the extent of the ideological (what is desirable), for much of the time the pragmatic has been constrained by the limits posed by the ideological. That is to say the overriding relationship has been that the possible may be pursued, as long as it does not fundamentally contradict the desirable (the ideological bases of the Revolution).

What this analysis has also demonstrated is that the balance between pragmatism and ideology has been further complicated by the shifting meanings of "ideology" in Cuba. As we have seen, at certain times ideology has meant either cubanía, socialism, or Communism (and, more often, a combination of any of these), but more importantly it has consistently and increasingly been equated with the Revolution. Indeed, as the pressures of the 1990s (tightened embargo, economic collapse, the forces of rampant globalization) increasingly constrained all action, the priority of defending the Revolution (i.e., the ideological) became paramount, allowing policy-makers to experiment with the most pragmatic of solutions for the most ideological of purposes—an explicit willingness to use means toward a desired end. Equally, the pursuit of an international identity and a global context in which to exist (a characteristic of various periods, as we have seen) has been both ideological and pragmatic.

Given the reality of Cuba's status as a small, developing economy based on either sugar or tourism, the international environment has played a significant role in shaping the subtle relationship between ideology and pragmatism. Cuba's freedom of action has been shaped predominantly by the Cold War (and above all U.S. hostility), as well as the rise of the "Third World" and something of a "South" consensus. Hence, with the end of the Cold War, Cuba curiously lost both its constraining parameters and its freedom of action, while the rise of a more actively hostile United States saw a new environment emerge, which, while limiting Cuba's economic freedom abroad, did give Cuban foreign-policy justification for a clearly ideological direction, in the form of both a historically legitimate nationalist resistance to U.S. hegemony and leadership of a perceived wider popular resistance to globalization. Thus, although the collapse of the Soviet Union changed things fundamentally for the Revolution, it did not necessarily change the delicate balance between the pragmatic and the ideological in foreign policy that seemed so much a part of the old patterns. In other words, Cuba may still be more of an exception than it seems or than one might expect.

NOTES

1. See Llerena, M. (1978), *The unsuspected revolution. The birth and rise of Castroism,* Ithaca, NY: Cornell University Press.
2. The Communists had long been an influential part of Cuban political culture, with thousands of members, substantial electoral support, two government ministers (1942–1944), a national newspaper (*Noticias de Hoy*) and radio station (*Diez Mil*), and a history of leading union activism, from the late 1930s through the Confederación de Trabajadores de Cuba (CTC).
3. See Kapcia, A. (2000), *Cuba. Island of dreams,* Oxford: Berg Publishers.
4. See Erisman, M. H. (1985), *Cuba's international relations: the anatomy of a nationalistic foreign policy,* Boulder, CO: Westview.
5. Otherwise known as the Council for Mutual Economic Assistance, CMEA.
6. This was in fact a Cuban (and not Soviet) response to the newly governing MPLA's request for military aid to repel a South African invasion. Cuba's immediate response was to send troops in a somewhat ramshackle operation (Operation Carlota), until Cuban persuasion obliged Moscow to begin supporting the operation logistically, allowing over 40,000 Cubans to be deployed at any one time.

7. In this process, the contribution of Casa de las Américas from early 1959 was fundamental, opening Cuban eyes and adding cultural depth to the new revolutionary activism.
8. Anderson, J. L. (1997), *Che Guevara. A revolutionary life,* London: Bantam, pp. 531–94.
9. See Dominguez, J. I. (1989), *To make a world safe for revolution. Cuba's foreign policy,* Cambridge, MA: Harvard University Press.

CHAPTER 11

NICARAGUA'S PRAGMATIC IDEOLOGUES

DAVID CLOSE

INTRODUCTION

Since 1979 the governments of Nicaragua have had clear ideological predispositions. When the Sandinistas (FSLN, Sandinista National Liberation Front) govern they tend toward the radical left, as witnessed between 1979 and 1990 and from 2006 until the present. During the intervening period, with the rightist administrations of UNO (National Union of the Opposition, 1990–1996) and the PLC (Constitutional Liberal Party, 1996–2006) in power, the tilt is toward the free-market right. In each case, ideological motives are clearly visible in domestic and foreign affairs, but generally more clearly on the domestic side. In foreign affairs Nicaraguan governments have been pragmatic ideologues.

This chapter examines the foreign policy of both the Sandinista and the conservative periods. It argues that since 1979 Nicaraguan governments generally have been pragmatists in international affairs. This does not mean that their programmatic or ideological preferences have played no part. Rather it suggests that the influence of ideological schemes on foreign policy in Nicaragua has been muted by the realities of being a weak state and the need to meet the demands of domestic politics. This latter point is particularly clear in the works of Carlos Escudé, Mohammed Ayoob, and JoAnn Fagot Aviel, which are discussed below.

Nevertheless, there are exceptions and these come less from the revolutionary government (1979–1990) or the first rightist administration

(1990–1996) than from the last conservative government (2001–2006) and the current Sandinista administration (2006–present). This is surprising because the current president, the FSLN's Daniel Ortega, was also president from 1984 to 1990, when a more pragmatic view predominated.

FRAMEWORK

The starting point for an analysis of Nicaragua's foreign policy is remembering that foreign policy is public policy. The same government that decides if it is better to spend more on health or raise lifetime capital gains exemptions also defines the state's national interest in world affairs. Thus it is misleading to separate state and governmental interests, because the government decides what is good for the state. Most governments claim to act pragmatically, in accord with the facts. However, most are also guided by some vision of what a good society would be; they are ideologues. Ideally, a government will steer a middle course. It will have principles but not be obsessed with them and will be flexible in the pursuit of those values without becoming opportunistic and rudderless. However, that is just the start.

Sometimes we forget that if there is a general consensus within the political elite, those few men and women who truly influence what a nation does,[1] changes in government need not produce stark changes in policy. Thus the state will appear to be governed pragmatically. When, however, the political elite is divided and there is little or no consensus on what should be done, a new party in office may tend to make dramatic changes that clearly reflect its values. This state appears to act ideologically.

Nicaraguan politics are polarized. Except for three decades in the late nineteenth century, the country has featured highly conflictive, two-party politics that leave little room for consensus. Even in the 1800s, this would occasionally spill over into foreign affairs. A new Liberal *caudillo* would strengthen ties with other Liberals in Central America, turning a cold shoulder to Conservative governments; and when the Conservatives returned they would undo what the Liberals had done. The Sandinista Revolution of 1979 made the ideological divide even starker, as a new two-party system, Sandinista v. Anti-Sandinista, emerged, but politics still revolved around two highly ideological, fiercely confrontational forces.

A further factor complicates determining to what extent Nicaraguan foreign policy may be pragmatic and/or ideological. Nicaragua has a weak state and the weak do what they must. This suggests pragmatism, though it might better be called resignation. However, weak states deal not just with stronger states but with each other, where they have more choices and base policies on different criteria. Further, weak states often align themselves with greater powers of their choice. The choice can reflect ideology (X shares our values) or pragmatism (Y gives us more for less), and should a state decide to diversify its links in order to lessen dependence on one country, as Nicaragua attempted to do in the 1980s, the mix of partners and protectors can reflect both ideological and pragmatic reasons. Nicaragua is a complex case.

Finally, there is the problem of knowing what pragmatic and ideological policies look like in practice. As defined in this collection, pragmatic politics value results over doctrine, while ideological politics tend to prioritize doctrine. As suggested above, what most call good policy has elements of both. One quick indicator of the balance between flexibility and doctrinarism is a foreign policy's pluralism.

This is more than maintaining diplomatic relations with states thought unacceptable (though it starts there). A pluralistic foreign policy sees a government doing business on a regular basis even with governments with whom it shares no philosophical affinity. On the other hand, an exclusionary or monistic foreign policy minimizes contact with states with uncongenial political profiles. These may be called rogues, pariahs, imperialists, or communists, according to the tastes of the government formulating the policy. Pursuing a pluralistic foreign policy does not imply approval of such states, only acceptance of the necessity of dealing with even unpleasant neighbors.

In seeking a way to conceptualize Nicaraguan foreign policy, the works of three analysts—Escudé, Ayoob, and Aviel—have special relevance, because all consider the effect of domestic political realities on the foreign affairs of a poor, weak state. Carlos Escudé of Argentina uses the concept of peripheral realism, which recognizes that power differences exist among states and that these influence behavior. As a result, a very few states, such as the United States since World War II, can set the rules; most have to follow the rules. Consequently, for peripheral states realism means avoiding conflict with great powers and defining the national interest in terms of development.[2] The concept helps explain why Nicaragua seeks privileged relations with a wealthier state, as this provides both a powerful interlocutor and a source of money for domestic projects.

Subaltern realism is associated with the Indian analyst, Mohammed Ayoob. The essence of this concept is that among weaker states, domestic concerns play a significant part in shaping international goals and postures. Ayoob thus stresses the interplay of domestic and international factors in explaining how the weak act in world affairs.[3] JoAnn Fagot Aviel puts the logic of Nicaraguan foreign policy this way: "Throughout its history, the primary goal of Nicaraguan foreign policy has been to obtain the resources the governing elite needed to remain in power."[4]

Accordingly, Nicaragua's foreign policy may be pragmatic or ideological and may search for opportunistic or principled outcomes, but it will always reflect domestic calculations. These may be based on the desire for development, the need to avoid conflict with more powerful states, seeking a powerful patron, or just to make sure that the government of the day is still the government tomorrow.

This chapter makes two points. First, as in many poor countries, domestic concerns shape Nicaraguan foreign policy to a substantial degree, whether that policy is made by a leftist or rightist administration. Second, it is the Sandinistas' revolutionary government of 1979–1990, that comes closer to the ideal of finding a middle way between the extremes of ideological obsession and pragmatic drift than the three conservative governments that followed them or the Sandinista administration elected in 2006. To make these points, this chapter analyses Nicaraguan politics and foreign policy, principally since 1979, in order to place Nicaragua's foreign policy among the four models presented in this collection.

NICARAGUAN FOREIGN POLICY 1979–2006

Although Nicaragua has never been a world power, its foreign affairs have always been complex. From independence in 1821 until 1893, the eastern half of the country was under British control. Between 1855 and 1858 all of Nicaragua was ruled by William Walker, a U.S. mercenary, who turned against those who had hired him to help them in one of the country's many civil wars. It took the combined forces of all the Central American states to finally expel Walker and restore Nicaraguan sovereignty. Then toward the end of the nineteenth century Managua's foreign policy centered on meddling in its neighbors' affairs and failing to convince Washington of the advantages of Nicaragua's trans-isthmian canal route.

The arrival of the twentieth century did not change Nicaragua's luck in foreign affairs very much. A 1909 rebellion, backed by the United States, brought the insurgents victory but also sparked a civil war. As a result, U.S. Marines were dispatched to Nicaragua in 1912, remaining until 1925. When their withdrawal sparked renewed conflict, the Marines returned, leaving only in 1933, after establishing the National Guard. The rise to power of Anastasio Somoza García in 1936 saw the United States gain an ally whom President Franklin Roosevelt called "our son-of-a-bitch."

In 1961, Somoza's son Luís, who had become president after his father was assassinated in 1956, let the United States use Nicaraguan airfields to launch the B-26s that were supposed to support the Bay of Pigs invasion. For its part, Washington stood by the Somozas until the family dynasty was toppled by the Sandinista Revolution in 1979.

Two patterns that persist into the present took shape the country's first 150 years as an international actor. First, Nicaragua's foreign affairs are more complicated than one might expect from a small, poor, peripheral state. Second, starting in 1909 the country has sought a special relation with a stronger partner. These traits do not make Nicaragua unique but are useful analytical benchmarks.

THE REVOLUTIONARY GOVERNMENT (1979–1990)

Nicaragua's relations with the world changed radically on July 19, 1979.[5] After being a close and reliable ally of the United States for seven decades Managua became a major source of concern for Washington. Obviously, the new revolutionary government needed a friend and the Soviet Union was the only state with the resources and disposition to help a young, semi-Marxist, revolutionary government find its feet. Yet we should not forget the coalition of states that supported the Sandinistas in their revolutionary struggle. Certainly Cuba was there but so were Costa Rica, under both social democratic and Christian democratic governments; Venezuela, under its social democrats; and Panama, under a populist strongman. And there were the many Sandinista support groups who met in church basements throughout the United States. Even before coming to power, then, the FSLN was developing a pragmatic foreign policy.

However, the Sandinista revolutionary government was in power during the last decade of the Cold War. Thus it found itself forced to take sides; and there was not much evidence that it wanted to steer a middle course. The FSLN's rhetoric of building socialism made it an anathema in Reagan's Washington. Moreover, the government's repeated references to protecting Nicaragua's sovereignty were a thinly disguised way of saying that Managua would chart its own course, no matter what. The trick was to challenge the U.S. government without provoking its ire. In this the revolutionaries failed. Viewed from this angle, the FSLN pursued an ideologically driven foreign policy that brought them into conflict with the United States.

Perhaps things would have been different if Jimmy Carter had been reelected in 1980. His administration had stressed human rights and struck a deal to turn the Panama Canal over to the Panamanians, so some accommodation with the Nicaraguan revolutionaries was not unimaginable. However, it was Ronald Reagan who won the White House in 1980, bringing with him the most resolutely anti-Communist foreign policy the United States had seen since the 1950s. More importantly for Nicaragua, President Reagan also came to office with the same taste for intervention that had characterized Washington's foreign policy in that period.

From this came the Contra (counterrevolutionary) War that raged in Nicaragua from 1981 until the Sandinistas left office in 1990, a bloody conflict that cost the lives of some 30,000 Nicaraguans, military and civilian. A natural consequence of the war was a shifting of national priorities to defense, which in turn demanded supplies of military materiel. The only source of arms easily open to the Sandinistas was the Communist Bloc and although aid and advisors came from throughout the Soviet Bloc, Havana and Moscow played the most significant roles.

Besides the war, Washington also squeezed Managua with an economic embargo from 1985 onward and pressured its allies to cut aid to the Sandinista state. Although Spain continued its assistance and Canada assumed an increasingly important role, the embargo made Nicaragua increasingly dependent on the Soviet Bloc for aid. Thus the revolutionary government's search for socialist partners and patrons should be seen as only partly voluntary and ideological. The alternative for the Sandinistas was, as President Reagan said, to "say 'uncle'," abandon power and leave the scene.

To see clearer evidence of the mix of ideologically driven and pragmatically oriented foreign policy, it is necessary to examine how Nicaragua got on with its Latin American neighbors between 1979 and 1990, focusing on two cases in particular. One of these is the FSLN's support of the FMLN (Marti National Liberation Front), which waged its own guerrilla insurgency in El Salvador throughout the 1980s. It is impossible to imagine the Sandinistas not supporting the FMLN, both materially and politically, even though this support gave Washington a pretext for launching the Contras.

The other dated from 1928 when Nicaragua ceded the Caribbean islands of San Andres and Providencia to Colombia, under pressure from the United States, which then had troops occupying Nicaragua. The issue lay quiet until 1978 when Nicaragua declared a 200-mile Exclusive Economic Zone (EEZ), which overlapped Colombian claims in the Caribbean. Then in February 1980, the revolutionary government—at that moment the JGRN (Governing Junta of National Reconstruction), which included Daniel Ortega—declared the 1928 cession null and void, and asked for the return of the islands. While this was partly a nationalistic gesture, it was also a practical attempt to secure control of a large maritime territory, and hence the right to exploit whatever resources might be found there.[6]

The most important diplomatic initiative of the revolutionary government dealt with seeking an end to the counterrevolutionary war. Throughout the 1980s civil wars–cum–guerrilla insurgencies raged not only in Nicaragua, but in El Salvador and Guatemala, as well. These wars involved some other states directly, Honduras in particular but also Costa Rica, and undermined stability and prosperity in the entire region. Faced with this crisis, the six nations of the isthmus, the five mentioned above plus Panama, began working among themselves to find a road to peace. The process evolved through a series of steps. Between 1983 and 1985, it was the Contadora Process, then in 1986 it became the Esquipulas Process and then finally in February 1987, President Oscar Arias of Costa Rica proposed a peace plan, which became the Esquipulas II Accord.[7]

Nicaragua's role in the process was critical, because it had to comply fully with the Accord's provisions. These included establishing a reconciliation commission, the termination of hostilities (the FSLN declared a unilateral ceasefire, which it had to abrogate in the face of heightened Contra action), democratization, free elections, halting assistance to irregular forces, and aiding refugees. Managua had the hardest part because the U.S. government refused to recognize the 1984 electoral victory of Daniel Ortega and supported the Contras' intransigence, thus complicating the Sandinistas' attempts to comply with the treaty. In the end, the Nicaraguan government did get agreement from its civil opposition, which permitted elections to be held. Although the FSLN lost badly at the polls (54 to 41 percent in the presidential contest), peace was finally at hand.

In retrospect, the foreign policy of the first Sandinista administration blended ideological and pragmatic elements. The ideological parts were plainest and involved the replacement of Washington by the Soviet Bloc as Nicaragua's foreign benefactor and protector. The revolution needed foreign support to survive and it sought this from the socialist superpower. If allying with like-minded states is ideological, then the first Sandinista government was ideological. However, if tailoring foreign policy in an attempt to guarantee the survival of a regime is pragmatic, the Sandinistas were pragmatists.

Discerning the balance between these pragmatic and ideological tendencies would be an interesting intellectual parlor game had the Sandinistas remained in opposition. However, they are not only back in power but they are still led by Daniel Ortega. Moreover, the practice of the first Sandinista government provides a useful background for viewing the policies of 16 years of conservative administrations.

THE ADMINISTRATIONS OF THE RIGHT

From 1990 to 2006 Nicaragua had three right-of-centre presidents: Violeta Chamorro,[8] 1990–1996; Arnoldo Alemán, 1996–2001; and Enrique Bolaños, 2001–2006. In some ways they were very different. Chamorro was politically weak and sought a nonconflictive foreign policy, Alemán's administration was politically powerful but his foreign relations were often confrontational and Bolaños combined political weakness with an ideologically provocative foreign policy. On the other hand, all rejected most of the Sandinista revolution, though Chamorro less so than her successors, and all three shared a commitment to neoliberal capitalism and their administrations embraced structural adjustment. In part, this reflected ideological preferences, although they also had three compelling practical reasons for signing on, forming closer relations with the International Monetary Fund (IMF) and World Bank.

First, the FSLN had already initiated a harsh austerity program in 1988 without any outside support—no concessional loans, just fewer and worse public services. Second, Nicaragua's economy was a wreck in 1990: five-digit inflation, high un- and underemployment and a real per capita income lower than before the revolution. Action was needed and any help was gratefully accepted. Finally, during the 1990s participation in a structural adjustment program signaled the government's good intentions to investors and donors. As there were no alternate sources of assistance that thought such a guarantee unnecessary, structural adjustment programs were really the only choice for a country like Nicaragua. The weak, after all, do what they must.

Another priority for the right in 1990 was returning Nicaragua to Washington's sphere of influence. Perhaps this was because no Nicaraguan leader could imagine the country without a powerful protector or it may have reflected gratitude for Washington's part in undermining the Sandinistas. In any case, President Chamorro restored the country's close ties with Washington, even though Washington lost interest in Nicaragua once the FSLN had been removed from power. President Alemán's ties with the United States were strained, because his behavior severely undermined U.S.-sponsored anticorruption programs. President Bolaños then restored good relations with the United States, but undermined his own presidency by doing so.

As the foregoing suggest, the differences among the three governments are more revealing than the common ground. To illustrate the most striking difference requires looking at each briefly.

THE CHAMORRO ADMINISTRATION

President Violeta Chamorro should have had an easy time managing Nicaragua's foreign relations. Unfortunately, being restored to the State Department's good graces was not enough to save the new administration from a rough ride. First, Nicaragua fell into a series of disputes with Washington, principally over the continuing presence of Sandinistas in certain government positions. Then Managua had to deal with multilateral lenders, whose conditions it could sometimes not meet, which produced delays in the disbursement of much needed loans. Only relations with Nicaragua's Central American neighbors returned to normal.

A good example of how Washington pressured the Chamorro administration concerned who would lead Nicaragua's army.[9] The Nicaraguan army inherited by Chamorro was the Sandinista Peoples' Army, the guerrilla force that the Sandinistas had transformed into a regular army. Although the armed forces successfully evolved into a professional, nonpartisan military, changing its name to the Army of Nicaragua in 1995, the most conservative wing of Chamorro's National Union of the Opposition (UNO) was joined by Washington in demanding the removal of the military's top commander, General Humberto Ortega, one of the nine Sandinista commanders of the revolution and the brother of Daniel Ortega. Chamorro did eventually dismiss General Ortega, but only in 1995, well after the initial furor had settled.

Chamorro acted pragmatically in her handling of this issue. Had she ceded to Washington's pressures, something a right-wing ideologue might have done, she could well have lost control over her nation's armed forces and provoked a coup. Here pragmatism in foreign affairs mirrored pragmatism in domestic affairs. Some of what Chamorro did, notably aligning again with the West, reflected her administration's ideological bent. However, she also acted in ways that reflected different values, most notably voting with the nonaligned bloc in the United Nations. The latter reflected Chamorro's dependence on Sandinista support to get her policies passed and was a pragmatic adjustment to domestic realities.

THE ALEMÁN ADMINISTRATION

Arnoldo Alemán was a political realist with an instinctive understanding of power and its use. In foreign policy this took two forms. One was to continue the foreign economic policy begun by President Chamorro. Although Alemán also had problems meeting the requirements of structural adjustment programs, he did steer Nicaragua into the HIPC

(Heavily Indebted Poor Countries) initiative, which permitted the nation to greatly reduce its foreign indebtedness.[10] Where he broke ranks with Chamorro was in his relations with neighboring states and even Washington.[11]

In dealing with neighbors Alemán did not shy away from conflict. His administration had diplomatic scrapes with Costa Rica over the Rio San Juan boundary and Honduras and Colombia over maritime boundaries in the Caribbean. The issues were straightforward but Alemán's responses were not. The Rio San Juan issue arose from Costa Rica's violation of accords governing the use of the river for its police patrols,[12] an issue that should have been a technical matter, resolvable through normal diplomatic channels, but the president transformed it into a grave international incident, perhaps to deflect attention from a growing corruption crisis. Much the same was true of the maritime dispute. When Tegucigalpa rejected Nicaragua's request to delay acting on the boundary until an appeal to the World Court was heard, Alemán imposed a 35 percent tariff on all Honduran goods entering Nicaragua and threatened to break diplomatic relations. Although the issue was of primary importance to Managua, Alemán's response was intemperate.

Alemán's dealings with aid donors were similarly testy. In relations with Washington and the international financial institutions (IFI) that funded Nicaragua's structural adjustment programs, Alemán (as the only alternative the United States had to the Sandinistas) was able to resist complying with requests from the State Department, International Monetary Fund, and World Bank for greater transparency in how their money was being spent. Other aid donors, private and official, complained of funds being diverted away from localities not governed by Alemán's Constitutional Liberal Party. And, most controversially, the president proposed taxing relief supplies sent in the wake of Hurricane Mitch in 1998, a position he later abandoned.[13] Although President Alemán acted pragmatically in defense of his domestic political interests, he did so in ways that provoked international conflict.

THE BOLAÑOS ADMINISTRATION

Enrique Bolaños was a hard-headed businessman and foreign-policy ideologue. On taking office in January 2002, he spoke of a new era in Nicaraguan foreign policy that would "convert the country into a clear political ally—serious, reliable and consistent—of the world's democratic nations in the fight against terrorism, drug trafficking and money laundering";[14] strong language but hardly exceptional four months after 9/11. Clearer evidence of ideological commitment was making

Nicaragua one of the 30-member Coalition of the Willing in the war in Iraq. Nicaraguan troops totaling 115, including sappers engaged in mine clearance operations, were committed to Iraq in 2003, but came home in February 2004, apparently due to lack of funds.[15]

It would be tempting to place the ratification of DR-CAFTA, the free trade agreement between the United States and five Central American states (Costa Rica, El Salvador, Guatemala, Honduras, and Nicaragua), plus the Dominican Republic, during Bolaños's mandate in the ideological column, too. Approved in October 2005 in a 49-37 vote that split the National Assembly along party lines, with the FSLN against and the parties of the right in favor, DR-CAFTA clearly brought Nicaragua even more fully into the neoliberal orbit. However, viewed practically, Nicaragua could hardly let its neighbors have tariff-free access to U.S. markets while it did not.

Bolaños was equally driven by principles in domestic affairs. Despite having been Alemán's vice-president and leading the PLC to power in 2001, his first big decision was to prosecute Arnoldo Alemán for corruption and see his former boss receive a 20-year sentence. This understandably cost him the support of the Liberals, resulting in Bolaños, like Chamorro before him, being forced to rely on Sandinista votes to govern. However, in 2003 Bolaños bowed to the U.S. secretary of state Colin Powell's pressure to break with Ortega.[16] Unsurprisingly, by 2005 the FSLN had turned against the president, seeking to force him from office. Since it took Washington's threat to suspend aid to Nicaragua to save Bolaños's presidency,[17] it is reasonable to suggest that his alignment with Washington paid off.

THE SECOND ORTEGA ADMINISTRATION

Between 1979 and 2006 several trends emerged. Nicaragua had governments with clear ideological identities. These influenced their foreign policies mostly in terms of defining like-minded states as their allies. Otherwise, domestic concerns—mainly development and preserving power—shaped foreign-policy agendas. There were, though, two outliers: Bolaños, who had an overtly ideological foreign policy, and Alemán who used foreign policy as a domestic political tool. In 2006, Daniel Ortega, who had been president from 1984 to 1990, returned to power, after 16 years and three failed attempts to retake the presidency.

Ortega's 2006 campaign stressed the theme of reconciliation and included the international sphere along with the domestic. In particular, it seemed that he would maintain good relations with the United States.[18] These expectations suffered a setback after Ortega's inauguration, as he emphasized ties with Hugo Chávez, Venezuela's president and one of Washington's most strident critics, as well as reaching out to Iran and Libya. Yet he also shunned Beijing, establishing diplomatic relations with Taiwan, doubtless because Taipei offered more material benefits than did the People's Republic of China. Ortega was acting like a good Nicaraguan leader and was being a pragmatic ideologue.

The ideological side of Managua's relations with Venezuela (and the other so-called Bolivarian states, Bolivia and Ecuador), Iran, and Libya is self-evident. It is almost as if Daniel was recreating a 1980s anti-imperialist alliance. And it is certainly true that associating with these states and their leaders will remind everyone of Ortega's revolutionary credentials. However, Venezuela promised massive aid, announced as US$385 million,[19] while Iran pledged US$350 million.[20] One estimate suggests that the money available from just one of several cooperation agreements with Venezuela "almost equals the total western foreign aid that Nicaragua gets in a year."[21] This lets Ortega finance a series of expensive social programs and thus appears remarkably pragmatic.

Nicaragua's membership of ALBA, the Bolivarian Alternative for Latin America and the Caribbean, which is Chávez's response to the Free Trade for the America's initiative sponsored by the United States, is also best seen as another decision that straddles the ideological-pragmatic divide. ALBA offers real economic benefits to its members in the form of technical assistance, liberalized trade, and privileged access to Venezuelan oil. Had Ortega withdrawn Nicaragua from DR-CAFTA and cast his nation's lot fully with Venezuela, Cuba, Bolivia, Dominica, and (temporarily) Honduras, it would have been an unmistakably ideological decision, for it would have turned Nicaragua's back on the U.S. economy. However, Ortega's decision to remain in DR-CAFTA, thus keeping a foot in both the radical and conservative economic camps, would suggest a sage pragmatism.

More plausible examples of ideology driving foreign policy were the Sandinista government's attacks on donor states, alleging that they sought to subvert the Ortega government. These began in August 2008 when the vice-minister of foreign affairs branded Swedish ambassador Eva Zetterberg "a devil"[22] for voicing concerns on television about "authoritarian signals" from the government, after two small parties lost the right to run in upcoming municipal elections. Then in October the administration charged "certain ambassadors" from countries of the European Union with "lending themselves to the political maneuvers of opposition parties to destabilize and overthrow the Ortega government."[23] Ortega's government also claimed that Oxfam UK was engaged in money laundering, along with two Nicaraguan institutions that were critical of the government.[24] Although squabbles with civil society groups is nothing new in Nicaragua, (the Alemán administration did it too) naming a British NGO suggested that the Ortega administration felt that Oxfam UK had overstepped its boundaries and impinged on Nicaraguan's sovereignty, just as Ambassador Zetterberg allegedly had.

Things got worse. The results of the 2008 municipal elections were rejected as fraudulent by the FSLN's opponents, leading to confrontations in which Sandinista supporters used violence. As a consequence, in 2008 the Budgetary Support Group (GAP[25]) withdrew the US$53.8 million it had originally committed to Nicaragua's budget.[26] Later, in 2009, the United States stopped disbursing Millennium Challenge Corporation funds to Nicaragua. Ortega first charged the EU and the United States with colonialism[27] and then called for donors to give Nicaragua money unconditionally.[28] Finally, the good relations that the Sandinista administration had maintained with Washington deteriorated, and in March 2010 the FSLN city councilors of León, Nicaragua's second largest city, declared the U.S. ambassador Robert Callahan persona non grata.[29]

It was Venezuelan money[30] that allowed Ortega to confront Nicaragua's donors. However, it would be a mistake to see the president's behavior as driven solely by ideology. He may have been telling his domestic opponents that foreign pressure would not make him renounce his allegedly ill-gained electoral victories of 2008. Ortega's decision to confront his country's foreign donors may thus have a pragmatic side that lets him keep power.

Although these confrontational positions reflected a domestic political logic related to mid-term, municipal elections, they are better seen as principled actions in which President Ortega declares Nicaragua's independence from the western alliance. Evidence of this was found in Nicaragua's rapid recognition of South Ossetia and Abkhazia, the first country after Russia to do so. This second edition of Daniel Ortega is, like the first, both an anti-imperialist and an unabashed Nicaraguan nationalist. However, this one pursues a less constrained foreign policy.

CONCLUSIONS

There are four issues that stand out as a form of conclusion to the case of Nicaragua. First, the balance between pragmatism and ideology has changed since 2001, with ideology now being more prominent. Since one conservative administration (Bolaños) and one leftist administration (Ortega) have followed this path, one might hypothesize that the specific blend of ideological and pragmatic elements in Nicaraguan foreign policy is contingent on the president's preferences.

Second, two factors most significantly affect the mix of ideology and pragmatism. The first was signaled above: the personal preferences of the president. However, conjunctive political opportunities and the immediate exigencies of domestic politics are also influential, as exemplified in Ortega's decision to join ALBA but remain in DR-CAFTA.

Third, until 2001 it would have been fair to say that pragmatism moderated ideology. However, since then and especially in Daniel Ortega's second administration, ideology has colored pragmatism. Fourth, the increasing complexity and fragmentation of the international environment has not led to greater pragmatism. On the contrary, with Washington's attention fixed on southwest Asia and with Venezuela benefiting from higher oil prices, Daniel Ortega had the opportunity to indulge ideological proclivities that he had to sublimate during the 1980s. When the great power cat's away, it appears that the weak-state mice will play. This condition may well persist for a while longer, since the new Obama administration has its hands full with the economic crisis.

Finally, there is one other question raised by this survey of Nicaraguan foreign policy. Since 1909 Nicaraguan governments have had a great power patron or, as now, a well-off friend who can be counted on for support. For most of the last century the United States filled that role, although from 1979 to 1990 it fell to Moscow, with assistance from Havana. Now it appears to have passed to Caracas, with help from Teheran. Is this a declaration of adherence to ideology or a pragmatic decision to cultivate a rich and powerful friend?

NOTES

1. One work estimates the size of a country's political elite at under one-tenth of 1 percent of the population. See, Michael Burton, Richard Gunther, and John Higley, "Introduction: Elite Transformations and Democratic Regimes," 1–37, in *Elites and Democratic Consolidation in Latin America and Southern Europe*, ed. John Higley and Richard Gunther, Cambridge: Cambridge University Press, 1992.

2. Carlos Esucudé, "An Introduction to Peripheral Realism and Its Implications for the Interstate System: Argentina and the Condor II Missile Project," in *International Relations Theory and the Third World*, ed. Stephanie Neuman, New York; St. Martin's Press, 1998, 55–76.

3. Mohammed Ayoob, "Subaltern Realism: International Relations Theory Meets the Third World," in *International Relations Theory and the Third World*, ed. Stephanie Neuman, New York; St. Martin's Press, 1998, 31–54.

4. JoAnn Fagot Aviel, "Nicaragua: Foreign Policy in the Revolutionary and Post-revolutionary Era," in *Latin American and Caribbean Foreign Policy*, ed Frank O'Mora and Jeanne A. K. Hey, 46–62, Lanham, MD: Roman & Littlefield, 2003, 46.

5. Information for this section is drawn principally from Aviel.

6. In December 2007, the International Court of Justice ruled that San Andres, Providencia, and a third island, Santa Catalina, did belong to Colombia; but it left open the question of maritime boundaries. See "U.N. Court Awards San Andres Islands to Colombia over Nicaragua, Rule on Others," *International Herald Tribune*, December 13, 2007, /www.iht.com/articles/ap/2007/12/13/europe/EU-GEN-World-Court-Nicaragua-Colombia.php; accessed October 1, 2008.

7. Jack Child, *The Central American Peace Process: Sheathing Swords, Building Confidence*, Boulder: Lynne Rienner, 1992.

8. Her proper name is Violeta Barrios de Chamorro.

9. For details, see David Close, *Nicaragua: the Chamorro Years*, Boulder, CO: Lynne Rienner Publishers, 1999, 45–48; 76–77.

10. David R. Dye and David Close, "Patrimonialism and Economic Policy in the Aleman Administration," in *Undoing Democracy: The Politics of Electoral Caudillismo*, ed David Close and Kalowatie Deonandan, 119–41, Lanham, MD: Lexington Books, 2004.

11. The following material comes from David Close, "The Foreign Policy of the Aleman Administration: A Small Country in a Big World," presented to the XXIII Congress of the Latin American Studies Association, Washington, DC, September 2001.

12. The riparian boundary between Nicaragua and Costa Rica is not midway between the shores but is located at the Costa Rican shore.

13. Nicaragua Network, *Hurricane Mitch Alert, No.1*, November 2, 1998, www.nicanet.org; accessed November 4, 1998.

14. Quoted in Nitlapan-Envio Team, "Our Place in the World," *Envio*, 262, May 2003, www.envio.org.ni/articulo/2090; accessed November 1, 2008.

15. Nitlapan-Envio Team, "Back from Iraq," *Envio*, 272, March 2004, http://www.envio.org.ni/articulo/2154; accessed March 19, 2009.

16. Nitlapan-Envio Team, "The 'Powell Effect' on Three Political Forces," *Envio*, 268, November 2003, http://www.envio.org.ni/articulo/2129; accessed October 29, 2008.

17. BBC News, "Deal to End Crisis in Nicaragua," November 11, 2005; http://news.bbc.co.uk/2/hi/americas/4329688.stm; accessed November 1, 2008. In 2000, Aleman and Ortega signed the Pact, a deal between the two parties to turn Nicaragua's courts, electoral authority, and comptroller's office into partisan instruments. The Pact reduced executive accountability and gave the Sandinistas and Liberals effective control over much of Nicaraguan politics.

18. Joseph Contreras, "All Signs Suggest Chastened Sandinista Firebrand Will Embrace Moderation," *Newsweek*, December 25, 2006–January 1, 2007, www.msnbc.msn.com/id/16241591/site/newsweek; accessed December 28, 2006.

19. A list of projects is found in Tim Rogers, "Ortega Balances Venezuelan Aid, IMF," *Nica Times*, April 27–May 3, 2007, www.nicatimes.net; accessed May 7, 2007; the US$385 million figure was reported by

Alfonso Martinez, "la ayuda de Venezuela asciende a 385 millones de dólares," *La voz del sandinismo*, 30 de enero de 2008, www.lavozdelsandinismo.com/nicaragua/2008-01-30/la-ayuda-de-venezuela-a-nicaragua-asciende-a-385-millones-de-dolares/; accessed November 1, 2008.

20. "Irán invertirá 350 millones de dólares en Nicaragua," *Tribuna Latina*, 6 agosto 2007, www.tribunalatina.com/es/viewer.php?IDN=3774; accessed November 1, 2008. There are no figures on disbursements available.

21. Ricardo Castillo Argüello, "La economía política de los petrodólares," *Confidencial*, 606 (19 al 25 de octubre de 2008), 14 [1, 13–14].

22. Nicaragua Network, "Two Foreign Interventions Draw Angry Responses from Government," *NicaNet*, August 19, 2008, www.nicanet.org/?p=548; accessed August 24, 2008.

23. José Adáan Silva, "Cayó como bomba en Unión Europea," *El Nuevo Diario*, 31 de octubre de 2008, www.elnuevodiario.com.ni/nacionales/31153; accessed October 31, 2008.

24. Rory Carroll, "Oxfam Targeted as Nicaragua Attacks 'Trojan Horse' NGOs," *The Guardian*, October 14, 2008, www.guardian.co.uk/world/2008/oct/14/humanrights-voluntarysector; accessed October 14, 2008. The formal basis for the charge was that Oxfam sent part of its program funds to CINCO, a research centre, which then gave part of that money to an organization (the MAM, Movimiento Autónomo de Mujeres) that was not legally incorporated and should not have received funds from Oxfam. The case was dropped without explanation in 2009.

25. Whose members are Denmark, the European Union, Finland, Germany, the Netherlands, Sweden, Switzerland, and the United Kingdom.

26. Some sources set the amount at $US62 million.

27. Blake Schmidt, "Ortega Accuses US, Europe of Colonialism for Freezing Aid," *Nica Times*, December 12–18, 2008, www.nicatimes.net; accessed December 12, 2008.

28. Lourdes Arróliga, "Shinishi Saito, Embajador de Japón: No existe cooperación sin condiciones," *Confidencial*, 622 (del 22 a 28 de febrero de 2009), 1, 4–5.

29. Eddy López, "Callahan 'non grato' en León," *La Prensa*, 26 de marzo de 2010, http://www.laprensa.com.ni/2010/03/26/departamentos/20316; accessed March 26, 2010.

30. *La Prensa* reported that for the first six months of 2009, Venezuelan aid to Nicaragua reached $US283 million, up from $US212 million for the same period in 2008; see, "Millones de dólares le llueven a Ortega," *a Prensa*, de 4 de diciembre de 2009, www.laprensa.com.ni/2009/12/04/nacionales/9505: accessed December 4, 2009.

CHAPTER 12

MEXICO'S FOREIGN POLICY UNDER THE *PARTIDO ACCIÓN NACIONAL*: PROMOTING DEMOCRACY, HUMAN RIGHTS, AND INTERESTS

ANA COVARRUBIAS

INTRODUCTION

The dilemma as to whether foreign policy is—or should be—determined by ideology or pragmatic interests is particularly interesting in the Mexican case, since for decades, Mexico's authorities—and academics—argued that Mexican foreign policy was essentially guided by "principles."[1] One might discuss whether in defending principles, Mexico was pursuing its national interests or not, but the idea of the righteousness of a policy of principles was broadly accepted and rarely contested.[2] Implicit in this position was Mexico's view of how the international system ought to be, however pragmatic its policy actually was. Pragmatism only became a more frequent—and rather pejorative—label applied to foreign policy during the presidential period of Miguel de la Madrid (1982–1988), as the Mexican economy underwent liberalization, and later when Mexico negotiated and signed the North American Free Trade Agreement (NAFTA) under president Carlos Salinas de Gortari (1988–1994). However, it was during Vicente Fox's presidential term (2000–2006) that the debate about the nature and goals of Mexican foreign policy took precedence. Various reasons explain this shift: the post–Cold War international agenda, the ascent to power of the right wing Partido Acción Nacional (PAN), and the personalities of Vicente Fox and his two foreign-policy secretaries, Jorge G. Castañeda and Luis Ernesto Derbez. Having defeated a party (Partido Revolucionario Institucional—PRI) that had been in power for over 70 years, President Fox had to be seen to break with the past, to clearly mark democratic "regime change," and to govern in accordance with the PAN'S principles of human rights and social justice. In a world free from the ideological tensions of the Cold War, Mexico finally found the legitimacy and the willingness to openly join the main currents in international politics: free trade, democracy, and human rights. Jorge Castañeda and Luis Ernesto Derbez understood the importance of so doing, not only because that was an agenda consistent with PAN'S positions, but also because it contributed to Mexico's own democratic transition and consolidation.

This chapter identifies changes and continuities in Mexico's foreign policy since Vicente Fox assumed power in 2000, with reference to the complex relationship between ideology, principles, and pragmatism. I will argue that the inclusion of values such as the active *promotion* of democracy and human rights abroad was new in foreign policy and rather than answer to Mexican interests in the international arena, it responded to domestic policy considerations and the beliefs of Mexican leaders during the first PAN government. President Felipe Calderón (2006–present) has taken a more cautious and moderate approach as far as the promotion of democracy and human rights is concerned, despite rhetorical continuity. On the other hand, very pragmatically, Fox's government recognized the need for closer relations with the United States, an approach also taken by President Calderón, despite continuing tensions over some areas, especially immigration.

In retrospect, the PAN'S foreign policy attempted to place Mexico as an advocate of democratic and human rights. This was clearly one of the priorities of the Fox administration, intended not only for external actors but, equally, for domestic audiences. In response to immediate— and to a certain extent, unexpected—events Fox's and Calderón's policies also attempted to project the image of a responsible nation: by cooperating with the United States in security matters in the case of the former, and by attacking organized crime, domestically and internationally, in the case of the latter, between 2007 and 2010. In pursuing their interests, both administrations resorted to the so-called democratic bonus, capitalizing on the 2000 elections as democratic, legitimate, and transparent. Furthermore, the Calderón administration has opted for formal and direct collaboration with the United States to fight organized crime.

As far as agency and process is concerned, Vicente Fox, Jorge G. Castañeda, and Luis Ernesto Derbez were key actors in the design and implementation of foreign policy, and their perception of what Mexico was and should be after the elections of 2000 defined their foreign-policy objectives. However Mexico's political opening resulted as well in a wider range of actors, including Congress, political parties, and civil society organizations, discussing foreign-policy issues. Thus, despite the persistent role of the president in Mexico's political system, different voices influenced foreign policy during the Fox administration. Calderón, however, appears to have reinforced the role of the president, and to a lesser extent that of the Ministry of Foreign Affairs, in foreign-policy making.

The context surrounding the PAN'S foreign policy has clearly been crucial, especially in terms of the deep economic, political, and social transformations that have occurred in Mexico since at least the 1980s. Equally important, however, is the fact that foreign policy has been implemented in a post–Cold War world, in the era of the "war on terror" and of a profound economic and financial international crisis. The first PAN government tried to join a liberal, post–Cold War order that abruptly changed with the events of September 11, 2001. The "war on terror" and the economic and financial crisis placed important constraints on foreign policy, limiting room for maneuver and moving Mexico toward an inevitable pragmatism in terms of foreign relations.

This chapter illustrates how Fox's government initially attempted to favor ideology over pragmatism by designing a foreign policy based on the promotion of democracy and human rights foreign policy, but eventually consolidated a pragmatic view—not value free—toward the United States. After September 11, foreign policy seemed to be guided in reaction to external events, and to a lesser extent by domestic pressures. In the final analysis, ideology generally seems to have accompanied pragmatism in Fox's *sexenio*. Not being a priority, Calderón's foreign policy so far seems to be mostly reactive to external and domestic events, and the field in which pragmatism has clearly prevailed over ideology.

The chapter is divided into four sections: the first will briefly describe Fox's foreign-policy project; the second part will analyze the two key issues of immigration and security in Mexican-U.S. relations; in the third, the more "ideological" aspect of Mexico's foreign policy, that of democracy and human rights promotion, will be examined; and, last, Calderón's first three years will be analyzed.

SETTING THE AGENDA: THE FIRST PAN
GOVERNMENT'S FOREIGN-POLICY PROJECT

President Vicente Fox and his first secretary of foreign relations, Jorge G. Castañeda, pursued an unambiguous foreign-policy project that underlined the idea of change: According to Castañeda,

> Our purpose is to respond, congruently and with vision, to the national, regional and world transformations as well as to the mandate of change implicit in the electoral victory of Vicente Fox. We wish to ensure the protection and promotion of the country's interests in the contemporary world.[3]

In concrete terms, Castañeda sought to implement a strategic relationship with the United States, as well as actively participate in the construction of a new normative international system. Only by attending to these objectives would foreign policy become efficient and relevant to satisfy the real needs of the country.

With respect to relations with the United States, Castañeda rejected the suggestion that Mexico had no option but to acquiesce to the demands of its neighbor, remain inactive or resort to a rhetorical defense. Instead, proximity to the United States also provided Mexico with valuable opportunities to deepen relations in three areas.[4] First, he sought to establish key areas for relations, with immigration becoming the most important "new" issue in the bilateral relationship. Second, bilateral relations would have to incorporate different actors in addition to the president of each country. Castañeda sought to identify and work with key actors in U.S. public life: Congress, state governments, the media, trade unions, key businessmen, and NGO'S.

Third, Castañeda sought to formulate a conceptual framework for a long term relationship with the United States and Canada to shape a North American economic community. This was not a totally new idea; despite the acknowledgement of significant cultural differences between Mexico and its northern neighbors, some academics such as Robert Pastor had already discussed the advantages of creating a sense of community between Mexico, the United States, and Canada. According to Pastor, the United States and Canada would be able to contribute to Mexico's development by creating some sort of structural funds, and closing the development gap, which in turn would not only strengthen the economic power of the North American bloc, but would also increase security in the area by improving the standards of living of Mexicans.[5] Considering that Mexico had proven to be democratic, and that social and economic integration with the United States was deepening—regardless of any governmental efforts to encourage it or not—Fox proposed a "Nafta plus," a project that would require an "open border": the free movement of citizens across the border, as well as of goods and services.[6]

Active participation in the international system was Fox's second foreign-policy objective, with the specific aim of contributing to the design of new rules to match the rapidly changing international system. With a policy emphasis on issues including human rights, indigenous rights, trade, disarmament, democracy, and the environment, Castañeda noted the change in the post–Cold War environment toward these issues:

> Some would have preferred that the international system of the 21st Century, after the end of the Cold War, had rested on the principles of non-intervention, juridical equality of states or the opposition to the use of force. But in reality the international system does not rely on those principles; for better or worse the fact is that the new rules that are being devised are interventionist, rather than anti-interventionist, particular, rather than general and concrete rather than abstract.[7]

The process of normative change in the international system would take place with or without Mexico, and Mexico had to chose between participating or remaining isolated and letting others decide. Furthermore, any new rules devised would be applied to Mexico. Given Mexico's long tradition in International Law codification,[8] the former path seemed clearly advantageous. The Mexican government's main decision in this sense was to compete for a nonpermanent seat in the Security Council.

Castañeda's quote demonstrates a clear desire to break with the PRI-dominated past, and to introduce new guiding values based on free trade, democracy, and human rights, that may be considered "ideological," at least in terms of how Mexico's foreign policy had been defined in the past. In his first annual report, President Fox confirmed this more ideological characterization of foreign policy, by setting out five "axis" that would guide his administration's foreign policy: (1) to highlight internationally the advances in terms of democratic institutions and the advance of democratic political culture, reflecting a plural, transparent, safe, and culturally vibrant Mexico; (2) to actively support and promote respect for and defense of human rights throughout the world; (3) to defend democracy; (4) to play a more active role in the construction of the international system of the new millennium; and (5) to promote continuous and sustainable international economic development.[9]

The Mexican government, however, did not necessarily perceive such positions as merely ideological but rather viewed them as responding to its need to strengthen the new democratic regime, and join the "international club of democracies." In Castañeda's words:

> The complex play between foreign policy and domestic change is manifested clearly by President Fox's commitment to the cause of human rights [. . .] The updating of our international obligations in the matter of human rights has prepared the political field to underpin respect for those rights in Mexico.[10]

According to Fox's second minister of foreign relations, there was no contradiction between Mexico's active participation in international politics and Mexico's traditional foreign-policy guidelines:

> In a world defined by globalization, the technological revolution, conflict and uncertainty, this government recognizes and appreciates the constitutional principles and foreign policy doctrines that have shaped our rich diplomatic tradition. However, the government of President Fox has taken the best of Mexico's diplomatic tradition and has adjusted it through its strategic "axis" to respond to the demands imposed by a globalized world.[11]

Coexistence between a "traditional" and a "new" foreign policy, as suggested by Fox's government, would not be easy. Interests, principles, international events, and domestic politics would contribute to making foreign policy one of Fox's most criticized areas.

MEXICAN-U.S. RELATIONS: THE SEARCH FOR PROGRESS

The agenda of Mexican-U.S. relations is extensive and complicated. For the purposes of this chapter, it is sufficient to analyze two events that demonstrate the intricate links between pragmatism and ideology in Mexican foreign policy: Mexican illegal immigration and the war on terror and the invasion of Iraq.

A bilateral agreement on immigration was Fox's main initiative in Mexico's relations with the United States. Mexico's proposal consisted of five points: (1) to regulate the situation of undocumented Mexicans in the United States; (2) to increase the number of permanent visas for Mexicans; (3) to implement a program for temporary workers; (4) to increase border security; and, (5) to institute regional compensation funds that included U.S. resources (public, private, or social) in order to promote economic development in those regions from which Mexicans emigrated most. According to Secretary Castañeda, the Mexican proposal had to be taken as a whole and no partial agreement was to be accepted. A "single undertaking" was the natural consequence of President Fox's idea of "shared responsibility" to solve the immigration problem between Mexico and the United States.[12]

Mexico's project seemed to make initial progress. During President Bush's visit to San Cristóbal (Fox's ranch) in February 2001, both governments approved the beginning of high-level conversations, and the Mexican government was highly optimistic about the feasibility of reaching an agreement and thus began active lobbying. In the United States, however, various actors were opposed to the initiative, and even before September 11, it was clear that the project was in trouble.[13] While some considered that the agreement would not have been reached even had September 11 not happened, most analysts on both sides of the border agreed that the terrorist attacks marked the end of any possible progress on the subject.[14] Indeed, after September 11 the initiative simply disappeared from the U.S. and Mexican agendas.

Despite its failure, it is worth briefly analyzing the initiative due to its implications for Mexican foreign policy. First, it must be understood in terms of President Fox's purpose of designing a "new" foreign policy that contrasted with that of the PRI. Mexico was attempting to change its passive and reactive position to an active one that took the initiative, while vicinity to the United States was to be an opportunity, rather than a problem.[15] Second, for the first time in many years, the Mexican government recognized illegal emigration to the United States as a concrete problem to be addressed by both countries, indeed as a priority in foreign policy. The Mexican government took the initiative to engage the United States in the search for a practical solution that would benefit Mexico as much as—or maybe more than—the United States. In this sense, it is worth mentioning that the issue of the Mexican proposal being interventionist in U.S. domestic politics was not raised; the key phrase of "principle of mutual responsibility" replaced nonintervention, as pragmatism prevailed over principles.

The War on Terror and, later, the invasion of Iraq in 2003 posed serious problems to a Mexican government whose foreign-policy priorities were to establish a "strategic relationship" with the United States, to participate actively in the construction of a rule-based international system, and to promote democracy and human rights throughout the world. The terrorist attacks of September 11 took place only a few days after President Fox visited Washington D.C., and President Bush declared that the United States "has no more important relationship in the world that the one we have with Mexico."[16] However, there was a widespread perception that Mexico's reaction to the attacks was "late, distant and ambivalent,"[17] even though the evidence to endorse this view is mixed. After September 11, Secretary Castañeda declared that Mexico should not deny any support for the United States, and that the U.S. government was right in taking reprisals against the perpetrators of the attacks.[18] President Fox sent Bush a letter expressing Mexico's solidarity, sorrow, condolences, and consternation for the loss of life and the destruction caused, as well as his government's disposition to help the people of the United States.[19] On September 13, Castañeda appeared before the Senate where he was accused by senators of the PRI, PRD and the Partido Verde Ecologista for surrendering sovereignty to the United States "in an absurd way," and thus endangering Mexico's security.[20] PRI senators questioned the government's commitments regarding the U.S. idea of creating a continental military force, and suggested that Castañeda's declaration regarding "not denying any support" for the United States demonstrated how far he was willing to go just to ingratiate himself with the United States, "even at the cost of generating total confusion in Mexico."[21] Castañeda simply stated that he intended to adhere to the declarations of the Security Council and the General Assembly and indeed, Mexico had already voted in favor of a Security Council resolution to collaborate in bringing to justice the perpetrators and sponsors of the terrorist attacks, as well as those responsible for granting them asylum.[22]

Fox visited Ground Zero in New York on October 4, 2001, but according to certain groups of U.S. public opinion, this was "too late" for a country that was also a "partner."[23] On that occasion, Fox reiterated Mexico's commitment to fight terrorism.[24] By December 2001, Castañeda had confirmed the government's stance:

> President Fox's position has been clear; we should support the United States because it has the right to self-defense, because the international community has joined the struggle against international terrorism prompted by such attacks, and because it is in our interest to construct a strategic relationship that necessarily implies a greater degree of solidarity.[25]

However, the criticism of some Mexican deputies and other sectors of Castañeda's "alignment" with the United States contributed to projecting the image that Mexico was not unconditionally aligned with the United States. Moreover, compared with the attitude of the United Kingdom, or even Cuba—which immediately offered the U.S. government medical assistance and the use of Cuban airports—Mexico's reaction was less supportive of the United States. In any case, it was clear that Mexico was no longer at the top of the U.S. agenda, and even less "the United States' most important relationship."

However, this did not mean that Mexico's reaction seriously damaged U.S.-Mexican relations. According to the former U.S. ambassador to Mexico, Jeffrey Davidow, the U.S. government sent Mexico a message stating that both countries had to find a way to guarantee maximum security without strangling the flow of people and goods across the border. September 11 increased problems in border crossing but the attitude of high-level officials in the United States toward Mexico was "friendly and helpful."[26] There was significant communication and the United States considered Mexico a "cooperative ally," even though this was not well communicated to the Mexican public.[27] President Fox's declarations during his visit to Ground Zero seem to confirm Davidow's position:

> Ever since September 11, we [the United States and Mexico] are in touch, minute by minute, day by day, in all that concerns security, not only with intelligence and information, but with investigation [. . .] And just today we agreed with President Bush to continue working in this way, with providing security and fighting terrorism as top priorities. At the same time, we will return to our normal bilateral agenda . . .[28]

Further agreements followed. In 2002, Mexico and the United States signed the "smart border" agreements to improve security along the border in the areas of infrastructure, and the flow of people and goods.[29] In July 2004, Mexican authorities announced that a new integral system of migratory operation would be implemented to track all legal visitors entering the country.[30] And in 2005, Mexico, Canada, and the United States signed the agreement for a Security and Prosperity Partnership (SPP). As its name indicates, the purpose of the SPP was to improve security and the standard of living of the peoples of Canada, Mexico, and the United States on the grounds that "our security and our prosperity are mutually dependent and complementary, and [this undertaking] will reflect our belief in freedom, economic opportunities, and democratic values and institutions."[31] The Mexican Ministry of Foreign Affairs declared that the partnership's goal was to "strengthen cooperation in the fight against criminal and terrorist activities across borders, and to guarantee safe, secure, humane and dignified repatriation of workers without legal documents in high risk areas."[32] The document underlined the Mexican government's expected benefits and strategic considerations: "Since security issues are intrinsically related to economic and trade flows these days, the SPP will assure that the new security measures implemented in the region will not become unnecessary obstacles to trade."[33]

Cooperation with the United States in the security sphere was not one of President Fox's initial foreign-policy interests, but it became unavoidable. One might argue that Mexico had no option given the predominant U.S. interest in security, but it coincided with Mexico's own interests as well; to improve national security, avoid any movement of terrorists across the U.S.-Mexican border, and as indicated above, protect bilateral trade. Pragmatism, therefore, was in the best interest of Mexico's security and trade, and of U.S.-Mexican relations, despite certain domestic resistance to "side" with the United States, based on concepts of defense of national sovereignty.

Despite bilateral cooperation in the security sphere, Mexico's partici-pation as a nonpermanent member in the UN Security Council (2002–2003) complicated relations with the United States. As tensions between the United States and Iraq increased in early 2003, and as a U.S. inva-sion became likely, the Mexican government had to define its position regarding Resolution 1441 and the U.S. claim that Iraq had violated it.[34] In March, the U.S. government tried to obtain authorization from the Security Council to invade Iraq, counting on Mexico's vote. According to Jorge Chabat, President Bush and Ambassador Tony Garza "sent messages" to the Mexican government stating that Mexico's support was expected, and that it should face the consequences if not granted.[35] Fox recognized that defying the United States would be difficult, but Mexico's stance regarding the invasion of Iraq had to be a "state decision," involving the consensus of the country's main political forces. Furthermore, public opinion polls showed around 80 percent of Mexicans to be opposed to military intervention in Iraq, and congressional elections were to be held in July of that year. Thus, the Mexican government declared that it would not endorse a UN Security Council resolution that authorized a U.S. invasion of Iraq. Moreover, an hour after President Bush announced that he would order the invasion of Iraq if Saddam Hussein did not leave the country in 48 hours, President Fox gave a speech transmitted by all radio stations and TV channels in Mexico, in which he reiterated that Mexico prioritized multilateral diplomacy to solve disputes and that the use of force should be, as stated in the UN Charter, a last resort to be taken only when other means had failed:

> We are a pacifist nation; we are a pacifist government, we have a clear vocation for peace and [endorse] the validity of the institutional mecha-nisms accepted by the international community [. . .] We share values, goals and purposes with the United States, the United Kingdom and Spain, but on this occasion we diverge on the timing and procedures. We maintain our belief that the diplomatic means to achieve it [disarmament] have not been used yet [. . .] In stating our position at the Council, we have clearly distinguished between bilateral issues on our agenda and our

multilateral commitments. Our relationship with the United States . . . should not change; we coincide with the fight against terrorism . . . as in many other issues, our shared objectives exceed our differences [. . .] when the countdown towards war has begun, it is time to strengthen our values of peace, plurality and tolerance.[36]

As a result, tensions between Mexico and the United States increased; as argued by Chabat, the Mexican insistence that if a vote had taken place at the Security Council, Mexico would have voted against it, was unnecessary "and only succeeded in chilling relations with the U.S. government."[37]

These two examples of Mexican-U.S. relations under Fox demonstrate various aspects of Mexican foreign policy. First, the Mexican government identified a concrete problem that needed to be addressed without relying on traditional principles: immigration. Second, external factors changed the course of Mexico's foreign policy and Mexico's response was mixed; on the one hand, the pragmatic view taken by Castañeda suggested that in order to maintain the government's agenda, and considering the consequences of any different path, it was in the country's best interests to support the United States after September 11. On the other hand, a significant section of public opinion resorted to more traditional positions—nonintervention, pacifism, multilateralism—thus reducing the government's margin of action. Third, as always, Mexico's policies were heavily influenced by U.S. interests and Mexico fully cooperated with the United States in bilateral security matters. Whatever the Mexican government's ideology or objectives—the PRI or PAN in power—Mexico's powerful neighbor remains a constraint and a great influence on Mexico's policies.

THE PROMOTION OF DEMOCRACY AND HUMAN RIGHTS: THE CONFUSION BETWEEN IDEOLOGY AND TRADITIONAL PRINCIPLES

The promotion of democracy and human rights is perhaps the most interesting area in which to examine the interaction between ideology and pragmatism in the PAN'S foreign policy. For the first time in the history of contemporary Mexico, the government identified value-oriented issues, such as democracy and human rights, as foreign-policy *priorities.*

As mentioned in the first part of this chapter, both Fox and Castañeda, and later Derbez, agreed that the promotion of democracy and human rights were legitimate foreign-policy goals. Indeed, Castañeda declared that Mexico recognized human rights as universal and indivisible,[38] a statement that clearly contradicted Mexico's previous understanding that democracy and human rights were "strictly domestic issues."[39] Reflecting this, activity in the fields of democracy and human rights increased: Mexico signed a technical assistance agreement with the U.N. Human Rights High Commissioner's Office, which helped to draft an assessment of the situation of human rights in Mexico; Mariclaire Acosta, a well-known human rights activist, was named undersecretary for human rights at the Ministry of Foreign Affairs; the government issued an open invitation to any appropriate U.N. body wishing to observe Mexico's human rights situation in situ; and Mexico endorsed the Declaration of Quebec City—which established that a democratic regime was an essential condition to join the hemispheric free trade area—as well as the Democratic Inter-American Charter, which provided the members of the Organization of American States with a specific procedure to deal with those countries where democracy was suspended. By the end of Fox's administration, Mexico had ratified three conventions, accepted the competence of six protocols and declarations, and partially withdrawn a reservation on article 25b of the International Covenant on Civil and Political Rights, concerning the vote of religious ministers. Regionally, Mexico had ratified one convention, accepted the competence of two protection mechanisms, and partially withdrawn a reservation of two instruments, also regarding the vote of religious ministers and the celebration of religious acts in public. Fox's government was also participating in the negotiation of five more human rights instruments.[40]

Mexico's human rights policy, however, did not necessarily strengthen Mexico's foreign relations, as reflected by the case of Cuba. As Mexico "became democratic" and used foreign policy to prove it, Cuba became the "test case." In the past, Mexican-Cuban relations had been conducted, at least officially, by complying with the key principle of nonintervention. By 2001–2002, however, relations had begun to radically change. In 2001 Castañeda announced the possibility that Mexico might vote in favor of the resolution calling on the Cuban government to improve human rights on the island at the U.N. Human Rights Commission, while in 2002 it actually voted for the measure.

Both votes in 2001 and 2002 produced an interesting discussion over the validity of human rights promotion. In 2001 the Congress, on the one hand, defended Mexico's foreign-policy principles of nonintervention and self-determination, and asked the government to abstain from voting, which the government finally did. By 2002, however, Mexico's position had altered and it voted in favor of the Human Rights Commission Resolution. The Mexican government justified such a drastic change in its position by arguing that "[Mexico's] concern about human rights in Cuba is legitimate because Cuba is a close and important country to Mexico."[41]

In February 2002 Fox visited Cuba and met well-known Cuban dissidents, among them Oswaldo Payá and Martha Beatriz Roque, at the Mexican embassy. According to Fox, he had notified Castro of this meeting, which was consistent with Mexico's general policy of defending human rights internationally.[42] From that year on, relations with Cuba became increasingly complicated. Mexico continued to vote in favor of resolutions requesting Cuba to take steps to improve the situation of human rights at the UN Human Rights Commission and, together with other incidents—such as a request by Fox that Castro leave the UN conference on "Financing for Development in Mexico" before President Bush arrived, and Cuba's deportation to Mexico of businessman Carlos Ahumada without following the appropriate procedure[43]—diplomatic relations became very strained. In May 2004, Mexican authorities declared a Cuban embassy official persona non grata, and requested that the Cuban ambassador leave the country, and that the Mexican ambassador to Cuba return to Mexico.

Relations with Cuba therefore are a very good illustration of the tension that existed between change and continuity, and of the influence of ideology in Fox's foreign policy. Cuba was an opportunity for Mexico to take a stance on democracy and human rights over the traditional principles of nonintervention and self-determination. It was clearly a governmental rather than state policy that almost led to a complete diplomatic rupture with Cuba, and it carried with it costs for Mexico's foreign and domestic politics. Cuba openly criticized the Mexican government and its foreign policy, and implemented an active diplomacy toward the opposition in Mexico, something that had not been the case when nonintervention was mutually respected.[44] Internal actors also criticized Mexico's policy toward Cuba, strongly questioning the validity of Fox's "new" foreign policy. The pragmatic position, of course, would have been to maintain relations with Cuba along traditional lines.

Another foreign-policy area where ideology and national interests did not coincide was that of the UN peacekeeping operations. Consistent with the government's ideas of implementing an active foreign policy in multilateral fora, supporting the construction of a new normative international system, and promoting democracy and human rights, the discussion was raised as to whether Mexican troops should participate in such operations, especially given the situation in Haiti in 2004. With one exception, Mexico had not participated in peacekeeping operations before,[45] but according to Secretary Derbez, Mexico, as the ninth largest contributor to peacekeeping operations was already supporting these operations: "If we are already funding them, the question that Mexican society should ask itself is whether we are not hypocritical by not providing personnel."[46] Despite the support of the Ministry for sending troops on peacekeeping missions, based on the fact that Mexico might gain international prestige, military training, influence at the Security Council, and reimbursement of its financial contributions to the UN, Fox finally rejected the proposal. To the Ministry, Mexico's participation in peacekeeping operations was a means to reiterate its commitment to democracy and human rights, and to strengthen the country's active role in international politics. But other actors in Fox's government, including the military, argued against this view on the grounds of Mexico's pacifist vocation and that, in sending troops abroad, Mexico would be violating the principle of nonintervention.[47] In this case, traditional principles were a very useful resource for those actors who opposed Mexico's participation in peacekeeping operations, and continuity in foreign policy prevailed.

FELIPE CALDERÓN'S FOREIGN POLICY: CONTINUITY OR CHANGE? PRAGMATIC OR IDEOLOGICAL?

Felipe Calderón's electoral platform promised that Mexico would contribute to reform multilateral institutions in order to construct "a world architecture with a human face," that Mexico would run for a seat at the UN Security Council, and that it would back all reforms of the Charter of the Organization of American States to reinforce the mechanisms to promote and defend the democratic institutions of the region.[48] The document also stated that Mexico would press for "special relationships" with Latin America, for a safer and more prosperous region in North America, and for a program of temporary workers with the United States.[49] The second annual report issued by the Ministry of Foreign Affairs begins by stating that foreign policy would promote Mexico's interests beyond its borders and identifies Mexico's active participation in the construction of a world order guided by the values and principles of democracy as a foreign policy "national objective" [sic].[50]

The foreign policy of President Calderón has been active although rather quiet, and to a certain extent successful in terms of both diplomacy and domestic politics (so far, foreign policy has not become the subject of domestic disagreement). The language of democracy promotion has not dominated the agenda, relations with Cuba have improved, and left-wing presidents such as Luiz Inácio Lula da Silva, Michelle Bachelet, Daniel Ortega, Rafael Correa, and Néstor Kirchner, among others, have visited Mexico. As during Fox's government, Mexico won a nonpermanent seat at the Security Council, and the president has made it clear that Mexican troops will not participate in peacekeeping operations.[51]

After two years in power, two of Calderón's foreign-policy initiatives are worth examining: relations with Cuba and the Mérida Initiative. The first case demonstrates a significant and pragmatic shift in Mexican foreign policy. With President Fox's foreign policy widely seen as an utter failure, Calderón sought to take a first step in rebuilding Mexico's so-called international prestige by improving relations with Cuba—a country that was clearly a special case given the significance of the Revolution for many in Mexico and the "special relationship" that the Mexican and Cuban governments had enjoyed until the end of the PRI regime. Once again, Cuba became the "test case" for a new foreign policy. Democracy and the promotion of human rights were quietly dropped from the agenda and communication between the governments renewed. New ambassadors were sent to each capital, the foreign ministers of each country visited each other, an invitation was issued to President Calderón to visit the island, and, according to the Cuban foreign minister Felipe Pérez Roque, relations were normalized.[52] The new bilateral agenda includes Cuba's debt with Mexico, human trafficking, and trade and investment, but not condemnation of human rights in Cuba, or democracy.

After the death of the prisoner Orlando Zapata in Cuba, in February 2010, the Mexican government issued a communiqué successfully balancing its concern for human rights, its respect for Cuba's sovereignty, and the principle of nonintervention. Mexico exhorted the Cuban government to take all necessary measures to protect the dignity and health of all prisoners, but recognized that no country had the right to judge how other countries protected and promoted human rights. Interestingly, the communiqué stated that Mexico's position was taken from a state rather than ideological perspective.[53]

Before turning to the Mérida Initiative, it is worth mentioning Mexico's policy toward Honduras after the coup in June 2009, since events challenged Mexico's policy of support for democracy and human rights. The Mexican government not only condemned the overthrow of president Manuel Zelaya and agreed with the OAS decision to suspend the Honduran government from participating in the organization, but invited Zelaya as head of state to visit the country in August, while not inviting Honduras to participate in the Latin American and Caribbean Summit that took place in Cancún, in February 2010. The Mexican government did not recognize the Honduran elections, or Porfirio Lobo as the new president.

Mexico's policy toward Honduras questioned the government's capacity to defend democracy abroad: Zelaya's visit to Mexico and the government's attempts to grant him asylum were unsuccessful, thus reanimating the discussion as to whether Mexico had the legitimacy, interests, and capabilities to promote democracy abroad.

The second case, the Mérida Initiative, reflects continuity with Fox's attempts to increase cooperation with the United States in order to solve shared problems. In an attempt to reduce violence, fueled by organized crime (especially drug-trafficking), Mexico and the United States agreed to strengthen cooperation. Formally, the initiative rests on three pillars: (1) the idea that each country will act in its own territory; (2) the implementation of bilateral cooperation; and, (3) the transfer of U.S. equipment and technology to Mexico, and the training of Mexican personnel.[54] The United States government agreed to grant Mexico US$400 million to fight drug-trafficking, and gave the first payment of US$197 million for training and technical equipment on December 3, 2008. The Mexican government has reiterated that the initiative will not allow the presence of U.S. troops, or any kind of police, on Mexican soil. Once again Mexico has recognized the need to cooperate with the United States, to ask for U.S. assistance but has been careful not to ignore principles, such as nonintervention and self-determination, and avoided "aligning" with the United States or surrendering sovereignty. Continuity and change, traditional principles, and new attitudes, therefore mix in Calderon's foreign policy.

CONCLUSIONS: THE DIFFICULT COEXISTENCE OF INTERESTS, VALUES AND IDEOLOGY

There is no doubt that the first PAN government introduced changes in Mexico's foreign policy, for better or worse. The projects of Fox and Castañeda were not free from contradictions, but they were clear and well designed. More importantly, Castañeda openly rejected Mexico's "old diplomacy" in favor of both a pragmatic and ideological foreign policy. Such an explicit opposition between an "old" and a "new" diplomacy (however accurate), and the differentiation between interests, values, and principles is what distinguished Fox's pragmatism-ideology formula from that of the past. The formula and the debate about it were openly recognized by the government.

In terms of the balance between pragmatism and ideology in Mexican-U.S. relations, Fox's initial approach was very pragmatic, as is Calderón's. The view first expressed by Carlos Salinas in the sense that vicinity with the United States was an opportunity, was reinforced during the first two PAN governments. In the case of Fox, however, September 11 presented significant obstacles to Mexico's approach, not only in terms of the immigration agreement—which may not have been signed anyway—but also in terms of Mexico's position regarding the U.S. security agenda and a foreign policy defined by unilateralism and preemptive war. Domestic politics and the legacy of a foreign policy of principles forced the government to take its distance from the United States. Pragmatism, as mentioned above, took precedence as a result of domestic concerns. Calderón has been more successful in reaching agreements with the United States because of the kind of issues on the table, especially organized crime. The Mérida Initiative reveals a highly pragmatic approach to a very serious problem without portraying the image of surrendering sovereignty to the United States. In sum, while pragmatism was the starting point for both administrations, in the case of Fox, it was overshadowed by domestic reactions to U.S. foreign policy, while in the case of Calderón, it has to a large extent prevailed over principles.

Both the issues of democracy and human rights and Mexico's participation in peacekeeping operations involved a conflict between ideology, principles, and pragmatism, as well as reflecting conflicting interpretations of the national interest. Secretaries Castañeda and Derbez argued that ideology and principles were in the end a manifestation of pragmatism, since in their view, to defend democracy and human rights abroad was to defend Mexico's domestic and international interests. However, many other actors, domestic and foreign (especially Cuba) strongly disagreed with this position, not only in terms of ideology, but also definitions of the national interest. Certainly regarding peacekeeping operations, the military and other domestic actors argued that in defending principles and not joining such operations, Mexico was protecting its national interests.

Given Fox's poor results in terms of foreign policy, Calderón has adopted a "state" view rather that a governmental one (as opposed to Fox, who wanted to mark a clear break with the PRI). Mexico's relations with Latin American countries governed by center-left and left-wing administrations have improved, and relations with the United States have responded to a common concern in the form of organized crime and security. Whether this is the result of a clear project, or of Mexico's very narrow margin for action is open to debate. Foreign policy clearly is not the priority it was under Fox, but this may be advantageous to Mexico's external relations.

NOTES

1. Such principles are nonintervention, self-determination, peaceful resolution of disputes, international cooperation for development, juridical equality of states, proscription of the use or the threat of the use of force, and the struggle for international peace and security. The Mexican

Congress approved the inclusion of these principles into article 89 (X) of the Constitution in 1988.

2. Ana Covarrubias, "Los principios y la política exterior de México," in Jorge A. Schiavon, Daniela Spenser, and Mario Vázquez Olivera (eds.), *En busca de una nación soberana. Relaciones internacionales de México, siglos XIX y XX*, Mexico, CIDE-SRE, 2006, pp. 387–422.

3. Jorge G. Castañeda, "Los ejes de la política exterior de México," in *Nexos*, vol. 23, no. 288, December 2001, p. 67.

4. Ibid., pp. 67, 69.

5. Pastor's final proposal was published as *Toward a North American Community. Lessons from the Old World for the New*, United States, Peterson Institute, 2001. He recognized that the European experience has been unique and is not possible to emulate in North America, but he suggests a community of a different kind was possible after all.

6. Fox suggested the "open border" idea even before he was elected president in July 2000. Jorge Chabat, "The Bush Revolution in Foreign Policy and Mexico: The Limits to Unilateralism," in Daniel Drache (ed.), *Big Picture Realities. Canada and Mexico at the Crossroads*, Ontario, Wilfrid Laurier University Press, 2008.

7. Castañeda, "Los ejes de la política exterior de México," p. 73.

8. Ibid.

9. Mexico, President Vicente Fox, *Primer Informe de Gobierno*, 2001, http://primer.informe.fox.presidencia.gob.mx. My emphasis.

10. Jorge G. Castañeda, "Política exterior y cambio democrático," in *Reforma.com*, June 12, 2002.

11. *La política exterior mexicana en la transición*, Mexico, Secretaría de Relaciones Exteriores-Fondo de Cultura Económica, 2005, p. 11.

12. Carlos Tello Díaz, "Jorge G. Castañeda. Todo lo que cambió," in *Arcana*, no. 8, December 2001, p. 21.

13. President Bush knew that granting amnesty to illegal immigrants would not be easily accepted. Jesús Velasco, "Acuerdo migratorio: la debilidad de la esperanza," in *Foro Internacional*, vol. 48, no. 1–2 (191–92), January–June 2008, pp. 160–61.

14. *Ibid.* pp. 151–52.

15. Velasco, "Acuerdo migratorio," *op. cit.*, p. 155. Castañeda, "Los ejes de la política exterior de México," pp. 87, 89.

16. "Remarks at a Welcoming Ceremony for President Vicente Fox of Mexico," *Weekly Compilation of Presidential Documents*, September 10, 2001, http://www.findarticles.com/p/articles/mi_m2889/is_36_37/ai_79210653, quoted by Chabat, "The Bush Revolution," p. 129.

17. Mónica Serrano, "Bordering on the Impossible: US-Mexico Security Relations Alter 9–11," in Peter Andreas and Thomas J. Niersteker (eds.), *The Rebordering of North Americas: Integration and Exclusion in a New Security Context*, New York, Routledge, 2003 pp. 46–47, quoted by Robert Pastor, "Después del libre comercio en América del Norte: cómo cerrar la brecha del desarrollo," in Ana Covarrubias (coord.), *México en*

un mundo unipolar . . . y diverso, Mexico, El Colegio de México, 2007, p. 133.

18. In Spanish: *no regatear apoyo.* "Apoyan represalias; hay razón y derecho," reforma.com, September 13, 2001, http://busquedas.gruporeforma/reforma/Documentos/printImpresa.aspx?DocId=1850.

19. Juan Manuel Venegas, "EU, bajo el fuego," in *La Jornada*, September 12, 2001, http://www.jornada.unam.mx/2001/09/12/023n1mun.html.

20. Andrea Becerril, "Acusan senadores a Castañeda de ceder soberanía a EU," in *La Jornada*, September 14, 2001, http://www.jornada.unam.mx/2001/09/14/023n2pol.html.

21. Ibid., and Jenaro Villamil Rodríguez, "*Evasiva* comparecencia de Castañeda en el Senado," in *La Jornada*, September 14, 2001, http://www.jornada.unam.mx/2001/09/14/024n1pol.html.

22. Andrea Becerril, "Acusan senadores a Castañeda."

23. Chabat, "The Bush Revolution," p. 29.

24. "Versión estenográfica de la entrevista de prensa concedida por el Presidente Vicente Fox Quesada, esta noche en la 'Zona Cero' de esta ciudad," Mexico, Presidencia de la República, October 4, 2001, http://fox.presidencia.gob.mx/actividades/?contenido=1935&imprimir=tue.

25. Castañeda, "Los ejes de la política," p. 73.

26. Davidow, *El oso y el puercoespín*, 356.

27. Ibid., p. 358.

28. "Versión estenográfica de la entrevista de prensa concedida por el Presidente Vicente Fox Quesada, esta noche en la 'Zona Cero'."

29. All 22 commitments may be found in Raúl Benítez Manaut, "La seguridad nacional en la indefinida transición: mitos y realidades del sexenio de Vicente Fox," in *Foro Internacional*, vol. 48, no. 1–2 (191–92), January–June 2008, pp. 191–92. Peter Andreas, "US-Mexico border control in a changing economic and security context," quoted in Mónica Serrano, "Integration and security in North America. Do good neighbors need good fences?" in *International Journal*, vol. 61, no. 3, Summer 2006, p. 618.

30. Chabat, "The Bush Revolution," p. 130.

31. Joint statement by President Bush, President Fox, and Prime Minister Martin, March 23, 2005, www.spp.gov.

32. Secretaría de Relaciones Exteriores, "Alianza para la seguridad y la prosperidad de América del Norte," www.sre.gob.mx.

33. Ibid.

34. As argued by Reynaldo Ortega, it is difficult to know whether the Mexican government acted in response to public opinion or whether public opinion encouraged the government to distance itself from Washington. In January 2003, a public opinion poll indicated that 82 percent of the people surveyed sustained that in case of a war between Iraq and the United States, Mexico should remain neutral; 14 percent thought that Mexico should support the United States, and less than 1 percent answered that Mexico should support Iraq. Reynaldo Yunuen Ortega Ortiz, "The United States-Iraq war and Mexican

public opinion," in *International Journal*, vol. 61, no. 3, summer 2006, p. 654; 657.

35. Chabat, "The Bush Revolution," p. 131.
36. Juan Manuel Venegas, "Vientos de Guerra. La fuerza sólo se justifica cuando las otras vías fracasan, dice Fox," in *La Jornada Virtul*/www.jornada.unam.mx/2003/03/18/014n1pol.php?origen=index.html.
37. Chabat, "The Bush Revolution," p. 132.
38. Tello Díaz, "Jorge G. Castañeda. Todo lo que cambió," pp. 22–24; Castañeda, "Los ejes de la política exterior de México," pp. 72–73.
39. Ana Covarrubias, "Los derechos humanos en la política exterior de México: ¿en defensa propia o de valores liberales?" in Covarrubias (coord.), *Temas de política exterior*, pp. 303–32.
40. *La política exterior mexicana en la transición*, pp. 142–44.
41. *La Jornada*, July 1, 2001, p. 8. In 2002, Fox's government argued that Mexico had not voted against any country, but had defended causes. Mexico, Gobierno de la República, "México vota a favor de causas y no en contra de países," comunicado, April 15, 2002, http://www.presidencia.gob.mx.
42. *Reforma*, February 5, 2002, www.reforma.com.
43. See Ana Covarrubias Velasco, "La política mexicana hacia Cuba a principios de siglo: de la no intervención a la protección de los derechos humanos," in *Foro Internacional*, vol. 43, no. 3 (173), July–September 2003, pp. 627–44. The most embarrassing incident was undoubtedly Castro's release to the press of his conversation with Fox, when the latter asked him to leave the country after lunch, before President Bush arrived, and not to attack the United States. A transcript of the conversation may be found in "Exhibe Fidel Castro charla de 'amigos'," *Reforma*, April 23, 2002, www.reforma.com.
44. Rafael Rojas, "México y Cuba, amigos desleales," in *Foreign Affairs en español*, vol. 4, no. 3, July–September, 2004, pp. 72–81.
45. The Mexican government sent a group of policemen to El Salvador in cooperation with ONUSAL after the civil war in that country.
46. "Versión estenográfica de la entrevista del secretario de Relaciones Exteriores, Luis Ernesto Derbez, a corresponsales mexicanos en el Hotel Ritz de Madrid," May 11, 2004, www.sre.gob.mx.
47. "Comentarios" sobre la minuta que reforma y adiciona la fracción III de3l artículo 76 de la Constitución Política de los Estados Unidos Mexicanos."
48. PAN, Plataforma electoral, http://www.presidencia.com.mx/plataformas/pan_plataforma2006.pdf.
49. Ibid.
50. Secretaría de Relaciones Exteriores, *Segundo Informe de Labores*, 2008, pp. 9, 11, www.sre.gob.mx.
51. Presidencia de la República, entrevistas, Leonardo Curzio, Enfoque 1a emisión, September 3, 2008, http://www.presidencia.gob.mx/prensa/entrevistas/?contenido=38363&impirmir=true.

52. Patricia Muñoz Ríos, "Con México se restableció el diálogo político: Pérez Roque," in *La Jornada*, October 20, 2008, http://www.jornada.unam.mx/2008/10/20/index.php?section=politica&article=015n1pol.

53. "México hace un llamado al Gobierno de Cuba a realizar las acciones necesarias para proteger la salud y la dignidad de todos sus prisioneros," comuniqué no. 074, March 15, 2010, http://www.sre.gob.mx/csocial/contenido/comunicados/2010/mar/cp_074,html.

54. Carlos Rico, "La iniciativa Mérida y el combate nacional al crimen organizado," in *Foreign Affairs en español*, vol. 8, no. 1, January–March, 2008, pp. 3–13.

CHAPTER 13

UNITY AND DIVERSITY IN LATIN AMERICAN VISIONS OF REGIONAL INTEGRATION

GIAN LUCA GARDINI

Outside Europe, Latin America is where regionalism has enjoyed the longest tradition and has arguably achieved the deepest and most sophisticated forms. In spite of different understandings of the essence and goals of regional integration, and different degrees of support for its deepening and enlargement, in Europe there is a convergence toward a unitary project, the European Union. Other regional initiatives are mostly subservient to, or at least compatible with, the EU scope and aims. However, in Latin America, regionalism, although meant to be an expression of unity and solidarity, has become a stark reflection of Latin American diversity and heterogeneity. Even in the presence of supposedly ideological affinities between a majority of the current left-leaning administrations, Latin American regionalism is characterized by a number of competing projects, whose rationales and agendas are often divergent, if not incompatible.

The long tradition of theoretical elaboration of Latin American regionalism dates back to the first half of the nineteenth century. In his 1815 letter from Jamaica, Simón Bolívar proposed the constitution of a federation of Hispanic republics as the only viable means to achieve continental political, economic, and social development. In Bolívar's initial formulation there was no anti-imperialist or anti-U.S. connotation (although by 1826 he was resisting the inclusion of the United States in the Congress of Panama), and Brazil was not even included in the project. In 1844, the Argentine intellectual and politician Juan Bautista Alberdi proposed the creation of a Latin American Union intended to foster economic prosperity and cooperation. In this formulation, an anti-U.S. and anti-imperialist character was present and Brazil was to be included in the venture.[1] By the mid-1800s, the three most fundamental and enduring questions and principles of Latin American regionalism were established: the relationship with the United States, the place of Brazil, and the quest for an aggregative development model.

This chapter will investigate how the Common Market of the South (MERCOSUR), The Bolivarian Alliance for the Americas (ALBA), and the South American Union (UNASUR) provide different responses to these three fundamental questions, and how their approaches reflect a different mix of ideological and pragmatic elements. Discussion will then focus on the tension between ideology and pragmatism when applied to regional integration as a concept and as a set of agreements and institutions. The chapter argues that MERCOSUR, ALBA, and UNASUR in their current formulation are not only incompatible, but also dysfunctional in terms of the objectives they purport to pursue.

MERCOSUR

ORIGIN, EVOLUTION AND CURRENT DEBATES

The history of MERCOSUR began well before its formal constitution. The diplomatic rapprochement between Brazil and Argentina in the late 1970s provided the necessary condition to eliminate security threats between the two countries and inaugurate a more cooperative phase.[2] The return of both countries to democracy in the first half of the 1980s produced a strong political motivation to strengthen bilateral cooperation with the aim of reinforcing the fragile democracies,[3] while the need to modernize the economy supplied an economic rationale for closer bilateral ties. Eventually, in 1986, Buenos Aires and Brasilia signed an industrial complementation deal based on a mechanism of sectoral, flexible, and gradual economic integration. With the triumph of neoliberalism and the Washington Consensus in the 1990s the Argentine and Brazilian administrations opted for a process of economic *apertura* (opening) to favor the insertion of the two countries in the globalized economy and attract foreign investments toward an enlarged regional market. Uruguay and Paraguay joined to form MEROSUR in March 1991.

From the outset MERCOSUR lost some of its initial political character. Instead it took on an essentially neoliberal economic direction,[4] adopting a universal, automatic, and linear removal of trade barriers, becoming a free-trade area with some elements of an incomplete customs union, while the aspiration to a common market has so far remained unfulfilled. Following the 1997 Asian crisis, the 1999 Brazilian unilateral devaluation and the 2001 Argentine collapse, combined with its inability to address asymmetries among members or endemic social problems, MERCOSUR has experienced a long period of self-reflection since the early years of this millennium.

Today, in a considerably different political scenario, both domestically and internationally, from the one in which it originated, MERCOSUR is in search of a new role and new guiding principles, as well as innovative forms of accommodation of its members' interests and agendas.[5] Argentina and Brazil still favor orthodox economic management, but have come to recognize the need to address some of the persistent asymmetries at the regional level and to complement trade liberalization with a public policy package. The vision inspiring MERCOSUR in this phase, if any such vision exists, is a reflection of these indications. The increasing dissatisfaction of Paraguay and Uruguay has also led to the creation of a small Economic Convergence Fund (FOCEM). Current challenges on the agenda include the completion of the customs union, the relaunch of international trade negotiations, and institutional deepening and enlargement. Most of all, in the context of the current redefinition of the roles of the United States and Brazil, and the questioning of neoliberal economics, MERCOSUR is attempting to reposition itself both in conceptual and geostrategic terms.

RELATIONS WITH THE UNITED STATES

MERCOSUR's posture vis-à-vis the United States has traditionally been ambivalent and remains such, but has never produced moments of great tension. During the Argentine-Brazilian bilateral period in the 1980s the United States did not pay much attention to the emerging bloc, while Buenos Aires and Brasília were eager to secure support in Washington for their democratic consolidation, debt rescheduling, and economic modernization. In the 1990s, with a varying degree of enthusiasm among its members, MERCOSUR aligned itself with the prevailing rules of the Washington consensus, encouraged by the United States. MERCOSUR became a model of open regionalism and its members welcomed the proposal of a Free Trade Area of the Americas (FTAA) in 1994. This initiative was expected to provide new market access for the agricultural and industrial production of the four associates.

In the twenty-first century, however, the U.S.-MERCOSUR relationship and agenda have become increasingly complex. The shift toward the Left in much of Latin America, the shortcomings of neoliberalism (upon which the FTAA was modeled), and a clear perception that the FTAA would benefit the United States more than their Latin American counterparts, led to its criticism and eventually abandonment at the 2005 Summit of the Americas. By then MERCOSUR had become the main focus of resistance to the FTAA project under Brazilian political leadership. What was rejected was not the principle of a mutually beneficial FTAA, but rather the form and terms of the draft. This posture, based on commercial interests rather than ideological principles, halted the original plan, but the United States simply altered its strategy through recourse to bilateral FTAs. At present, Brazil and Uruguay seem happy to entertain a kind of privileged relation with Washington. The former has developed affinities in the bio-fuel sector and in multilateral forums, such as the WTO, while the latter plays the U.S. card to advance its own demands within MERCOSUR and threaten the partners with an even closer association to Washington.[6] As a result, MERCOSUR is the only area in Latin America with no preferential trade agreement with the United States. Whether this is ideologically negative is a matter of opinion, but the practical realities of trade are not questionable.

THE ROLE OF BRAZIL

During the Argentine-Brazilian bilateral integration and in the first years of MERCOSUR the political initiative largely stemmed from Buenos Aires with Brasilia offering a calculated level of support for the venture.[7] Since 2000 this pattern has been reversed. Brazilian economic preponderance and its ascendance to the status of an international power forced a redefinition of roles. Brazil now sees MERCOSUR, and indeed the rest of South America, as a platform to boost its claims to international power.[8] Since Brazil intends to present itself in multilateral forums as the regional representative of South America or at least MERCOSUR, regional leadership is seen as a strategy, or even a necessity, to achieve global recognition. This leadership however is far from uncontested.[9] On the one hand, this leaves the bloc without a clear lead or shared project, while on the other it preserves space for debate and dialogue within a group in which one member has about 70 to 80 percent of the population and the GDP. Brazil itself seems to divide its leadership credentials and commitment between MERCOSUR and the newly created UNASUR (which will be discussed later). MERCOSUR thus finds its fate precariously linked to Brazil's own choice and vision of itself and the region.

THE DEVELOPMENT MODEL

MERCOSUR accepts the capitalist model of production and favors open economies and export-based growth. No regional redistributive mechanism, with the exception of the small FOCEM, is in place.[10] However, where a revision of orthodox neoliberalism may emerge is in the quest for greater attention to social issues and the rectification of the democratic deficit. Overall, the development model adopted by MERCOSUR remains relatively close to the original neoliberal paradigm. Indeed the current debate on the development model is not about different ways to implement the same principles, but rather hinges on very different visions. On the one hand is the idea to return MERCOSUR to its original economic and trade objectives, while an even more adventurous step in this sense would be to advocate a dilution of the members' commitments, and to allow them to negotiate FTAs with third parties. On the other hand is the proposal to deepen the political content of MERCOSUR, pushing forward the Parliament of MERCOSUR and the broader involvement of civil society. What the two have in common is a claim to a return to the true origins of MERCOSUR, which are still disputed,[11] and a consensus on the necessity to complete some institutional deepening, at least to allow the free-trade area to produce the expected benefits for its members.[12]

ALBA

ORIGIN, EVOLUTION, AND CURRENT DEBATES

While MERCOSUR is the legacy of the idea of open regionalism of the 1990s, the twenty-first century has brought with it a substantial degree of novelty in terms of regionalism. The questioning of neoliberalism and a quest for international autonomy and multipolarity led to renewed vigor with regard to integration, and the emergence of both ALBA and UNASUR, which are largely political projects with a marginal economic dimension.[13] ALBA is essentially a tool of President Hugo Chávez's regional activism and agenda. Attempting to distance his country from the United States, Chávez first attempted to consolidate a leading role in the Caribbean, and then among the poorer Andean countries. The first application of ALBA's principles materialized with the Venezuelan-Cuban agreement of 2004, while Bolivia, under the presidency of Evo Morales, joined in 2006. At present, Nicaragua, Dominica, Ecuador, San Vicente and the Grenadines, and Antigua and Barbuda are also full members of ALBA.

More than anything else, ALBA is a concept.[14] Its associates are inspired by the Bolivarian ideals of Latin American political unity, solidarity, and endogenous development, but these principles remain loosely codified or institutionalized. It is also primarily a political project and is ruled by the preeminence of the political over the economic.[15] Its key objectives are the fight against poverty and the pursuit of social development, and it was in fact created as a reaction against neoliberal economics and as an alternative to the existing and proposed integration schemes based on neoliberal foundations. It opposed the U.S.-sponsored Free Trade Area of the Americas (FTAA), and also opposes those Latin American integration schemes, such as MERCOSUR and the Andean Community (CAN), that share the U.S. preference for free trade, privatization, and deregulation. The result is a strongly ideological vision. On the one hand, only those countries strictly adhering to the Bolivarian ideology are welcome to join, while on the other, a confrontational stance toward those not sharing these principles is almost inevitable. This means that the grouping is not attractive to a majority of Latin American countries; it is also potentially divisive as it exacerbates the dichotomy between supporters and nonsupporters of the project.

RELATIONS WITH THE UNITED STATES

ALBA was conceived as an alternative to the U.S.-sponsored FTAA.[16] Its aim is explicitly "counter-hegemonic" in that it offers a model to counter what is perceived as a U.S.-dominated, if not imposed, scheme of regional relations.[17] Indeed President Chávez emphatically declared that the goal of ALBA is "to bury the FTAA and the imperialist, capitalist economic model."[18] While this strong posture owes much to President Chávez's own ideology, it also hides a pragmatic strategy designed to underpin Venezuela's claims to regional leadership in Latin America. Complementary projects emanating from ALBA are also intended to diminish U.S. influence in the region while promoting that of Venezuela. Petroamerica in the oil sector is intended to decrease Venezuelan dependence on crude exports to the United States, which currently account for about 60 percent of Caracas's oil exports.[19] The Banco del ALBA aims to limit the influence of the World Bank and the International Monetary Fund, which—according to a *chavista* view—simply reproduce and perpetuate neoliberal economic models and represent an expression of U.S. power.

Besides rhetoric and ideology, the Chávez government has a clear vision of a new Latin American order, reflected in three points that Chávez expressed in 2000.[20] First was the assertion that neoliberalism was the "path to hell." Second was the proposition that Latin American unity is the only hope for survival in a globalized world. Third was the prediction, and prescription, that the world in the twenty-first century must be multipolar, itself a challenge to U.S. hegemony since it implied a reconsideration of the U.S. role in Latin America and beyond. Opposition to the United States is not only a question of rhetoric and populist opportunism, but stems from a negative evaluation of the last thirty years of development policies in Latin America. Above all, the Bolivarian stance is a reaction to the failure of neoliberalism in Latin America, especially in terms of a widespread decrease in salaries, a rise of the unemployment, lower standards of labor rights, and the boom of the informal sector. ALBA is not only politically opposed to U.S. hegemony in Latin America, but also to the economic and social values that Washington embodies and promotes. It is thus essentially ideological.

THE ROLE OF BRAZIL

Both Brazil and Venezuela conceive of subregional integration (MERCOSUR and ALBA, respectively) as a means to project their influence through Latin America and to implement their vision of regional unity and order. However, it is apparent that these efforts to form a "global southern coalition" are competing rather than complementary.[21] While there is no official clash between Caracas and Brasilia, this does not mean that there are no tensions either, but the two countries seem to have found a compromise to focus on common interests and delay addressing contentious issues. Ultimately Chávez is willing to recognize Brazilian power and to accommodate it, as long as he is able to influence the regional agenda.

This is in part due to the fact that Chávez has sought a rapprochement with Brazil, especially in the period of 2002–2006. This was for a number of reasons: the 2002 attempted coup convinced him of the necessity to gain the support of the major regional player, Brazil and the major regional bloc, MERCOSUR; the two countries held a shared vision of South America, as opposed to Latin America, as suitable geostrategic space for global insertion; and Caracas saw in Brasilia a potential ally on energy issues (the creation of Petrosur put together the state oil companies PDVSA of Venezuela, ENARSA of Argentina, and PETROBRAS of Brazil, following a scheme that ALBA had already introduced with Caribbean and Andean countries). On the Brazilian side, Venezuela's accession to MERCOSUR represented an opportunity to check Chávez's initiatives and at the same time show goodwill to those countries (Paraguay and Uruguay) calling for a rebalance of structural asymmetries within the bloc. However, to date, Venezuela's accession is on hold due to the pending ratification by Paraguay and Venezuela itself, which casts doubts on the real will and feasibility of this enlargement. These dealings reflect no particular ideological affinity. Ultimately, the

Brazilian-Venezuelan deal is based on a quid pro quo between Caracas' acquiescence to Brazilian regional preeminence and Brasilia's tolerance of the Bolivarian efforts to drive the regional agenda.

THE DEVELOPMENT MODEL

Consensus among members is sought essentially on political direction rather than economic formulas, the latter following and reflecting the goals set by the former. This is a reassertion of the political over the economic and also an attempt to regain a central role for the state.[22] Preference for endogenous development means a model based on local needs and conditions, and not a general theory applied or adapted to a case study. The recognition that Latin America is characterized by very different levels of development led to the adoption of the principle of different treatment for different member states, with different rather than reciprocal commitments in the cooperation agreements including special clauses. For instance, the contributions of Venezuela and Cuba to ALBA are tailored to the resources of the two countries, with Venezuela pooling technology and energy resources and Cuba providing health and education assistance.

ALBA prioritizes a number of sectors deemed essential for development. Social development is given a central position, with successful state-sponsored social projects run and equipped by regionally pooled resources targeting specific areas with serious health, education, or sanitation deficiencies.[23] Energy is also a key sector for development. Once again, opposition to the U.S.-sponsored Hemispheric Energy Initiative (HEI) has prompted a reaction that materialized in the creation of PetroAndina, PetroCarribe, and Petrosur. A major tenet of the ALBA development model is the role of the state as a central force, as opposed to markets and private investors.

Finally the ALBA development model rejects not only the U.S. approach to integration as embodied in the FTAA but is in opposition to all those models such as MERCOSUR and CAN that accept a neoliberal matrix. The complexities of ideology and pragmatism emerge when one considers that Venezuela itself is seeking membership of MERCOSUR and has joined UNASUR (see below).

UNASUR

ORIGIN, EVOLUTION, AND CURRENT DEBATES

Sometimes labels, slogans, and "concepts that have a high media impact, but are hard to pinpoint in a concrete manner" are used.[24] Such is the case of UNASUR. Often described as the union or convergence between MEROSUR and CAN, it is a different and distinct project altogether: it is essentially political in character and for the time being lacks the economic dimension of the other two. Most of all, UNASUR is the result of Brazil's vision to create "South America" as a cohesive and politically active community. Yet UNASUR's status and true nature remain relatively undefined. The ratification of the constituent treaty is still pending and therefore the organization has not formally come into existence.[25] Paradoxically, meetings of its organs take place and it challenges the principle of noninterference in the domestic affairs of member states.[26] Furthermore, idiosyncrasies among members are so noticeable that they may hamper any further institutional or political development. Indeed, the question of whether UNASUR is a proper regional integration process or a mere instance of interstate coordination and cooperation has yet to be answered.[27]

The notion of a South American common space has a long history but its political and economic construction is much more recent, and was given significant momentum and a more political content by President Cardoso in the First South American Summit in 2000.[28] The 2004 Cuzco summit created the Community of South American Nations (CSN), which marked the launch of a South American political project bringing together all twelve South American countries under Brazilian leadership, while the 2008 Treaty of Brasilia established UNASUR. In principle, UNASUR represents the world's fifth economic bloc (the fourth in terms of acknowledged market economy) with an annual combined GDP of US$2.915 trillion and a total population of over 380 million people.[29]

The strengths of UNASUR may well simultaneously prove to be weaknesses. First, the fact that it is the product of a Brazilian initiative provides the bloc with a designated, or self-designated, leader, with an obvious interest in a return from the success of the organization. At the same time, Brazilian preponderance generates resistance and makes the success of the group overdependent on Brazil's own domestic and international preferences. Second, the fact that UNASUR pretends to represent a new regional entity, South America (as opposed to Latin America), on the one hand, makes the grouping geographically well defined and geostrategically less elusive, but on the other, leaves aside a player like Mexico, whose trade and cultural importance to the region cannot be underestimated. Third, the fact that all twelve South American countries joined the group may give it a certain legitimacy and weight, but also creates problems of coordination and compatibility.

RELATIONS WITH THE UNITED STATES

Brazil's self-perception and aspiration to be a regional as well as global power, as well as its prioritization of South America, are crucial in understanding the competitive but low-level tensions in relations between UNASUR and the United States.[30] In its quest for a global role, Brazil portrays itself as the representative of a significant region, be this MERCOSUR, South, or Latin America, but cannot afford confrontation with the United States, especially as it shares with Washington several interests in multilateral forums.[31] The "South Americanization" of important political issues is a relatively low-risk, cost-sharing, and return-maximizing device for Brazil's international insertion.

This strategy is relatively articulated. UNASUR is primarily an instrument for political and security coordination. It has the function to resolve regional differences and tensions and thus to diminish reasons for U.S. interference. Internal wars (Bolivia), interstate conflict (Ecuador-Colombia-Venezuela), threats to democracy (Honduras), drugs trafficking (Colombia and the Amazon basin), and the arms race in Latin America are concerns shared in Brasilia and Washington. It is in the interest of both to solve them, and in the case of Brazil to solve them without U.S. involvement, which would challenge Brazil's regional status. As a corollary, UNASUR is meant to displace the Organization of the American States (OAS), often seen as an instrument of the United States, as the central stage to address South American conflicts. The 2008 Bolivian crisis showed that successful UNASUR action would result in the reinforcement of the Brazilian position and a loss of standing of the United States and the OAS, as its hemispheric coordination device.[32]

As stated earlier, emphasis on South America has led to the exclusion of Mexico from the project. The direct effect is to eliminate the only credible competitor of Brazil in terms of demographic and economic size and cultural power. The indirect effect is to exclude Mexico as the U.S. "Trojan Horse" in Latin America. By placing Mexico, and for this sake Central America and the Caribbean, into the North of the continent, Brazil also responds to the expansion of U.S. bilateral FTAs by trying to diminish their appeal as well as the cost of exclusion to South American nations. The project of a South American Free Trade Area to be linked to UNASUR can be seen this way or, alternatively, as a device for Brazil to negotiate its own FTA with Washington on better terms.[33] While the presence within UNASUR of close U.S. allies in trade (Chile) or security (Colombia) clashes with vociferous U.S. critics (Venezuela and other ALBA countries), the "South Americanization" of key issues allows the bloc to challenge the United States without endangering relations with Washington.

THE ROLE OF BRAZIL

UNASUR is a Brazilian creation and as such reflects the limits surrounding Brazilian claims to regional leadership. It is strictly intergovernmental, decisions are taken by consensus and require national incorporation, and its objectives are broad enough to accommodate a wide range of interests. Within UNASUR Brazil would acquire enlarged markets, energy supply, and access to the Pacific, as well as a platform to support its global aspirations. Chile sought new markets, access to energy resources and a venue to address frictions with its neighbors. Bolivia would find new markets for its gas and easier access to port facilities. Peru would strengthen its role as a gate to Asia and profit from energy integration. Colombia could regionalize its internal problems and diffuse tensions with neighbors, and Venezuela saw an opportunity to advance its Bolivarian agenda at the regional level, while all other members saw some advantages and opportunities.

Still, coexistence has been problematic as differences tend to prevail over commonalities. UNASUR's viability currently relies on loosely defined and scarcely codified commitments and the marginalization of critical issues such as trade and development. Also political and security coordination is elusive and overall Brazil's leadership and agenda are far from uncontested. President Chávez considers UNASUR as another alternative to neoliberal-type integration, while Brazil and other associates see MERCOSUR and CAN as the pillars of the forthcoming UNASUR economic dimension. The influence of Chávez's ideological stance can be detected in the proliferation of goals, now totaling twenty-one specific objectives.[34] Venezuela is increasingly able to complement Brazil's agenda, as the growing emphasis on social issues and the rejection of an accelerated tariff reduction have demonstrated.[35] This exposes the tension between resources available and declared objectives, as well as between Brazil's and Venezuela's preferences and styles, which in turn reflect tensions between pragmatism and ideology.

As the above reflects, Brazilian leadership has not gone uncontested. Even the evolution and role of the South American Defense Council might be in doubt, as it is not clear that a majority of South American countries prefer to rely on a Brazilian-sponsored defense scheme rather than a U.S. one. For example, in spite of signing up for the Defense Council in 2009 Colombia has concluded an agreement for the United

States to use military bases in its territory, thus undermining the Brazilian objective of eliminating the U.S. military presence from South America. In short, UNASUR adds to the debate between those who consider Brazil a "leader without followers"[36] and those who see in Brasilia a new form of "constructive leadership."[37]

THE DEVELOPMENT MODEL

UNASUR is a very peculiar form of integration, mostly in that it has no proper trade dimension, given the lack of consensus in this area. Ironically ideological differences have resulted in a pragmatic compromise: in the absence of any consensus on concrete instruments and policies, the issue has simply been left aside. However, sooner or later this will have to be addressed, and will be a decisive test for the viability and survival of UNASUR. At the regional level, MERCOSUR and CAN promote a broadly neoliberal agenda of trade barrier elimination, export-growth economies, and integration within global markets, while ALBA rejects neoliberal recipes and places emphasis in terms of trade on solidarity, compensation, and barter. At the national level, Chile adopts very low tariffs and has concluded free-trade agreements with countries across the world including the United States, which would be unthinkable in the case of Venezuela. Peru and Colombia are following the Chilean model, while Ecuador, Bolivia, and Venezuela tend to regulate and restrict foreign trade and are converting to largely state-dominated economies. Brazil and Argentina are in their own ways somewhere in the middle. What is clear is that no real economic integration is possible without trade-policy convergence.

IDEOLOGY AND PRAGMATISM
AT THE REGIONAL LEVEL

A distinction has to be drawn between the concept of regional integration on the one hand, and its concrete implementation in agreements and organizations on the other. In the former case, ideology largely prevails over pragmatism. In the latter, a tension between the two elements best captures the current scenario. Regarding the term and its use, the rhetoric of integration captures hearts and minds, the media's attention, and votes; its actual content and implementation, including pragmatic compromise and bargaining, do not. The rhetoric of integration serves the interests of politicians and the media and nourishes civil society's sense of belonging to the great Latin American family. Integration could mean almost anything at the discursive level, but its operational meaning is a different thing altogether. In what has been described as the "great escape forward," when Latin America is unable to address the current limitations of its integration, it simply creates yet another scheme that suffers from the same problems and tensions as its predecessors.[38]

The prevalence of ideology over pragmatism in the understanding of integration is also evident in the "double gap" between declarations, or the wording of the treaties, and their implementation on the ground.[39] The first gap is between declarations by politicians and press reports on the one hand, and what is actually being discussed at the technical level on the other. The second gap is between what is agreed upon at technical level on the one hand, and what is in fact either incorporated into national law, or applied in practice on the other. MERCOSUR is a good example. The internalization of regional norms remains quite low, thus weakening the application of regional law within domestic jurisdiction.[40] Also, regional rules that are put into force may be simply disregarded in practice, as occurred with the disruptions to intraregional trade caused by the Argentine-Uruguayan dispute over the construction of a paper mill.[41]

When it comes to the implementation of integration through actual agreements and organizations, a mix of ideology and pragmatism emerges. This should not be confused with the gap between rhetoric and reality that largely remains valid. The five factors identified in this volume can be used to analyze the choice of a country to join or reject a given integration bloc and the way in which putting this decision into practice forms an integral part of foreign policy. Since there is no supranationality in MERCOSUR, ALBA, or UNASUR and all three are strictly intergovernmental, the external projection of each bloc (its "foreign relations") can also be directly related to its member states. In this sense, the five factors can be applied to two dimensions: a country's position vis-à-vis one or more integration options; and the behavior of the integration organization and the role of individual members to determine its posture in external relations.[42]

First, ends and purposes that members confer to a given organization determine its pragmatic or ideological stance. When the bloc is used to alter the regional or international order (ALBA), ideology may prevail, but when the association is designed to attain greater international insertion within a largely accepted framework of norms (MERCOSUR) a more pragmatic style tends to emerge. Second, the available means determine the bloc's capacity to produce effects. ALBA largely functions thanks to Venezuelan oil resources. What is interesting is that none of the three schemes possesses its own resources and entirely depends on member states' contributions, thus reinforcing the leverage each associate has on the group. As occurs at the level of individual countries, an ideological stance can be a resource in itself, as ALBA illustrates. Third, on agency, both member states and individual leaders may act as an agent and affect the style of the organization. This is reinforced by the intergovernmental nature of the processes and by strong presidentialism, which is transposed at the regional level.[43] Latin American regional organizations tend to replicate the style of their stronger members. Fourth, by a similar token, the intergovernmental nature of the decision-making process largely influences the combination of ideology and pragmatism. Theories of "groupthink" also apply (ALBA), while pluralism seems to produce institutional paucity and policy inconsistency rather than pragmatism (MERCOSUR and UNASUR). Fifth, policies, including regional integration, do not emerge in a vacuum, but reflect the values and constraints of their historical and political context. The questioning of regional and global orders and paradigms, together with the partial retreat of the United States from the continent in the twenty-first century has opened up space for political and economic innovation. This has taken the shape of both ideological and pragmatic solutions. Overall, the ideological or pragmatic connotation of Latin American blocs is to be sought more at the level of national interests and agenda, rather than at the level of regional norms and institutions.

CONCLUSION

In terms of contemporary Latin American regional integration, three tensions emerge.[44]

(a) Between change and continuity. The more new formulas and projects for regional integration proliferate, the more unlikely is the attainment of the goal and the more probable is continuity in the form of ineffective regionalism.

(b) Between unity and diversity. The overabundant production of regional institutions, bodies, and norms is meant to signal a unity of intent at the regional level, but in fact reflects the plurality (incompatibility) of views, interests, and agendas.

(c) Between ideology and pragmatism. Declarations, principles, and solemn intentions, as well as emphatic discourse, have to face the reality of diplomatic practice and structural constraints. Resources are finite and accommodation is generally more rewarding than confrontation in political praxis.

MERCOSUR, ALBA, and UNASUR are the product of different political logics and visions and give very different responses to three fundamental foreign policy questions for all members. The relationship with the United States varies from mildly competitive in commercial terms (MERCOSUR), to inconsistent or elusive (UNASUR), to ideologically confrontational (ALBA). The place of Brazil is not clearly defined either. ALBA represents a challenge to its regional leadership aspirations and approach, UNASUR is a Brazilian creation designed to promote Brazil's role regionally and globally, but its leadership is subject to significant limitations, and Brazil's leadership of MERCOSUR is not only contested, but Brasilia itself seems lukewarm and is certainly more interested in its own agenda. Finally, the models of development range from open economy and free trade (MERCOSUR), to rejection of free trade in favor of compensation and barter (ALBA), to the impossibility of adopting any model due to divergences between members (UNASUR).

In this context, it is hard to see how one single integration project may gradually prevail over or absorb the others. They might be able to coexist, depending on the persistence of the gap between discourse and practice, and on the maintenance of low-level integration, characterized by loose commitments, diffused and flexible roles and rules, and tolerance of ideological differences. A slightly more optimistic view would envisage an accepted division of labor, whereby ALBA would put forward the continental social agenda, MERCOSUR would somehow define the economic and trade scenario, and UNASUR would deal with political and security coordination. Still, if there is no consensus on either what or how to integrate, then integration will remain a concept with no real content. The panorama is not conducive to any deepening of Latin or South American integration, especially as the economic dimension is crucial. With overlapping membership and divergent rationales and agendas, MERCOSUR, ALBA, and UNASUR are not only incompatible in their current format, but dysfunctional in terms of the objective of continental unity, solidarity, and economic and social development.

Regarding pragmatism and ideology and how they may characterize regional integration, a clear distinction has to be made between the actual concept of regional integration and its translation into agreements and integration schemes. In the former case, ideology largely prevails over pragmatism. In the latter, a tension best describes the current picture as exemplified by ALBA and UNASUR. In the case of ALBA, to formally abide by Bolivarian principles may sometimes appear as more important than the realities of diplomacy and economic convenience. This ideological stance limits possibilities for enlargement and international support. However, single members in practice have pursued more pragmatic foreign policies,[45] and ALBA itself can be ironically viewed as a pragmatic marriage of convenience: Venezuela uses it to advance its position in the region and the other members obtain cheap oil and financial assistance. UNASUR started very pragmatically. It could count on the support of the main regional power, concentrated on a limited number of issues, and left aside sensitive questions. Still, practice unmasked ideological differences. The weight of Brazil has led to resistance, the items on the agenda have proliferated to accommodate ideological claims, and crucial steps such as the adoption of a development model have been delayed for essentially ideological reasons.

Ultimately, Latin America is divided between a rhetorical, almost theatrical, support for continental solidarity and integration and a strong, practical preference for national sovereignty and interest, accompanied by a traditional aversion to supranationality. Regional positioning and integration choice are a core part of national foreign policy, and as a result, the tension between ideological and pragmatic aspects of Latin American regionalism has to be understood with reference to national agendas and dynamics.

NOTES

1. Simón Bolívar, *Escritos Políticos*, Alianza Editorial, Madrid, 1969; Gerardo Oviedo, "Pensamientos sobre la integración latinoamericana: un corpus textual," *Cuadernos Americanos*, No. 126, 2008, pp. 53–72; Peter H. Smith, *Talons of the Eagle. Dynamics of US-Latin American Relations*, Oxford University Press, Oxford and New York, 2000, especially pp. 87–92; Norberto Galasso, *América Latina. Unidos o Dominados*, Ediciones Instituto Superior Dr Arturo Jauretche, Buenos Aires, 2008.

2. Rosendo Fraga, "La Experiencia Histórica en Brasil y Argentina desde 1966 hasta 1983: Cominenzo de la Convergencia," in José Maria Lladós and Samuel Pinheiro Guimarães (eds.), *Pespectivas. Brasily Argentina*, IPRI-CARI, Brasilia and Buenos Aires, 1999, pp. 367–85.

3. Roberto Russell, *Cambio de Régimen y Política Exterior: El Caso de Argentina, 1976–1989*, FLACSO, Documentos e Informes de Investigación, No. 88, 1989, Buenos Aires.

4. Gian Luca Gardini Gardini, "Who invented Mercosur?" *Diplomacy and Statecraft*, 18:4 (December 2007), pp. 805–30.

5. Andrea Oelsner, "The Institutional Identity of Regional Organizations, or Mercosur's identity crisis," paper presented at the VI General congress of the ECPR, Potsdam, September 2009; Romeo Perez, "El Mercosur antes su Extraña Crisis," CLAEH working paper, Montevideo, November 2009.

6. Roberto Porzecanski, *No Voy e TREN. Uruguay y las perspectivas de un TLC con Estados Unidos (2000–2010)*, Debate—Random House Mondadori & Editorial Sudamericana Uruguaya, Montevideo, 2010.

7. Gian Luca Gardini, *The Origins of Mercosur*, Palgrave Macmillan, New York, 2010.

8. Miriam Gomes Saraiva and Andres Malamud, 2009, "Argentina and Brazil between continuity and change," paper presented at the ABRI-ISA Joint Conference, Rio de Janeiro, July 2009. See also the chapter by Miriam Gomes Saraiva in this volume.

9. Andrés Malamud, "Leadership without Followers: The Contested Case for Brazilian Power Status," in Estevão C. Rezende Martins and Miriam Gomes Saraiva (eds.), *Brasil, União Europeia, América do Sul: Anos 2010–2020*, Konrad Adenauer Foundation, Brasilia, 2009, pp. 126–48; Sean W. Burges, "Without Sticks or Carrots: Brazilian Leadership in South America During the Cardoso Era, 1992–2003," *Bulletin of Latin American Research*, 25:1, 2006, pp. 23–42; José Antonio Sanahuja, "La construcción de una region: Suramérica y el regionalismo neoliberal," in Manuel Cienfuegos and José Antonio Sanahuja (eds.), *Una Región en Construcción: UNASUR y la integración en América del Sur*, CIDOB, Barcelona, 2010, pp. 87–134.

10. Olivier Dabène, *The Politics of Regional Integration in Latin America. Theoretical and Comparative Explorations*, Palgrave Macmillan, New York, 2009.

11. The debate is whether the original project is the more political one conceived by the first democratic administrations of Alfonsín of Argentina, Sarney of Brazil, and Sanguinetti of Uruguay who launched the integration process in the mid-1980s, or the more economic and commercial one as understood and implemented by the 1990s administrations that in fact did sign the 1991 Treaty of Asunción. On the point, see Gian Luca Gardini, *The Origins of Mercosur*, pp. 100–102.

12. All concur that the adoption of the common customs code, the elimination of the double tariff, an effective mechanism of dispute resolution, and the coordination of trade policies would be positive and indispensable steps.

13. In this sense, it is questionable whether ALBA and UNASUR are to be considered schemes of integration, cooperation, or coordination. See a debate on definitions in Dabène, *The Politics of Regional Integration in Latin America*, chapter 1. For a strict definition of regional integration, see Philippe Schmitter, "Change in Regime Type and Progress in International Relations," in Emanuel Adler and Beverly Crawford (eds.), *Progress in Postwar International Relations*, Columbia University Press, New York, 1991, pp. 89–127. For an understanding of regional integration as one dimension of regionalism, see Andrew Hurrell, "Regionalism in Theoretical Perspective," in Louse Fawcett and Andrew Hurrell (eds.), *Regionalism in World Politics*, Oxford University Press, New York, 1995, pp. 37–73.

14. Thomas Fritz, *ALBA contra ALCA*, Centro de Investigación y Documentación Chile Latinoamérica (FDCL), April 2007.

15. Nayllivis N. N. Soto, "Alternativa Bolivariana para las Américas: Una Propuesta histórico política al ALCA," *Geoenseñanza*, 2004, 9:1, pp. 57–73.

16. Carlos N. Oddone and Leonardo Granato, "Los nuevos proyectos de integración regional vigentes en América Latina," *OIKOS Revista de economía heterodoxa*, 2007, 6:7, pp. 29–50.

17. Alberto Montero Soler, , "ALBA: avances y tensiones en el proceso de integracion popular bolivariano," *Revista Agora*, 3 (2007):5.

18. Speech by President Hugo Chavez at the 4th Summit of the Americas, Mar del Plata, November 2005, in Zuleima Centeno, "Participación de Venezuela en Mar del Plata," Ministerio del Poder Popular para la Comunicación y la Información de la Republica Bolivariana de Venezuela, November 11, 2005, available online at http://www.minci.gob.ve/reportajes/2/5660/participacion_de_venezuela.html (last accessed March 27, 2010).

19. Thomas Fritz, *ALBA contra ALCA*.

20. Ministerio de Relaciones Exteriores de la Republica Bolivariana de Venezuela, *Boletin*. Oficina de coordinación de Prensa, Caracas, 2001.

21. Sean Burgess, "Building a Southern Coalition: The Competing Approaches of Brazil's Lula and Venezuela's Chavez," *Third World Quarterly*, 28:7 (2007), pp. 1343–58.

22. Soto, "Alternativa Bolivariana para las Américas."

23. Fernando Ravsberg, "Cumbre del ALBA en Cuba," BBC Mundo, December 13, 2009, available online, http://www.bbc.co.uk/mundo/economia/2009/12/091213_0626_cuba_alba_gm.shtml (last accessed March 27, 2010).

24. Felix Peña, "Strategic Partnerships and Trade Preferences," International Trade Relations Newsletter, March 2010, http://www.felixpena.com.ar/index.php?contenido=negotiations&neagno=report/2010-03-strategic-partnerships-brasil-mexico (last accessed May 7, 2010).

25. At the time of writing, only Ecuador, Bolivia, Venezuela, Guyana, and Peru have ratified the constituent treaty. Four more ratifications are needed for it to come into force.

26. Gian Luca Gardini, "Verso una nuova guerra fredda?" *Affari Internazionali*, 24 settembre 2008.

27. Isidro Sepulveda Muñoz, "Introducción," in Ministerio de la Defensa, *La Creación de UNASUR en el Marco de la Seguridad y la Defensa*, Centro Superior de Estudios de la defensa nacional, Documentos de Seguridad y Defensa No. 29, Madrid, January 2010. See also note 13 about the debate on definitions. For the reasons to include UNASUR in this work, refer to the discussion on definitions in Dabène, *The Politics of Regional Integration in Latin America*, pp. 5–11.

28. Carlos Piñeiro Iñiguez, *La Nación Sudamericana. Del imperativo histórico-cultural la realización económico-politica*, NuevoHacer Grupo Editor Latinoamericano, Buenos Aires, 2004. See also the section on Brazil and

UNASUR later on in this chapter. The 1st South American Summit was also accompanied by an academic forum promoting the geostrategic concept: Instituto Rio Branco, IEPES, IPEA, BID, "Seminario sobre America do Sul: A Organização do espaço sul-americano," Brasilia, July 31–August 2, 2000.

29. Author's elaboration based on World Trade Organization, *Trade Profiles*, available on http://stat.wto.org/CountryProfile/WSDBCountry PFReporter.aspx?Language=E (last accessed August 5, 2010). Figures based on consolidated data 2008.

30. Luis Claudio Villafañe Santos, "A America do Sul no discurso diplomatico brasileiro," *Revista Brasileira de Política Internacional*, 48:2 (2005), pp. 185–204, p. 201. Sergio Caballero, "Brasil y la integración regional sudamericana: entre el liderazgo regional y el global player," paper presented at the VI CEISAL Conference, Toulouse, June–July 2010, pp. 4–5. See also the chapter by Miriam Gomes Saraiva in this collection.

31. Alfred P. Montero, *Brazilian Politics*, Polity Press, Cambridge, 2005, chapter 7.

32. José Antonio Sanahuja, "La construcción de una región: Suramerica y el regionalismo posliberal," in Manuel Cienfuegos and José Antonio Sanahuja (eds.), *Una Región en Construcción. Unasur y la integración en América del Sur*, Fundació CIDOB, Barcelona, 2010, pp. 87–134, p. 119.

33. Romeo Perez, Director of CLAEH, interview with the author, Montevideo July 13, 2010.

34. Treaty of Brasilia, art. 3.

35. See, for instance, the creation of a South American Energy Council and a South American Health Council.

36. Andres Malamud, "Leadership without Followers: The Contested Case for Brazilian Power Status," in Estevao Rezende Martins and Miriam Gomes Saraiva (eds.), *Brasil, Uniao Europeia, America do Sul: Anos 2010–2020*, Brasilia, Konrad Adenauer Foundation, 2009, pp. 126–48.

37. Marcel Fortuna Biato, "La Politica Exterior de Brasil. ¿Integrar o dspegar?" *Politica Exterior* 23:131, pp. 45–58.

38. Sergio Abreu, Minister of Foreign Affairs of Uruguay (1993–1995), interview with the author, Montevideo, July 20, 2010.

39. Marcel Vaillant, formerly member of the Mercosur Technical Assistance Sector (SAT) and currently Professor of International Trade at the Universidad de la Republica, Uruguay, interview with the author, Montevideo, July 5, 2010.

40. With no established and undisputed primacy of communitarian law over national law and generally with no direct applicability, MERCOSUR, ALBA, and UNASUR regulations all need incorporation into national law. See Andrés Malamud, "Mercosur Turns 15: Between Rising Rhetoric and Declining Achievement," *Cambridge Review of International Affairs*,

2005, 18:3, pp. 421–36; Alejandro D. Perrotti, *Tribunal Permanente de Revisión y Estado de Derecho en el Mercosur*, Konrad Adenauer Foundation-Marcial Pons, Buenos Aires, 2008; Olivier Dabène, *The Politics of Regional Integration in Latin America*, chapter 4.

41. For an exhaustive study of the case and its legal implications, see Didier Opertti Badán, "Las Plantas de Celulosa: Cronología de un Conflicto," *La Ley*, forthcoming, November 2010.

42. However, when applied to this second dimension, the five factors need some flexibility and adaptation as no bloc has its own foreign policy, not even of an infant EU-type, and variance and inconsistency among the associates' positions may be significant.

43. Andrés Malamud, "Presidential Diplomacy and the Institutional Underpinnings of Mercosur. An Empirical Examination," *Latin American Research Review*, 40:1 (2005), pp. 138–64.

44. Gian Luca Gardini, *L'America Latina nel XXI Secolo*, Carocci, Rome, 2009.

45. Venezuela, for instance, following calculated political cost-benefit analysis, has joined MERCOSUR and UNASUR trying to advance its own agenda. Ecuador has denounced the FTA agreement with the United States but has actively campaigned for the renewal of the ATPDEA that grants preferential access to the U.S. market to most of its exports. Nicaragua has joined ALBA and at the same time has ratified the Dr-CAFTA free-trade agreement with the United States.

Conclusions

Gian Luca Gardini and
Peter Lambert

The use of ideology and pragmatism in twenty-first century Latin American foreign policies has an original connotation that makes it qualitatively different from the past. Ideology and pragmatism are defining elements of any political behavior and policy choice, including foreign-policy design and implementation, and the eleven country case studies contained in this volume confirm their complex coexistence and interrelationship throughout the first decade of the new millennium. However, the analysis suggests that what is significantly innovative in this combination, as compared to the past, is what we highlighted in the introduction as the "considered and calculated variety in intensity, circumstance, purpose and arena of the mix of ideology and pragmatism."[1]

Indeed, ideology and pragmatism appear to be deliberately employed by Latin American administrations with a lucid awareness of the possibilities and constraints that the two have to offer. Ideology is not accidentally, clumsily, or dogmatically applied, nor is pragmatism selected by default or imposed by size or circumstance only. Nor is their combination the result of mere contingency or external structures and conditions. Their adoption and combination are instead carefully and purposefully calculated and adjusted depending on the audience, the venue, and the circumstance. This has resulted in a conscious and intelligent combination of ideological and pragmatic styles, discourse, and actions, which helps make sense of apparently contradictory goals and behaviors. Far from signaling incoherence or inconsistency, the case studies indicate that such a combination generally expresses diplomatic and political acumen in the pursuit of the national interest and international autonomy.[2] Ideology and pragmatism may be used both to describe foreign policy and, more interestingly, as an operational tool of foreign policy. It would appear that over the past decade they have evolved from essentially descriptive features into systematic and sophisticated instruments of foreign policy, the combination of which gives rise to an assertive international stance aimed at altering—more or less radically—existing global and regional orders.

One of the main purposes of this volume was to explore the possible motives, locate the possible sources, and identify the possible agents of ideology and pragmatism in contemporary Latin American foreign policies. To this end, Chapter 1 established an analytical framework based on five factors: ends and purposes of foreign policy; means and resources available; agency and the role of the human factor; process of foreign-policy formation; and historical and political structures. Given the steady erosion of the barriers between domestic and international politics, we opted for this quite specific analytical model rather than a more traditional level-of-analysis approach, since it could be applied to all case studies and produce different and comparable analytical results regarding ideology and pragmatism. National differences and peculiarities were expected and indeed emerged, but overall a number of commonalities and trends are identifiable.

ENDS AND PURPOSES

As predicted in the analytical model, empirical studies confirmed that when the purpose of a given foreign policy is to challenge the existing order, a significantly ideological stance is often employed either in discourse or in practice, as witnessed in the case of Venezuela and its ALBA project. Conversely, when the goal is to join a club, pragmatic elements tend to prevail, as witnessed by the same country in the case of its relationship with Mercosur. This simultaneous and parallel use of ideology and pragmatism by Venezuela in its regional relations, is just one example of many in this volume of the complexity of the two elements and the interplay between them.

With regard to the purpose of foreign policy in terms of the target audience, what emerges strongly from the analysis by Malamud, Birns and Sanchez, Kapcia, and Raby on Argentina, Bolivia, Cuba, and Venezuela, respectively, is that more ideological features, essentially discursive, tend to come to prominence when the target audience is domestic and when foreign policy is used as an instrument to further internal objectives. In this case, a more assertive international discourse, and at times action, may serve to rally internal consensus, diffuse domestic discontent, divert attention away from domestic concerns, or steal political and media space from the opposition. In the international milieu, however, very assertive or even harsh behavior may be counterproductive, and tends to be more unusual.

AVAILABLE MEANS

The resources at a country's disposal clearly contribute to shaping its international posture and style. This may have several dimensions. First, the availability of natural resources may provide a country with an excellent tool for international insertion and dynamism. In the case of Venezuela, oil largely finances the regional aspirations and projects of Caracas, and ALBA is almost entirely based on Hugo Chavez's oil diplomacy. Were it not for Venezuelan oil wealth, the entire Bolivarian project would have a much lower profile and be perceived as less attractive or threatening by its supporters and detractors, respectively. Second, the presence of natural resources, when coupled with other factors, may contribute to determine the posture of a given country vis-à-vis foreign partners. As Birns and Sanchez explain in the chapter on Bolivia, recent clashes with Brazil and the consequent combination of ideology and pragmatism adopted by the Morales administration is closely related to the nationalization of the gas fields, a development mirrored in Fernando Lugo's attempts (which combine both pragmatism and ideology) to reassert Paraguayan sovereignty over the Itaipú hydroelectric dam it shares with Brazil. Third, means or assets may be understood in terms of international mentors and support. Cuba's ideological foreign policy was related to the support it received from the Soviet Union, a stance that clearly had to be modified (although not abandoned) in the 1990s following the collapse of the Soviet Bloc and the consequent need for Cuba to adopt a more pragmatic line in order to survive. Finally, in the absence of any other significant resource, ideology itself could be a useful asset to raise the international profile and bargaining power of a country. This is exemplified by Nicaragua's pragmatic ideologues and in particular by Daniel Ortega's second administration, in which Bolivarian discourse and aspirations converged with the reality of free-market policies, in a not-so-unusual combination of ideology and pragmatism, designed to benefit from regional initiatives (for example ALBA and DR-CAFTA).

AGENCY

This is a key element in all of the chapters. On the one hand, an emphasis on the importance of agency reinforces the belief that politics is made by human beings for human beings; on the other, it points to the theoretical approach of the English School that suggests that individuals and their actions have to be understood in the framework of their historical context and experience. In Latin America, the prominent role of the president and his/her inner circle owes something too to the presidential system of government in place.

The emphasis on the human factor is particularly strong in the chapters on Venezuela (Chávez), Peru (especially Fujimori and Toledo), Nicaragua, and Paraguay (all presidents). This suggests not only that where individual leaders wield more personalist, centralized, and authoritarian forms of power, they will have a particularly strong influence on foreign policy, but also that in poorer, more underdeveloped countries, such as Paraguay and Nicaragua, presidents tend to hold greater potential influence over foreign policy. Of course, in such situations if the presidency is weak, then foreign policy may well drift, as was the case in Paraguay in much of the 1990s.

In contrast, where foreign-policy institutions and bureaucracies are stronger, more developed, and more efficient—often in more developed countries—the role of the individual leader and his/her ability to determine foreign policy are reduced. Thus, in spite of President Lula's charisma and personality, Miriam Gomes Saraiva pays more attention to the role of currents within the foreign ministry, Itamaraty, than on the policies of the president, while Joaquin Fermandois, in the case of Chile, is more concerned with the priorities of the governing coalition than with the personal preferences of Ricardo Lagos or Michelle Bachelet. This is not to relegate the human factor, which still remains a centerpiece of foreign-policy-making and its ideological and pragmatic dimensions in all case studies. Rather it is to emphasize that individuals and their power to dictate or influence policy are tempered by the environment in which they operate.

PROCESS

Agency is closely related to the process guiding the formulation of foreign policy, which also affects its combination of ideology and pragmatism. Not surprisingly, where foreign-policy bureaucracies and mechanisms are more articulated and function more effectively, foreign policy tends to be more consistent and prevailingly pragmatic. In the case of Brazil, Miriam Saraiva emphasized the importance of the correlation of forces within Itamaraty, Ronald Bruce St. John identified the strong and professionalized diplomatic corps in Peru as one the main reasons for the country's continuity in international relations, and Peter Lambert suggested that Paraguayan foreign policy has become more pragmatic and coherent with the gradual professionalization of the foreign-policy bureaucracy from 2003 onward.

In contrast, the domination of foreign policy by the executive in Argentina led to erratic foreign policies that were not state, but rather essentially administration policies. This may be the case too in Bolivia and Venezuela, where congressional majorities have facilitated the implementation of new directions in foreign affairs, confirming that the process (institutional procedures and mechanisms, timing, and participating actors) does matter in the construction of the content and style of foreign policy.

STRUCTURE AND CONTEXT

No event, strategy, or policy exists in a vacuum but is rather situated in place, time, and context. Indeed from the analysis of all the case studies in the volume, the structural context is a factor that clearly emerges as a dominant influence on the combination of ideology and pragmatism.

Latin America's proximity to the United States, and its role (perceived or real) as part of a U.S. "sphere of influence" during most of the twentieth century, especially during the Cold War, has been a highly relevant factor in the formulation of foreign policy in all Latin American countries. Indeed, the pervasiveness of the U.S. political, economic, and cultural presence in Latin America is such that one cannot understand certain prevalent stances or policies without specific reference to Washington. As Ana Covarrubias argues, Mexican foreign policy is essentially reactive to both external and domestic events, while Diana Raby stresses the paradoxical centrality of the United States to the Bolivarian project. Especially during the Cold War, in most of the countries studied, from Chile to Colombia to Cuba, the United States played a highly influential role in domestic and foreign policy, at times representing the overwhelming contextual influence on politics. In the case of Nicaragua, as David Close argues, a history of dependency, U.S. intervention, and structural weakness of the state propelled the country into the forefront of the Cold War in the 1980s, thus limiting its foreign-policy options. External events, such as the fall of the Soviet Union and the emergence of the Pink Wave have also been central (although not predominant) in the shift between ideology and pragmatism in Cuban foreign policy.

Of course, structure and context go far beyond the role of the United States or other external actors. Peter Lambert and Joaquin Fermandois both argue, in the cases of Paraguay and Chile, respectively, that the legacies of authoritarianism and the transition to democracy are central contextual explanatory factors in any analysis of the convergence between ideology and pragmatism during the 1990s. Meanwhile, in the case of Argentina, the overwhelming element of continuity, according to Andrés Malamud, is that of Peronism and its tendency in terms of foreign policy to respond to immediate domestic demands and priorities above and beyond any coherent medium or long term foreign policy in the national interest.

Overall four conclusions and one open debate can be drawn from the case studies contained in the volume. Our first conclusion is that *the prolif-eration of issues on the international agenda and the multiplication of actors at all levels on the international scenario have resulted in greater opportunities for the development of both ideology and pragmatism within foreign policy.* The increasing complexity of international relations and the interconnections between countries have opened new spaces and opportunities for innovative and creative foreign-policy solutions in Latin America. The ability to develop relations simultaneously with, for example, the United States, Russia, Iran, China, the European Union, and most Latin American neighbors, simply did not exist twenty years ago. Similarly, the new opportunities offered through regional development (ALBA, UNASUR, etc.) or even global development (the G-20 and the Group of Cairns within the WTO, the new financial and economic G-20, the BRIC, IBSA, etc.) significantly increase the number and scope, quantity, and quality of potential venues for negotiation and bargaining, and alliances.

With this expansion of international partners, relations, and opportunities, more ideas, policies and relations may be explored, without causing disproportionate objections, prejudice or reprisals. In this environment both ideology and pragmatism have been able to thrive. The twenty-first century also offers more space to diffuse tensions, to negotiate compromises, to bargain and to move away from a zero-sum game toward a situation characterized by issue-based coalitions and agendas. Precisely because of this increase in international interaction and opportunities, ideology may still be prevalent in discourse and rhetoric, but pragmatism appears to be prevailing in terms of action and practice.

Second, *the combination of ideology and pragmatism is largely deter-mined by the actors working within the structural constraints in which they operate.* While it would appear that agency tends to predominate over structure, it is also apparent that the latter presents crucial limitations as well as opportunities that define the choices and alternatives available. This is entirely consistent with the English School perspective, which places the human factor at the center of foreign policy and international relations, but which has tried to balance this with the importance of the national and international context, the legacy of historical experience and the role of interests and ideas. Moreover, the increase in the number and variety of agents and the parallel rise in the intricacy and sophistication of context and structure make the whole agency-structure debate ever more complex. The result is the need for more complex, multidimensional, and pluralistic explanations,[3] including of the multiple tensions that characterize the international environment: ideas versus interests, justice versus order, and—ultimately—ideology versus pragmatism.

Third, almost as a natural consequence, *the world of today is character-ized more by coexisting tensions than by dichotomous positions or clear-cut differences* as was arguably the case in a Cold War bipolar world. The tensions between ideology and pragmatism are accompanied by and closely related to another set of three interlinked and crosscutting tensions.[4] In the first place, there is a clear tension between discourse and practice. All the case studies have highlighted how, while ideology may stand high in the realm of discourse, the actual practice of diplomacy gives way to far more pragmatic and less confrontational stances. A second tension emerges between unity and diversity in Latin America. While discourse privileges continental commonalities and a rhetorical support for cohesiveness and solidarity, the evidence suggests that national interests and agendas are often divergent if not competitive and make use of ideology and pragmatism according to convenience. The tension between unity and diversity and the problems it creates apply equally well to definitional labels such as the "Pink Tide," or the "progressive administrations," and to their operational tools, such as foreign policy. Finally, a tension between elements of change and continuity characterize the foreign policies of contemporary Latin America, a point we will return to when discussing the open debate resulting from this investigation.

Fourth, *foreign policy, especially in Latin America, increasingly seems to be a continuation of domestic politics by other means.* As suggested by a leading Latin American scholar in the field of International Relations, international politics is after all politics and can be understood with the same analytical categories as any other form of politics.[5] It would be a mistake to try to isolate International Relations and Foreign Policy as if they were governed by unique norms and rules disconnected from other realms. Indeed the country case studies in this volume have clearly demonstrated how foreign policy is not an isolated sphere of policy, but is intimately connected with economic and societal interests, debates, and actors. In particular, the cases of Peru, Nicaragua, Argentina, Cuba, Paraguay, and Bolivia reveal the significant influence of different aspects of domestic politics on the nature and content of the country's external relations. Finally, the return of the state at the domestic level is accompanied by a regained centrality of the state as the key promoter of regional development and projects, as discussed by Gian Luca Gardini in his chapter on regionalism.

Returning to the discussion regarding the tension between change and continuity, this remains an open-ended debate. This book has dealt with two aspects. First, to what extent do the foreign policies adopted by the Latin American administrations in the first decade of the new century represent an actual break from the past? Our contributors have argued that the Fox administration in Mexico, Hugo Chávez in Venezuela, post-1990 Cuba, Duarte and Lugo in Paraguay, the Concertación in Chile, and Evo Morales in Bolivia have all represented clear departures, in one way or another, from the past. The degree to which the positioning along the ideology-pragmatism continuum and/or the calculated use of a combination of the two elements have been decisive to this change may be open to discussion, but there has clearly been a qualitative element of change. Brazil, Colombia, Peru, and Nicaragua, in very different ways and each with their national specificities and nuances, seem to have experienced a greater degree of continuity in foreign-policy style and orientation, but each has also experienced elements of considerable change. Argentina, with its paradoxical continuity in terms of erratic solutions and Peronist style remains a particularly special case, but both of the Kirchner administrations clearly reflect the tensions between ideology and pragmatism, and the regional political developments which are central to this volume. In our view therefore, despite some elements of continuity, the 2000s bear such striking differences from the 1990s as to represent a significant change in Latin American foreign policies.

The second aspect concerns the contingent or enduring nature of the features that currently define Latin American foreign policies, especially in terms of ideology and pragmatism. Some structural elements are seemingly long-lasting ones, but the international milieu is currently in a process of significant change. The influence of the United States in the region is declining relatively to the growth of other states (China, India) and nonstate actors (social movements, drugs trafficking, and other criminal gangs), although of course it remains a significant actor. The emergence of new countries as global economic—and increasingly political—players (not only the BRIC, but also South Africa, South Korea, and Mexico) will reinforce the challenges to the existing regional and global order, especially in its philosophical and normative content. And the proliferation of forms of international governance at the regional and global level will propel a continuing expansion of issues, interests, and stakeholders in the international arena.

For Latin America all of this means that the changes in structural factors that shaped the specific new context that allowed the Pink Tide to emerge will probably continue: the reassertion of Latin American autonomy and nationalism, the questioning of globalization and U.S. economic and political dominance, and the redefinition of models of development and international interaction are all issues that are likely to continue to open up new opportunities for Latin America. What may change of course is the political orientation of the administrations in Latin America. With a significant round of presidential elections between

2009 and 2011, the term "Pink Tide" may well become redundant, or at least less widely used as a term of reference. Agency after all, remains crucial in terms of change and/or continuity in domestic and foreign policy. However, we would argue that given the emerging new international environment mentioned above, the principle issues, tensions, and trends analyzed in this book not only define a key decade of Latin American foreign policies but, regardless of the outcome of forthcoming elections, will continue to strongly influence Latin American international relations in the near future.

NOTES

1. Gian Luca Gardini and Peter Lambert, "Introduction" to this volume.
2. An entirely different question is how the notion of national interest is constructed and adopted, shared or contested, and by whom.
3. For a discussion of pluralism of theories and methods in the social sciences, see Donatella Della Porta and Michael Keating, *Approaches and Methodologies in the Social Sciences: A Pluralist Perspective*, Cambridge University Press, Cambridge and New York, 2008.
4. We borrow this conceptual framework from the theory of tensions conceptualized by Gian Luca Gardini, *L'America del XXI Secolo*, Carocci Editore, Rome, 2009.
5. Maria Regina Soares de Lima, speech at the Round Table "Relaciones Internacionales en la América Latina del Bicentenario," V Congress of Latin American Political Science (ALACIP), Buenos Aires, July 2010.

INDEX